The Polynesians voyaged hundreds of miles
across open wat
for the most part
currents. Their
their own nake
knowledge of th

THEY WERE THE CHILDREN OF TANGAROA, GOD OF THE SEA, and their eastward expansion to the islands of the Pacific represents the last great movement of people into the only remaining unpopulated area of the habitable world.

Tapping the scientific resources of archaeology, oceanography, botany, zoology, geology, and physical anthropology, ROBERT C. SUGGS reconstructs the prehistory of the Polynesians—perhaps the greatest mariners the world has ever known.

He traces their origin to Eastern Asia, and step-by-step, he follows their migrations to the scattered islands of the Polynesian triangle. He studies the warfare, the agriculture, the religion, family life, sexual customs, political and social organization of these adventurous people who journeyed into the unknown centuries before Columbus set sail for the New World.

THE ISLAND

CIVILIZATIONS OF

POLYNESIA

Robert C. Suggs

Mentor: Ancient Civilizations

Published by THE NEW AMERICAN LIBRARY

O Ta'aroa te tupuna o te mau atua ato'a; na'na te mau mea ato'a i hamani. Mai tahito a iuiu mai o Ta'aroa nui, Tahi-tumu.

Tahitian Creation Chant
from *Tahiti Aux Temps Anciens,*
by Teuira Henry, Paris, 1951

Tangaroa was the ancestor of all the gods;
by him were all things made.
From ancient times, great Tangaroa existed,
the source of all.

SECOND PRINTING

Library of Congress Catalog Card No. 60-14723

MENTOR TRADEMARK REG. U.S. PAT. OFF. AND FOREIGN COUNTRIES
REGISTERED TRADEMARK—MARCA REGISTRADA
HECHO EN CHICAGO, U.S.A.

*MENTOR BOOKS are published by
The New American Library, Inc.
1301 Avenue of the Americas, New York, New York 10019*

PRINTED IN THE UNITED STATES OF AMERICA

Contents

Acknowledgments

I wish to express my deep gratitude to Dr. H. L. Shapiro of the Department of Anthropology, American Museum of Natural History, and to Mr. and Mrs. Cornelius Crane of Ipswich, Massachusetts, who made possible my anthropological research in Polynesia that served as a nucleus for this work. I am also indebted to Dr. K. P. Emory and Mr. Yoshiko Sinoto of the Bernice Bishop Museum in Honolulu, Mr. J. Golson of the University of Auckland, New Zealand, and Professor Dr. T. Barthel of the University of Tübingen, Germany, for their cooperation in the exchanging of scientific views, which has greatly stimulated my research. Dr. Walter Fairservis of the American Museum was very helpful in discussing Asian-Oceanian relationships. None of the above are responsible for my views, but their help has been most kind.

Mr. Nicholas Amorosi has contributed the illustrations, charts, and maps.

My Polynesian friends brought their talents to serve the ends of modern science in the exploration of their past, and they too deserve mention.

Finally, my wife, Rae, has helped much in this as in all my work. My thanks could but poorly repay her contribution.

Plates

(Plates will be found in a complete section between pp. 128 and 129.)

Figures

1

Polynesia

During the Age of Discovery, the great European nations began to extend their reach into the eastern Pacific in search of new worlds to conquer and new sources of wealth, and discovering in their search the island world of Polynesia. The tales brought back by the mariners and scientists who accompanied these first expeditions set aflame the imagination of a jaded Europe. Here, truly, were marvelous islands, like emeralds on the blue velvet of the sea, inhabited by a noble brown-skinned race of tall, muscular men and well-formed, receptive women. The strange culture of this race, with its colorful ceremonies, weird idols, and seemingly idyllic existence in the midst of apparent plenty, fascinated the Europeans, awakening an interest that has never been extinguished through the years. In our time, the numerous tourist tales and travelogues, not to mention the efforts of the film industry, have created a version of Polynesian culture that bears practically no relation whatsoever to reality. It is this absurd image that has been most often impressed on the mind of the modern tourist who spends his Polynesian sojourn trying to "go native" among the "happy, carefree people" of the islands, only to find that this is the quickest way to self-abasement before the natives, who are no more happy and carefree in actuality than any comparable group in contemporary American society.

The misplaced emphasis and complete distortion which characterize the current view of Polynesia is unfortunate because it entirely obscures many of the more interesting aspects of Polynesian culture. If the casual visitor to Polynesia could but realize, he is being constantly confronted with the living monuments of one of the great epics of the human race, the Polynesian migrations.

The language spoken by the Tahitians in the streets of Papeete, the ancient skull found in a dark rock crevice in some secluded valley of Hawaii, the swift outrigger canoes racing in the lagoon of Aitutaki, and the silent, weed-covered stone platforms of the Marquesas Islands, all speak eloquently of the Polynesian past to those who can hear and understand.

The trained linguist with tape recorder, note pad, and pencil will capture and analyze the sounds, words, and grammar of the Polynesian dialects and can tell much about their position in relation to the other languages of the Pacific and Asia, thus helping us to reconstruct the point of origin, as well as the route of the Polynesian migrations.

The physical anthropologist, calipers in hand, rounding up a group of natives, will measure the dimensions of their bodies, take note of their hair form and eye color and "type" samples of their blood. He will also poke around the burial caves and old temple sites, collecting the often fragmentary skeletal remains of ancient Polynesians for painstaking reconstruction and measurement. The data collected from the living Polynesians together with that obtained from the skeletons of their revered ancestors will indicate their racial affiliations and the course of their racial development, thus contributing greatly to our knowledge of Polynesian prehistory.

The ethnographer will observe the functioning of native social groups, noting such things as their kinship systems, land tenure, and ceremonies and carefully cataloguing the tools and techniques that constitute the native technology. From these data parallels can be drawn to other native groups, and distributions of various tools or customs can be worked out in attempts to reconstruct previous stages of Polynesian culture and show the processes of its evolution.

While these technicians are all hard at their absorbing tasks the archaeologist will begin to clear the brush from what everyone had previously taken for a deserted beach and with his spade and trowel will exhume the remains of ancient houses littered with the tools and debris left by long-departed inhabitants. With these tools the interrelationships of ancient Polynesian island cultures can be most accurately drawn, and another dimension will be added to the complex problem of Polynesian antecedents.

Research similar to that described above has been going on in Polynesia for years, having begun almost simultaneously with the arrival of the Europeans. Previous scientists have placed us in their debt for their great accumulation of knowledge concerning Polynesia, preserved within the libraries and museums of the Western world. The research is by no means at an end, for new techniques are being developed which will allow us to derive more information from our data than ever before. In archaeology, techniques of stratigraphic excavation are making great contributions, as is the well-known radioactive-carbon time clock for dating archaeological remains. The physical anthropologists are turning their attention more and more to human characteristics that are controlled by known genetic mechanisms, such as blood typing. Linguists have recently applied the technique of glottochronology to languages of Polynesia for the first time with encouraging results. New vistas for scientific research are constantly opening to the students of Polynesian anthropology.

In the pages ahead we shall utilize the salient facts derived from the years of research conducted by archaeologists, linguists, ethnologists, and physical anthropologists to reconstruct the prehistory of the Polynesians. In addition to this anthropological data, other areas of scientific research, such as geology, paleontology, zoology, botany, and oceanography, will be tapped for the considerable contributions which they can make to the problems of Polynesian origins.

As in all science, such facts alone are insufficient to any but the most well-informed specialist. Therefore the facts must be ordered in an interpretive framework if they are to have any meaning. The interpretations in this book are mine, whether they agree or disagree with currently accepted thought, and they have been made to the best of my ability. They are, however, conditional on the appearance of new evidence and in no way represent a dogma. At all times I have attempted to restrict myself to those areas of the problem that are of major importance and in so doing avoid the numerous minutiae of small significance to the general reader, despite their interest to the scientific community.

In tracing the movements of the Polynesians we shall not be dealing with the representatives of a mighty civilization, such as those of the valleys of the Nile, Indus, or the Tigris and Euphrates. Unlike the Egyptian, Indian, and Mesopotamian societies of antiquity, the Polynesians have not left their imprint on the mainstream of Western civilization through contributions in arts and science. Nevertheless, the migrations of the Polynesians are among the greatest achievements of the human species, spanning the entire Pacific and four millennia of time. The technical problems that had to be surmounted to make way for such an achievement were of an appalling magnitude, quite comparable to many of the architectural and scientific wonders of the Mediterranean world that are far better known. The Polynesian migrations represent the last great movement of people into the only remaining unpopulated area of the habitable world. The actors in this drama were possessed of amazing maritime ability, born of long acquaintance with the sea. They were inured to the hardships and dangers of voyaging hundreds of miles across open water in mat-sailed wooden canoes held together by pegs and cord, without the benefit of any navigational aids besides the naked eye and their own empirically derived knowledge.

The successes that crowned these voyages are obvious. To them we owe the present-day populations of the islands of Polynesia. Of the failures encountered in the course of the long trek from Asia to Easter Island we will never know; they are hidden forever in the Stygian depths of the Pacific with the remains of thousands of lost canoes and their crews who sailed into the unknown, either by design or by accident, and did not return.

In conclusion, I hope that this book will convey to the reader a feeling for the accomplishments of science in probing the mists of the Polynesian pasts, as well as an appreciation of the methodology and techniques of anthropology. Finally, I will be most grateful if I have been able to impart in some measure the significance of one of the greatest events the sea has ever seen, the coming of the Polynesians.

2

The Sea and the Islands

The island worlds of the Polynesians lie scattered across the mid-eastern Pacific like a galaxy of stars in the depths of a brilliant blue cosmos. In compact groups or in awesome isolation, these little dots in the immense, teeming ocean were each and every one a home for a group of daredevil Polynesian voyagers, microcosmic worlds that contained all the necessities for the support of life as Polynesians knew it. Yet the Polynesians were often not content to remain on the safe beaches of a newly discovered home, but willingly committed themselves to the waves again, pushing farther east, north, and south until all the eastern Pacific islands capable of supporting colonies had been colonized, and even tiny desert islands bore the traces of Polynesian explorers in the form of crude temples, broken tools, and wrecked canoes. Voyaging through the vast reaches of this sunny sea, one can only agree that the Polynesians are more than deserving of the appellation bestowed on them by the late Sir Peter Buck: "Vikings of the Sunrise." Truly these Polynesians, at a much earlier epoch of human history, quite surpassed the seafaring abilities of the hardy Norsemen.

The Polynesian islands lie in a broad triangular area in the middle and eastern Pacific, extending from Hawaii, north of the equator, to New Zealand on the southwest corner and Easter Island on the southeast. Within this triangle three major divisions are made, based on cultural and geographical criteria. The islands of Samoa and the Tongan group are known as "Western Polynesia," and those of

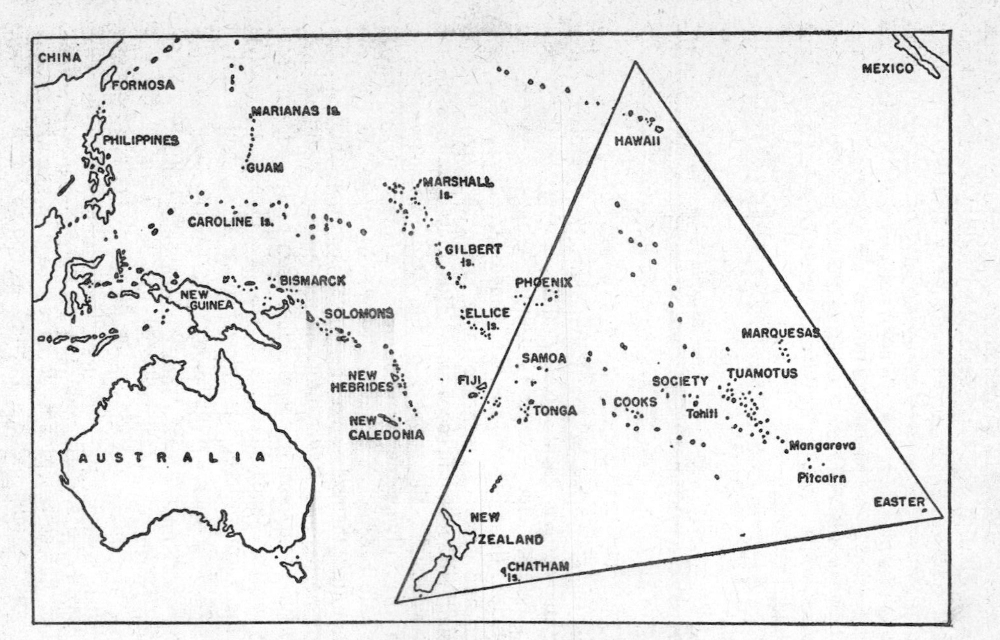

Fig. 1. Map of Oceania showing Polynesian triangle

the Society Islands, Hawaii, Cook Islands, and the Australs are known as "Central Polynesia." The third division, "Marginal Polynesia," comprises the Marquesas, Easter Island, Pitcairn, and New Zealand. A fourth division is sometimes referred to. It is made up of a scattering of small islands outside the western periphery of the Polynesian triangle and called the "Polynesian Outliers." These are small islands in Melanesia or on the Micronesian fringe settled (or invaded) by wandering Polynesian groups, examples of which are Ontong Java, Rennell Island, Tikopia, and Kapingamarangi.

The Polynesian triangle is located between the large continental-shelf areas of Indonesia and Papuasia on the west and the abyssal 2,000-fathom eastern Pacific. To the northwest are the islands of Micronesia, and to the south increasingly colder, stormier waters gradually merge into the bleakness of the Antarctic Sea.

The ocean currents and winds that sweep through the Polynesian triangle render the navigation feats of the Polynesians more astounding, as they run mainly from east to west, contrary to the direction of Polynesian migrations. In the Southern Hemisphere a cold current sweeps up from the Arctic Ocean along the west coast of South America, bringing with it giant rays and hordes of squid and whale. This is the famed Humboldt Current, renowned to game fishermen and marine biologists throughout the world for the variety and number of the marine creatures that it bears with it. The coolness of this current has lowered the temperature of the coastal winds of Peru and Chile to such an extent that the entire coast is an arid desert, extending into southern Ecuador. At about this point, the Humboldt veers westward, striking out across the Pacific south of the equator, cutting through the apex of the Polynesian triangle and bringing some of its marine fauna into the marginal regions of Polynesia. North of the equator, the Japan Current, bringing warm, moist air, has traversed the coastal regions of the Canadian northwest and continues south along the California coast to Mexico, at which time it also turns westward following a path northward of the equator. We thus have currents running toward the equator along the coasts of North and South America, and crossing the Pacific in a broad band on either side of the equator. In the equatorial regions, however, the equatorial countercurrent moves from west to east at an appreciable rate in a band of seasonally varying width.

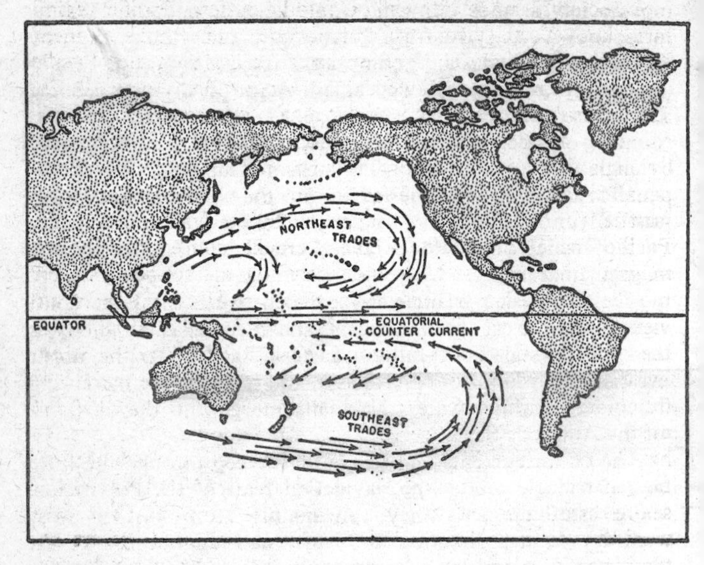

Fig. 2. Prevailing currents of the Pacific

The winds of the Polynesian triangle are those well known as the southeast "trade winds" that the European mariners used to pick up after their arduous fight around the Cape of Good Hope to convoy them safely into the depths of the Pacific, whether for whales, teak, chinaware, or souls. These winds blow much of the year, reversing themselves annually, however, for a period of several weeks, during which the northwestern winds blow quite strongly.

The geological history of the Polynesian islands is for the most part a relatively short one, speaking as the geologists do in multiples of millions of years.[1]

The two great New Zealand islands are oldest, with a past stretching well back into the age of reptiles, perhaps 100 million years ago. Most of the other islands of Polynesia either date back to the early Pleistocene, Pliocene, or Miocene at most. The majority of the islands are volcanic; formed by outwellings of lava from submarine vents and fissures produced by warping upheaval and depression of segments of the basaltic crust beneath the ocean floor in the never-ending sequence of tectonic movements going on throughout the earth. Apparently there was a marked increase in such movements in what is now the middle-eastern Pacific region in the late Tertiary or early Pleistocene, and a huge segment of the ocean floor along the eastern margin of the Pacific sank, forming the dark depths known as the Pacific Basin. This subsidence produced contingent movements in the surrounding areas as the earth's crust attempted to compensate by expansion, compression, torsion, or warping. The compensatory fluctuations resulted in systems of cracks appearing gradually in the basalt crust in the ocean floor west of the Pacific Basin, and through these cracks poured the molten magma from the earth's center, forming the foundations for most of the islands of Polynesia. Many more islands than are visible today died stillborn in that remote period long before the onset of the great ice age. These islands are now becoming known through their profiles on the fathometer graphs of the oceanography ships that have plowed trails across the area in recent years. Many of these drowned islands may have been exposed in the past when the tremendous absorption of sea water into the glaciers of the ice age lowered the sea level round the world by 200 feet or more, but they were subsequently inundated by the glacial melt waters returning the ocean to its original level. Other submarine mountains simply never attained the size necessary to rise more than a short distance above the sea bottom, or having risen, succumbed to the incessant pounding of the sea and disappeared again.

By geological criteria three main types of island may be distinguished in the Polynesian triangle. Each of these types is characterized by a different environment in terms of flora and fauna, and as we shall see later, the differing environments played a causative role in producing some of the cultural diversity among Polynesian cultures.

The first main type that we will discuss is the "high island." Islands of this type are composed generally of basalt in the main, although occasionally a few sedimentary rocks of various types occur. They are elevated to impressive heights above sea level, the best example coming to mind is the towering Mauna Loa on Hawaii, poking its head 13,000 feet through clouds and visible 100 miles away at sea. This, however, is extreme, for most of the other high islands rarely reach more than 6,000 feet. Soil is usually thick and rich and water is abundant. These islands have a relatively rich flora, usually divided into a series of successive zones of altitude. Thus there will be grass and vines of various types and palms on the beach. Up farther in the valleys these will disappear, and hardwood such as casuarina will be found. On the plateaus forming the island roof, tree ferns, low ground ferns, and wind-gnarled shrubs festooned with xerophytic plants will appear. An equally rich group of insects accompanies the floral population. Most high islands are surrounded by reefs which provide havens for numerous varieties of edible fish and also handy shallows and vantage points for the fishermen who seek them. Some high islands, such as Easter Island or the Marquesan group, lack reefs completely, owing to the temperature of the ocean and the bottom conditions.

Low islands are the coral atolls represented in Hollywood versions of Polynesia as idyllic paradises, and they are beautiful to behold—although one's impression from the sea often changes abruptly on landing, when clouds of flies or mosquitoes may appear. Many atolls are quite as large as the high islands in area, but are often no more than ten feet above sea level. The great naturalist Darwin believed that such atolls were formed by the outward, upward growth of a coral reef around a gradually subsiding volcanic island. Total subsidence resulted in submergence of the entire volcanic core around which the reef had formed; but as the core sank, the reef continued to build up, keeping its elevation and finally remaining as the only thing above water long after the central volcanic island foundation had disappeared, its place being filled by the lagoon of the atoll. Alternative theories have been proposed, many of which have validity in some cases, but it appears that Darwin was basically right. Borings taken on Pacific atolls since World War II have proven the existence of basaltic foundations deep beneath the lagoon.[2]

Newell, an authority on the biology of coral reefs, has said of their marine life: "The biological exuberance of a flourishing coral reef with its innumerable ecologic niches and many hundreds of species is at least suggestive of the tropical rain forest ashore." Besides the coral polyps, billions of organisms—one-celled animals and marine algae, sea slugs, spiny urchins, and a great variety of fish—are integrated into a functioning interacting community within the structure of a coral atoll. Although the marine life is abundant, varied, and brilliant, the terrestrial flora and fauna are far from that, being quite impoverished. Part of this is due to a lack of water, rain water providing the best and often the only source. Plants capable of surviving on the desiccated coral sand and shingle are few, and it is only with difficulty that the Polynesians managed to cultivate the plants needed for their existence. Even then, famines in these atolls were a continual threat. Add to the danger of famine the far more terrible menace of tidal waves, capable of sweeping over these low islands as though they were non-existent, and the idyl of atoll dwelling loses some of its sheen. Examples of islands of the atoll type are those of the Tuamotu group in French Polynesia. More famous, but outside the Polynesian triangle, are the Micronesian atolls of Bikini, Eniwetok, and Tarawa, identical with their Polynesian mates to the east.

The third common island type is that known by a Polynesian name, *Makatea.* Makatea is actually an uplifted coral atoll on the northern fringes of the Tuamotu group, but its name has been bestowed as a type designation on all uplifted coral islands of the Pacific. These islands are characterized often by a steep, occasionally undercut shore, while the surface of the island is extremely rugged owing to pits and differential erosion of the coral rock. On older islands the pits may have filled in with soil that accumulated as a result of decaying vegetation, or, as on *the* Makatea, may have been filled with guano. The vegetation of such islands is generally more abundant than that of the coral atolls and grows in great profusion.

The mention of the island types and their flora and fauna naturally raises several questions. How did the vegetation and insects originally get to these isolated islands? Where did they originate? The establishment of life on the volcanic islands may have begun soon after they rose above the surface of the sea, even before they were completely cool. An example of how quickly life can establish itself on a fresh volcanic cone was given by the 1883 explosion of the island group of Krakatoa. The blasts were heard 3,000 miles away and an estimated 18 cubic miles of dust and debris were hurled to an altitude of 17 miles, ultimately circling the earth. Over 1,000 villages and 36,000 people were wiped out by the tidal waves following on this catastrophe, and not a living thing remained on the small fragments of the original island group still above water. *Within two weeks, however, insects as well as plants had been naturally reintroduced,* some by wind, others arriving on jetsam or in the feathers of birds that began to frequent the still smoldering heaps of volcanic debris.[3]

The rapidity with which the inhospitable new volcanic cone was reseeded was probably matched by the coral atolls and *makatea* islands. As soon as they rose high enough above sea level to present a dry surface, they were hosts to a rain of spores, seed-carrying birds, and floating debris that soon brought about marked changes in the landscape. The spores of ferns, orchids, and related plants are microscopic and are carried to substantial altitudes by winds. Many descend into the sea and destruction but others fall onto island soil and grow. The common beach plants of Polynesia have seeds and fruits that can float for long periods of time, retaining their viability. These have been disseminated by drift. Other plants bear fruits that are eaten by birds, after which the seeds, carried in the birds' intestinal tracts, are deposited later at other locales. Further, many plants bear seeds in pods having hooks or a coating of a sticky substance that will attach itself to the feathers of a bird and thus be carried long distances. Many insects are disseminated in the same ways as plants.

Fish and shellfish are free to swim where they may within the limits of depth, water temperature, salinity, and other environmental factors imposed on them by nature. The shellfish and shore fauna of Polynesia also have spread by drifting, many of the animals in question going through free swimming stages at some time during their development. Some Polynesian forms have managed to drift as far east as Clipperton Island, off the coast of Mexico.

In the ways so briefly outlined above, the islands of Polynesia received their first "settlers" long before the foot of man ever printed the tide lines of their beaches. New Zealand, of course, received many floral and insect migrants in this fashion, but the main body of its flora and fauna is apparently derived from the larger land mass to which it was once connected. The large ostrichlike moa birds and the atavistic *tuatara* lizard (a hangover from the age of reptiles 100 million years ago) are only part of this continental heritage. The rich virgin forests of New Zealand bear more abundant witness to the past connections of the now isolated islands.

The sources of the earliest plants and animals of Polynesia, including the fish and shellfish, are unanimously to the west, on the old continental areas of Sundaland and Papualand, now engulfed by the rising sea in postglacial time.[4] The unsubmerged portions of these two continental areas are the archipelagoes of Indonesia and Malaya on the one hand and Australia and the New Guinea–Papua area on the other. These areas contributed the flora and fauna of Polynesia, despite the fact that the dissemination by natural means took place against both wind and ocean currents. Although the coast of America is as close to Polynesia as the Sunda–Papualand area, practically no plants or animals of New World origin arrived in Polynesia. Those that did are minor and inconsequential, many of them possibly having arrived with the Europeans when they discovered Polynesia. The paucity of New World migrants in Polynesia is probably due to the same factor that halted the flow of Old World marine life moving from west to east. This was the deep Pacific Basin, a chasm whose width made passage of even the toughest seeds or planktonic creatures impossible, as it required more time to span the abyss than these life forms could afford.

The most important aspect of the Polynesian environment, however, is that comprising the plants and animals introduced by the Polynesians in their exploration. Among these plants are the breadfruit, coconut, taro (both wild and domestic), yam, sweet potato, sugar cane, pandanus, and the *terminalia,* as well as a number of less important fruits. The domesticated animals of the Polynesians were only three in number, the pig, dog, and jungle fowl. Inadvertently the rat and some species of lizards may have been carried, but they were not truly domestic animals. We know from ancient Polynesian legends, backed by the hard-won evidence of archaeology, that the Polynesians brought their animals and food plants, or cultigens, along with them on their canoe voyages so that should an island be discovered, the discovering party would have all the necessities for establishing the sound economic basis of the new colony. In the study of the Polynesian food plants and domestic animals we obviously have many a clue to the origin of the Polynesian people, a fact that has not escaped unnoticed. Unfortunately, the literature on the botanical problems has been especially clouded by a host of weird and ill-based theories often displaying the lack of the authors' breadth more than their erudition. Botanists apparently have a weakness for "land bridges"—hypothetical sunken bodies of land once connecting now isolated islands—as these have featured prominently in theories of the origin and dispersal of Polynesian plants, with the result that if all the proposed land bridges were traced on one map, Polynesia would look like a map of the track system at Grand Central Station in New York. Other botanists have proposed transoceanic migrations in 3000 B.C. (skipping all intermediate islands). Still others have insisted that all Polynesian plants have originated in the New World, invoking drift, and more recently, Peruvian Indians as the transportation means.

The problem of Polynesian plant origins, although still possessed of minor uncertainties, was considerably cleared up in an extremely important study done by the well-known Pacific botanist E. D. Merrill. Merrill had spent a lifetime in the study of Pacific flora and had often assailed with vigor the irrational "theories" of many of his colleagues. He devoted the last years of his life to a study of the botanical collections made by the scientific staff of the expeditions of Captain Cook, whom we shall often mention in the course of this book, as they made many "firsts" in the name of science throughout those remarkable voyages of discovery. Sir Joseph Banks, Solander, and the Forsters, botanists aboard the *Endeavour* on her first and second voyages, had made outstanding plant collections in Tahiti and on most of the other islands that they visited. Tahiti had been little touched by European intruders before that time and therefore these collections are of the greatest value. They give us an excellent view of the native flora of Polynesia before the introduction of European or American plants by the whites.

Although the attention of the *Endeavour* scientists was naturally directed to the food plants of the Polynesians, they collected everything available, including the lowly weeds, which are also of anthropologic importance since they are often accidental human introductions, brought in with other cultivated plants, and hence are often good indicators of contacts with outside cultures.

Merrill was able to make a detailed study of the *Endeavour* botanical collections, still preserved in Great Britain since 1767, when they were collected. He examined the scientists' notes and journals as well and finally published his verdict: "The botanical evidence clearly indicates that, as of 1769, all the cultigens in the Pacific Islands, with possibly one exception, and all the more numerous weed species, with possibly two or three exceptions, were brought in purposely or inadvertently from the *west* by the early people who occupied the Polynesian triangle." [5]

(Italics are mine.) The work of Cook's brilliant scientists is thus still proving its value after almost two centuries! The exceptions mentioned by Merrill are interesting, especially in the case of the cultigen that is the sweet potato (*Ipomoea batatas*), claimed recently to be of American origin by Thor Heyerdahl in his *Kon-Tiki* "theory." The basis for this claim is that one of the names for the sweet potato in Quechuan (a Peruvian Indian language from the Andean region) is *kumar,* while the Polynesian sweet potato is called *umara* (Tahiti), *kuma'a* (Marquesas), *kumala* (Fiji), *umala* (Samoa), etc. Heyerdahl takes this as proof that potatoes originated in the home of the Peruvian Indians and were carried by them to Polynesia. This is similar to maintaining that Coca-Cola originated in Arabia because Arabians now use the word; obviously one can read the argument in the opposite direction quite easily. The word *kumara,* and related forms, is found in all Polynesian languages, therefore indicating that it was part of their language before the Polynesians dispersed so widely. It is found in only one language in Peru, however, which indicates that it is probably an introduction there. Merrill's opinion on the sweet potato is that it is probably of African origin. Studies of cell structure and genetics, as well as sweet-potato insect parasites, indicate Africa or South Asia as its probable source.[6] Skottsberg, a well-known Scandinavian botanist who worked extensively on Easter Island, supports Merrill's opinion, pointing out that no wild possible progenitors of the sweet potato are found in South America and that the Quechuan word in common usage for the sweet potato is not *kumar* but *apichu,* while *kumar* may be European-introduced.[7]

Merrill believes the American weeds in Polynesia to be the result of contact with some of the Europeans who sailed the Pacific previous to Cook's voyages and introduced these weeds in the course of their visits to various islands.[8]

There can be no scientific doubt, therefore, of the origins of the Polynesian food plants. The breadfruit, pandanus, yam, and sugar cane are all of Southeast Asian origin. The coconut is likewise, but seems to have been carried by ocean currents or Polynesians to the coast of Central America, where the early Spaniards found a few on the beaches. The taro probably originated in upland southern Asia or India.[9] The sweet potato as we have seen is probably of African origin.

What of the animals that the Polynesians carried with

them? The most important of these was the pig, *Sus Cristadus,* a native of Asia, well represented in extremely ancient archaeological remains in China.[10] Accompanying the pig was the dog, about whom little is known scientifically in the way of species differences. We do know that the dog originated in the Old World and was only brought to the New World from Asia by the ancestors of the American Indians. In addition to the pig and dog, a more proud and stately but less economically important passenger on the Polynesian voyages was the strikingly beautiful jungle cock (*Gallus gallus*), with his drab mate, of course, also a native of Asia.[11] The beautiful gun-metal and gold plumage of this bird was utilized for feather headdresses and ornaments, hence his inclusion in the Polynesian economy. With these purposely transported animals traveled some others of a far less desirable nature, in the capacity of stowaways. These were the ubiquitous rat (*Rattus concolor*) and species and genera of the lizards known as geckos and skinks. *Rattus concolor* is distributed at present from Asia to the Marquesas, and therefore is an Oceanian form. Wild forms of this species occur in the Philippines and Indonesia.[12] The Polynesian skinks and geckos are more closely related to Asian forms than to those in the New World, indicating an Asian origin for them also.

We have covered a span of 100 million years of natural history in a very short chapter, and a summary is definitely indicated after such a trip. We have seen that the islands of Polynesia, excepting New Zealand, are relatively recent arrivals on the geological scene. Long before the arrival of man, these islands were supporting a flora and fauna of Indo-Malayan origin, transmitted by natural means across the Pacific from west to east. The Polynesian discoverers of the islands brought with them more plants and weeds of Indo-Malayan or mainland Asian origin, as well as Asian domesticated and human symbiotic animals.

To conclude, if one were to formulate a hypothesis of the origin of the Polynesian people on the evidence of botany and zoology alone, one could not, without great intellectual dishonesty, escape the conclusion that the Polynesians originated somewhere on the coast of Asia or the adjoining islands.

3

The Men

The Polynesian race was first known to the Western world through the medium of sailors' journals, in which one must always allow for the highly understandable human factors affecting the writers, who had been subjected to incredible hardships in their voyages to the South Seas. Their descriptions dwelt mostly on the beauty of the Polynesian female, and today we are heritors of this emphasis (transmitted through such well-known sources as Melville and O'Bryan), in the Hollywood version of the Polynesian beauty in well-fitted "uplifts."

Science presents a different picture of the Polynesians, however. For an objective view of the living race we must go to the large amount of anthropometrical and serological data available. Analysis of this information, when taken together with archaeological data from the Asian coast and from within Polynesia, can allow us to draw some very reliable conclusions concerning the origin of the Polynesian race.

As a beginning, one may set forth the characteristics of the Polynesians as they exist today. A few qualifying remarks are necessary as a preface to our discussion of racial characteristics to indicate the difficulties under which such studies are made in Polynesia.

First, in all of Polynesia, but more especially in the eastern islands, Polynesians have been mating with non-Polynesian visitors since the first white men appeared in the sixteenth century. The results of such racial crosses are obviously of no value for determining the characteristics of the original Polynesians, but how does one identify them? In Polynesian society sexual customs were and still are extremely permissive, and contacts are frequently of an orgiastic nature. Sexual hospitality was common, as were institutionalized secondary mates. Determining parenthood under these conditions is difficult. Genealogies might be of assistance, but they only express *sociological* parenthood and not *biological* or actual physical parenthood, which, given the sexual customs of society, might be quite different. In addition to their unreliability, the genealogies are hard to come by in most of Polynesia today, since cultures are breaking down or have already collapsed, and genealogies, once the pride of every individual, and the basis of property, ceremonial rights, and obligations, have become a useless cultural appendage, already disappearing in a large area of Eastern Polynesia.

In selecting individuals of pure ancestry one also has to cope with very human factors, such as pride and prevarication. Often a native will claim pure ancestry simply because he is ashamed to admit to his beachcombing American grandfather, or because he enjoys kidding the white man along. Why does the white man want to pry into a man's ancestry, anyway?

It is obvious that Polynesians of pure ancestry must be selected with remarkable care for the sample to yield reliable results. Despite the seemingly insurmountable difficulties such studies have been carried out, mostly under the auspices of the Bernice P. Bishop Museum of Honolulu, by H. L. Shapiro and Louis Sullivan, the leading students of Polynesian physical anthropology.

They provide a firm body of carefully gathered data from which we may define a Polynesian racial type and its main subdivisions, and formulate some hypotheses concerning the origin of the Polynesian race.

(There is no "pure" Polynesian race, in the true sense of the word, just as there is no pure race of any type. A race is actually only a statistical scientific abstraction of a number of hereditary characteristics possessed by a group, distinguishing it from other groups. These characteristics should be nonadaptive, that is, they should not have any value, whether positive or negative, for individual survival. All members of all races differ from one another, and all races, hence, contain quite a wide range of variation.)

As a whole, the Polynesians are characterized by a height that places them among the tallest peoples in the world.[1] They are broad and muscular in structure, with a tendency to corpulence. Their skin color is yellow-brown, and their wavy hair is black with a rare reddish tinge. The cephalic indices range from dolichocephalic (long, narrow head) to brachycephalic (shorter, broader head), with the majority of living inhabitants falling into the latter group. Their faces usually are wide, with projecting cheekbones covered with some fatty padding. The nose is long, broad, and high, with a straight profile and a depression at the root. The nasal wings are full but do not flare markedly. The eyes are deep-set with heavy lids that sometimes have a slight internal epicanthic or Mongoloid fold. Eye color is medium to dark brown. The lips are full but not Negroid, and body hair is sparse but more marked than in the Mongoloid or Negroid primary races.

Recently a rising interest in serology has been evident in circles of physical anthropology because the various blood types (A,B,O, M,N, Rh, etc.) can be precisely identified in the individual and also have been found to occur in significantly different proportions in different races. More important, we know the genetic mechanism whereby these characteristics are inherited. They are not controlled by a complex group of genes as are such traits as cephalic index, height, and so on, but are the manifestations of single factors on the human chromosomal threads. They are therefore believed in many circles to hold more promise for the identification of racial groups and for racial-history studies than the old revered body measurements of classical physical anthropology.

Serological work in Polynesia reveals that the Polynesians are characterized by high percentages of types O and A.[2] Types B and AB are present in Western Polynesia in a sizable amount, but are found only in small amounts in Eastern Polynesia, and their presence there is seldom free from the suspicion of miscegenation. The M factor is generally high in Polynesia, as is the R^2 gene of Rh types. A newly discovered factor in blood chemistry, the "Diego" antigen, is completely lacking among the Polynesians, as well as the Australian aborigines and the natives of Papua. It is found in amounts varying between 2 and 50 per cent in South American Indians and pure Mongoloids. More than any other factor, it is the blood-type distributions of Polynesia that have served as a foundation for the widely publicized popular theory of Polynesian origins, proposed recently by Thor Heyerdahl.[3] According to this "theory," the fact that the Eastern-Central Polynesians and the South American Indians both have high percentages of type O, low percentages of type A, with the absence of types B and AB, indicates that the Polynesians and Peruvian Indians are originally of the same stock. On the face of the matter, the similarity between the two groups is surprising, but one must look deeper into the literature of serology to evaluate the significance of this similarity. Upon even a brief survey of the available data it is obvious that Heyerdahl is grasping at straws to bolster his theory—as the great Harvard anthropologist Hooton [4] pointed out so clearly, peoples of the most physically diverse and unrelated races have similar blood types. The Eskimos of Labrador have blood-group frequencies practically identical with the aborigines of Australia. Pygmies of the Ituri, Russians, and Iranians also have similar frequencies and so on, ad infinitum. Any ex-service man need only look at his dog tags to see how fallacious are arguments based on similarities of blood-type frequencies for postulating migrations. My own type is O. Am I therefore Polynesian or Peruvian Indian? Could my Anglo-Saxon ancestors voice their opinions on my racial heritage, their ideas might be couched in terms somewhat less scientific but far more to the point.

The distribution of various types of diseases in Polynesia is quite interesting and reveals other characteristics of the Polynesian race for which there is little or no explanation, but which nevertheless separate it from other racial groups in the adjacent areas of Oceania and the New World.

A striking feature of disease distribution in Polynesia is the complete absence of malaria, which is found in Melanesia to the west in endemic proportions and also in the New World in Mexico and Central and South America in the forest regions. The anopheles mosquito, vector of the malaria parasite, is present in large numbers on all Polynesian islands, but the malarial parasites are just not there.

One of the most dreaded scourges of the islands of Oceania is the filaria parasite, which produces the cruelly disfiguring elephantiasis. Like malaria, the filaria parasite is introduced into the blood stream by mosquitoes (of the *Culex* or *Aëdes* genus) and goes through a life cycle in the human carrier, settling finally around the lymph nodes in the elbows, knees, or genitalia, completely blocking the small lymph ducts, which ultimately calcify. The resulting swelling in the affected area is likely to produce limbs that look like those of an elephant, heavy and stumplike, with thick sausage fingers and toes sprouting from hands and feet that are almost hidden by the swelling of the adjacent limb and the folds of barklike, discolored skin that covers them. In the case of unfortunate males who have been infected in the genital area, the scrotum may ultimately reach the ground when the victim is in a standing position and it may be necessary to arrange some sort of sling or other carrying measure to permit locomotion. This disease is found in Polynesia, Melanesia, and Papua and was known to the natives since precontact times, as legendary records and ethnological evidence indicate. It is not found prehistorically in the New World tropical areas, however, despite the fact that the insect vectors are present in swarms. Whites are apparently especially prone to this disease and many colonials have contracted it in French Polynesia, where it remained unchecked until about 1950.

Leprosy is another disease that apparently was found among the Polynesians upon arrival in their present habitat, and is spread throughout Melanesia, Papua, Micronesia, the Philippines, and Southeast Asia. It was not present among American Indians before Columbus, however, and appears to have been introduced into the New World across the Atlantic by the early voyagers from Europe, where it was a recent arrival from the East.

Venereal disease was unknown among the Polynesians before the arrival of the Europeans, who acted as the intermediaries in transmitting this *strictly American Indian disease* to all parts of the civilized and noncivilized world within a short time. Researches by Dr. Robert Proper, of Albuquerque, on Indian skeletons from various areas of North America, Mexico, the Caribbean, and the Pacific coast of South America indicate that venereal diseases were endemic in the prehistoric Indian population. Skeletal specimens provide the most conclusive proof in the form of the bubbly areas of bone where syphilitic lesions have left their mark. More graphic proof is found in the artistic works of the Peruvians and Mexicans, especially in the ceramic arts, where the syphilitic's saddle-bridge nose and venereal lesions are depicted often quite clearly. Had any contact occurred between the American Indians and the Polynesians, there would have been a subsequent introduction of this disease into Eastern Polynesia, and it would perhaps have preceded the Europeans by many centuries. As it happened, however, the venereal diseases were introduced by Europeans after the conquest of the New World, for we read in the earliest historic sources that no such diseases were present in Polynesia at its discovery. Once introduced, the diseases made very rapid progress and contributed greatly to the depopulation that occurred in most island groups of Polynesia in the mid-nineteenth century, and the effects of these diseases are still quite evident. In the Marquesas islands in 1957–58, collecting female reproductive histories from the women, we found numerous cases where complete barrenness was traceable to an early venereal infection at age fourteen to sixteen, and there is no reason to suppose that the Marquesans are atypical in this respect. The remedies which the natives themselves devised for the venereal diseases were successful in a few instances. In other cases, however, they only proved to be efficacious in banishing some of the more displeasing symptoms while the disease continued to rage internally.

At present, the discontinuous distribution of the various types of venereal diseases in Polynesia is rather interesting, suggesting that either genetic survival factors, historical factors, or a combination of both have played a part in dissemination of the maladies. In Eastern Polynesia, tropical chancre and gonorrhea are common with occasional cases of syphilis. In Western Polynesia, yaws is prevalent, with cases of gonorrhea and tropical chancre being more rare.

Now that we have an acquaintance with the Polynesian race as it is today, we may enter into the more knotty problems of its origin and the source of its variation.

The Polynesian race is a perfectly modern group of Homo sapiens. There are no traces of any earlier, more primitive inhabitants anywhere in the islands of the Polynesian triangle. Indeed, as we have seen, these islands are so isolated that they would have been impossible for Paleolithic men, such as Pithecanthropus or Solo man, to attain with their low level of material culture. Perhaps more important is the fact that during the ice age many of the islands were still forming and were uninhabitable. It was only much later in human history, when boats and navigation techniques had developed on the mainland of Asia, that these islands were brought within the reach of man. By then, such human fossil forms as the Java man, Peking man, and the relatively more recent Solo man had long departed from the face of Asia, and were replaced by groups of men substantially the same as modern types.

To get the proper perspective on Polynesian racial history, we must go back to the late Pleistocene, when the glaciers were withdrawing and the upper Paleolithic cultures of Eurasia were well past their peaks. At this time, much of the Asian mainland was occupied by a Paleo-Caucasoid people, similar to the Ainu of Japan. Southern Asia was occupied by Negroid and Australoid groups. It must be remembered that in this epoch the islands of Indonesia were still not completely separate from the mainland, although the rising sea level, caused by the glacial melt, was already beginning to encroach on the land. The populations of what is today mainland Asia on the one hand and Indonesia on the other were still able to maintain contact without sea voyages, and the Australian continent was peopled during this final glacial epoch by groups traveling on foot. In North Asia, the Mongoloid race, as we know it today, was developing its distinctive characteristics as a result of environmental pressure during the final glaciation.[5]

The Polynesian race is a result of the intermingling on the Asian mainland of elements of three main races, the Caucasoid, the Negroid, and the Mongoloid, in the coastal area of South China in the period after the end of the last glaciation.

The main contribution to this racial admixture was probably from the Amurian or Paleo-Caucasoid group, traces of which have now been completely obliterated except in the archaeological record and as personified in the few remaining Ainu.[6] Hooton has stated that the white component in the Polynesian mixture is much stronger than either the Negro or Mongoloid, based on comparisons made with crosses of Negro and white and Mongoloid and white individuals. Persistent Negroid features that ordinarily are characteristic of Negro-white crosses are not common among Polynesians, nor are the Mongoloid features commonly found to persist in offspring of Mongoloid-white unions. Crosses of Polynesians with Caucasoids are much more Caucasoid, however, than would be ordinarily expected if the Polynesian race did not already contain a large Caucasoid element.[7]

The Negro element in the racial background of the Polynesians was probably contributed by the Oceanic Negro race, which is different in many respects from the African Negro. Oceanic Negroes, in contrast to their African genetic relatives, have hair that ranges from black to brown or reddish and may be wavy or curly. The lips of the Oceanic group are only moderately thick, and body hair is much more pronounced than in the African Negro. The nose form of the Oceanic Negro varies, but the flat, thick-tipped African Negro nose is scarcely ever found. The Oceanic Negroes were present on the mainland of Western Asia in very early times and may themselves have evolved from a mixture of dwarf Negrito population with some Caucasoid and Australoid groups.[8] The marginal distribution of the pygmy Negrito in the Asian-Oceanian area indicates that they are perhaps one of the earliest races of Neoanthropic man to appear in the area.

In early postglacial times some of these Negrito groups seem to have penetrated as far east as Australia, where their presence at least 12,000 years ago is recorded by radiocarbon dating. Other Oceanian Negro groups probably moved into their present homes in Melanesia and Papua simultaneously, aided by land bridges still not inundated by the postglacial rise in sea level. Still other Negro groups pushed up into what is now the Indochina, South China coast area where they met and mingled with groups of the Paleo-Caucasoids. The presence of a dark-skinned population in this area is recorded at an early date in Chinese historical documents, which also show that remnants of this dark-skinned group, who were incidentally excellent seafarers, remained on the south coast until as late as T'ang dynasty times (c. A.D. 700). Archaeological evidence from Indochina [9] indicates that the earliest known Neolithic populations of that area were dolichocephalic, short groups referred to by the Chinese archaeologists as "Paleo-Melanesian."

As Shapiro remarked as early as 1940,[10] it is no longer possible to draw a clear-cut line between Polynesian and Melanesian since many Melanesian groups, such as the Fijians, have been infiltrated by Polynesian elements. The presence of Polynesian elements within a Melanesian population may also be the result of an early common heritage, submerged in the course of independent evolution over several millennia. Although there is no reason whatsoever for language, physical type, and culture to go together, we know now that all Polynesian languages make up a subgroup of a larger linguistic family of which Melanesian languages are principal members, within the larger category of the Malayo-Polynesian language family. Certain cultural similarities in the early culture of the Polynesian Marquesans in the second century B.C. indicate a possible convergence of some aspects of Polynesian and Melanesian culture as one goes back in time. We may also look for a convergence in physical type once skeletal material from Melanesian archaeological sites becomes more available.

The Mongoloid component of the Polynesian is as weak as the Negroid relative to the overwhelming Caucasoid contribution. Evidence has accumulated [11] to show that the Mongoloid race is a rather new participant in the pageant of human development and that it evolved after the last glaciation in Siberia or East Central Asia and spread north and south from there. By the second millennium B.C. the inhabitants of Honan and Kansu were "essentially oriental in character," according to Davidson Black,[12] who studied the archaeological skeletal collections from that area. From then on, the Mongoloid race spread southward into the area where the Negro and Paleo-Caucasoid population was probably already present and subsequently introduced a number of Mongoloid characteristics into this group. This movement, like most primitive "migrations," should not be thought of as either a single movement of a large body of people or a number of successive migration waves, but as a long-term process involving much individual infiltration of each group by the other as well as migrations of larger groups.

The mixture of Caucasoid, Mongoloid, and Negroid elements was welded into a stable genetic unit on the mainland of Asia, according to H. L. Shapiro.[13] In the past, others have theorized that the Polynesian race was a result of either successive migrations into the Polynesian triangle by discrete racial groups, or the migration of a Caucasoid group through Indonesia and Melanesia, picking up genetic characteristics of the Mongoloid and Negroid groups en route.

Shapiro's thesis, however, seems far more in accord with what we know of the mechanics of racial differentiation and the cultural factors involved and will probably be largely borne out by further work.

Archaeological evidence from within Polynesia itself that sheds light on the earlier stages of the Polynesian race is not present in the quantity that we should like. Native sentiments have naturally militated against any extensive collecting of human skeletal material from their burial caves and temples of the pagan past, and excavation has usually been impossible. Collections have been made, but they were largely obtained by rather dubious means without location and association data, thus making it impossible to date the collections in any way at all, or often, even to know where they were made.

Recently, however, modern archaeological field work in New Zealand, Hawaii, and the Marquesas has provided us with a large corpus of skeletal material precisely dated by archaeological associations going back to the earliest settlements of each of those island groups. The Marquesan collection contains a large number of burials from the oldest known archaeological site in Polynesia, Site NHaal on Nuku Hiva, where Polynesians were living in the second century B.C. Together with the New Zealand Moa-Hunter burials from the Wairau Site and the Hawaiian collections from such sites as South Point, these burials put our knowledge of early Polynesian physical anthropology on a much firmer footing and shed much light on previous theories. For example, based on anthropometrical studies of living Polynesians, it was postulated that the earliest population in Polynesia was a dolichocephalic group,[14] since dolichocephaly is found in all the living marginal groups of Polynesia today (Easter Island, Marquesas, New Zealand, Hawaii) and is far more prevalent there than in Central or Western Polynesia, where the populations are markedly brachycephalic. A few dolichocephalic skulls recovered from burial caves in Central Polynesia tended to support this hypothesis, indicating the presence of longheadedness in the earlier population.

Now, with the evidence on hand in the form of burials in indisputable archaeological contexts, we can affirm this and state definitely that the early Polynesians were longheaded when they arrived in Eastern Polynesia and that the inhabitants of Western and Central Polynesia were also longheaded, in the case of the latter area, at least as late as A.D. 1000. The present predominance of shortheadedness in Central and Western Polynesia was seen in the past as the result of successive migrations of the same Polynesian population from the coast of Asia. According to this view, these migrations penetrated the central area but did not reach the margins. It now seems wiser to discard this theory of successive migrations to account for the complementary distribution of the traits of dolichocephaly and brachycephaly in Polynesia and attribute the present differences to the processes of population differentiation proceeding at varying rates.

To summarize the picture up to this point, we have seen that the Polynesians probably developed on the southeast Asian coast from a melange consisting of a preponderant Caucasoid element with some Negroid and Mongoloid influence. At some time after the genetic characteristics of the group had been stabilized by inbreeding, the Polynesians began to filter out into the Pacific, gradually pushing farther and farther until they arrived in the area where they presently are found. The groups which first arrived in the Polynesian triangle were dolichocephalic, much like those who had once inhabited the coast of China.

There is certainly no need to suppose that the first Polynesians were a physically perfect homogeneous group in every respect, for human groups all display a range of variation in all characteristics, quantitative or qualitative. The range of variation displayed by island populations of Polynesia vis-à-vis each other today, however, is probably much greater than that displayed by the original population. Some of this variation has already been mentioned: i.e., the B blood type's being absent or present in negligible quantity in Eastern Polynesia, while it is present in very sizable amounts in Western Polynesia; the complementary distribution of the physical traits of dolichocephaly and brachycephaly; and also occurrences of various diseases. There are many other differences expressed in more minute characteristics which are nonetheless important and should not be overlooked. For example, the Easter Islanders, who are free from European genetic admixture, have markedly longer heads than other Polynesian populations,[15] and yet they are a distinctively Polynesian group in over-all terms. Again, the Polynesians of the little atoll of Pukapuka, isolated on the northern rim of the Cook group, are distinguished by a marked decrease in stature, quite below the uniformly high standards of other groups.[16] Sullivan's study of the Marquesan data [17] (collected by E. S. C. Handy) revealed that the Marquesans were a much more heterogeneous group than the inhabitants of any other archipelago in Polynesia. There were definite differences between the populations of the various islands within the Marquesan archipelago, and there were also a great range of individual variations within each of the island populations. The Moriori of the Chatham Islands have long been thought to exhibit very unusual features of skull conformation for a Polynesian group, such as a fossa praenasalis, loaf-shaped skulls, receding massive brows, and long, narrow palates.[18]

What is the cause of variation of this nature and what significance should we attach to it? Earlier workers in Polynesian physical anthropology were prone to interpret variation as the result of discrete migrations of physically different populations or actual races. Thus, the dolichocephalism of Easter Islanders was attributed to a contact with a Melanesian population. The unusual characteristics of the Moriori or Maori were attributed by various researchers to influence from Australoid, Melanesian, or Fuegian Indian.

All of these hypotheses ignored the role of microevolution in producing population differentiation, and their theories suffer because of this oversight. The conditions for microevolution are: isolation by natural geographical or social boundaries and environmental differences. Mutations are the main factors in producing this "short-term evolution," as it might be called. Are conditions in Polynesia permissive of such differentiation? The island groups are widely scattered, the distances between prohibiting anything but infrequent contact. Social class distance within an island population was marked in many instances, so that breeding would not be random. Environmental differences obtaining between such islands as those of the Hawaiian chain and the Tuamotu atolls are extremely great and were the source of adaptive pressures upon the gene pools.

It is obvious that the geographical and cultural conditions present in Polynesia were ripe for microevolution to take place. We will now attempt to spell out in more detailed terms exactly how such group differentiation occurs.

Each one of the islands of Polynesia was settled by a group of people who may or may not have constituted a representative sample of the population on the islands whence they came. The odds are greatly against a migratory group's encompassing the full range of variations of the parent population. Exigencies of voyage may have further reduced the genetic "treasury" of such a group before they arrived in their new home. Once established on another island, a small group of this type becomes what geneticists call a "breeding isolate," that is, a breeding group effectively separated by natural (or social) barriers from contact with other breeding groups. In such small populations it is known that particular gene combinations or mutations have a chance of survival greatly above that of similar combinations or mutations in other larger populations. These genetic "accidents" not only tend to survive but to spread evenly throughout the population, although even in small groups some are extinguished. Through this effect, known as "genetic drift," a small breeding isolate tends gradually to accentuate the differences between itself and the parent group from which it derived. Isolation is therefore a major factor in evolution, and it is undeniable that the Polynesian island societies were isolated before the coming of the Europeans. Although there was a great deal of voyaging, both intentional and accidental, the contacts of this type were insufficient to alter radically the gene pool of any population and counteract the tendencies of genetic drift.

There is an additional factor to be considered besides isolation as an important cause of differentiation of island groups. This is the effect of an environment that operates selectively on the gene pool of a population.

Placed in a given environmental niche, say a coral atoll, a population of migrants from a high volcanic island would have numerous adjustments to make. Water would always be scarce, as would many types of plant food. The reef lagoon marine biota would differ radically from that around a volcanic island. Over a period of time, those individuals would tend to survive whose genetic heritage had somehow endowed them with resistance to desiccation and to deficiencies in various vitamins or other nutritional factors that their new diet imposed. This would of course tend to conserve the genes of the more adapted individuals within the gene pool, while their less adapted fellows gradually contributed less and less.

To these factors must further be added the factors of social selection, the tendency to marry within certain limits imposed by society thus inhibiting random mating and the growth of a homogeneous group. Class distinctions were quite marked in societies such as those of Hawaii and Tahiti, and the tendency for the various ranks to inbreed would produce a series of subpopulations within a society whose differentiation might well become accentuated. One only has to look at the royal houses of Europe to see the results of microevolution operating through social selection. Sexual selection also plays a part in mating within a population, but it is somewhat of an imponderable in Polynesia and need not be gone into here.

In summary, on the basis of archaeological evidence bearing out the hypotheses of leading authorities in Polynesian physical anthropology, the Polynesian race originated on the coast of Asia as a composite made up of a large Paleo-Caucasoid population element and small elements of Negroid and Mongoloid groups. The same parent group may also have produced some of the Melanesian populations of such areas as Fiji. After mating had produced a genetic strain that was stable and bred true, the group filtered into the Pacific (for reasons that will be discussed later) and ultimately arrived in the Polynesian triangle. The original longheaded population arriving in Western Polynesia was probably endowed with a normal range of individual variation. Through the mechanisms of non-randomly selected migratory groups evolving in isolation under widely variant ecological conditions in societies that were often highly class-structured, more pronounced variations arose among the populations and were accentuated through time to give the diversity displayed in Polynesian physical anthropology today. This diversity is nonsignificant in face of the overwhelming similarities expressed in the majority of quantatitive and qualitative criteria known to anthropology.

4

The Language

The Polynesian language has been called the "Italian of the Pacific" because of its soft-flowing vocal qualities and beautiful intonation. Like Italian, it is a language that seems to lend itself well to music, as attested by the long-time popularity of many Hawaiian song hits; and because of a strange charm it seems to have for Westerners, other languages have borrowed from it. In the forefront of Polynesian borrowings is the word *tabu* (forbidden) immortalized by the French perfume manufacturers (and also by Sigmund Freud in a title of one of his early works). A word commonly used in the anthropological fraternity is *mana* (supernatural power). Other less-known borrowings used by geologists are *'a'a* and *pahoehoe,* to designate two particular types of volcanic lava. The word *mako* is known to every marine angler as the name of the vicious blue shark. In Hawaii the borrowings are particularly numerous, and the inhabitants of our fiftieth state, whether Oriental, Portuguese, Scandinavian, old Hawaiian, or "mainlander," all use such words as *puka* (hole, tunnel), *pali* (cliff), *luau* (feast), *hukilau* (fish drive), *kai* (toward the sea), *uka* (inland), and many others. New arrivals are often hard put to understand long-time residents who suggest a "drive over the pali and back through the puka."

The Polynesian languages are members of the Austronesian or Malayo-Polynesian language stock. Also included in the Austronesian family with the Polynesian languages are those of Micronesia, Melanesia, Indonesia, the Philippines, and some of the languages of Madagascar, which forms the western limit of the huge expanse of ocean over which the speakers of these languages have spread, the opposite terminus being tiny Rapa Nui or Easter Island, 3,000 miles from the coast of Chile. The Malayo-Polynesian languages (which have the same status as the Indo-European language family of which our language is a member) are further related to a group of languages on the coast of Asia, called generically the Thai-Kadai family. Among these are the languages of the Thai and Kadai of Siam and the Li dialects of the Formosan aborigines. Thus the linguistic evidence points in the same direction as the evidence of physical anthropology for the point of origin of the Polynesians, the coast of Southeast Asia.

The history of the study of the Polynesian and other Pacific languages and the efforts leading to the present classification of Malayo–Polynesian languages as stated above is a fascinating story, beginning, as do so many other aspects of the history of science in the Pacific, with the great Polynesian expedition of Captain Cook. Although a relationship between certain of the Austronesian languages had been postulated as early as 1706,[1] the first good opportunity for collecting comparative material fell to George Forster, the young naturalist attached to the second Cook expedition. This opportunity by no means escaped the roving and extraordinarily perceptive Forster, who collected a series of basic vocabularies on the various islands of Polynesia and Melanesia visited by the *Endeavour* in the years 1772–75. The similarities between the words recorded on various Polynesian islands for such commonplace entities as pig, fish, or man, and abstract concepts, such as numerals and various verbs, were very striking, but no such similarity was noted in the New Caledonian and New Hebridean vocabularies. In addition to these linguistic similarities and differences, Forster noted the obvious physical differences between the Melanesians and the Polynesians and later published some of his data and his opinions, declaring that there were two races in the Pacific. One, the Polynesian, was light-colored, tall, athletic, and "of benevolent temperament," speaking languages related to Malay. The other, a race of darker, slighter, and shorter people of rather nasty personality, spoke languages unrelated to each other or to anything else; these were the Melanesians.

Despite the fact that he missed the Melanesian-Polynesian

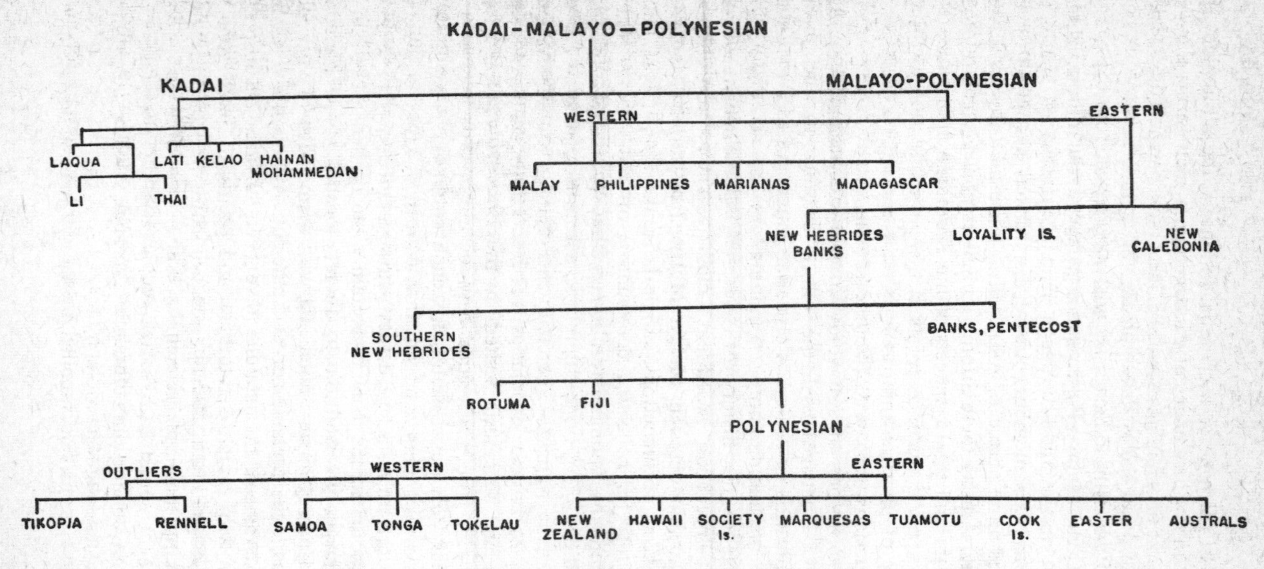

Fig. 3. The Malayo-Polynesian languages (after Greenberg, 1950, and Grace, 1955)

connection, Forster's direct methodology of comparison (later to become a standard in historical linguistics) and the very fact that he felt the need to compare is quite remarkable, not to mention the most important result, that he saw a relationship which has since been well substantiated by science.

After the initial discoveries in Polynesia, missionizing began quite rapidly. These naked, uninhibited natives of rather pleasant and receptive dispositions led an enormously sinful (and absorbingly interesting) life and presented a convenient, safer outlet for the well-known Christian urge to uplift than the more sanguine American Indians or Africans. An immediate by-product of "uplift" was the production of numerous word lists, dictionaries, grammars, and ultimately Biblical or liturgical translations into the vernacular, printed by the various missionary societies. Simultaneously, similar missionizing was going on in Melanesia. The totality of this material allowed more extensive linguistic comparison, and soon further attempts at broader classifications of Pacific languages were published. Müller, between 1876 and 1888, published a classification in which he went so far as to group Malay, Melanesian, and Polynesian together as members of a single language family. The famous Pater Wilhelm Schmidt, founder of the Vienna School, published similar classifications stressing the relationship of Melanesia and Polynesia. Other authorities, such as Ray and Churchill, attempted to deny the relationship of Melanesian and Polynesian as members of a single language family, but this most often seemed to be caused by an inability to see past racial differences and to put the darker, and one gathers less desirable, Melanesians in any kind of classification with the "attractive" Polynesians. All of these studies had certain common defects, however. They were generally based on comparisons of certain quite limited aspects of the languages involved. To prove relationship a few phonological features might be selected with a small list of vocabulary items, and it was felt to be sufficient. Although the relationship was one that should have been obvious on inspection of a fair sample of sources and seems to have gone unchallenged among the upper echelons of the world's linguists, it required a scientific methodology working on a broad basis of sound data to present acceptable quantified proof of the connection between Polynesian, Melanesian, and Indonesian languages.

This proof was supplied by the German, Otto Dempwolff,

who between 1934 and 1938 published a series of articles of profound importance.[2] To determine whether, in fact, there was a genetic relationship between these languages or not, and if so, to determine what degrees of relationship existed, Dempwolff first attempted to reconstruct the state of the early Indonesian language from a detailed study of three separate Indonesian dialects: Javanese, Tagalog of the Philippines, Toba-Batak of Borneo. Starting with a classification of the various types of words or "roots" according to their consonant-vowel structure, Dempwolff was able to work out a system of sound correspondences for the various positions within each type of word. By a study of these sound correspondences, he was able to establish, tentatively, the phonetic or sound system of the early or "proto" Indonesian language from which the present-day languages had diverged. A similar study of shifts of meaning between cognate words in the three languages used as his base allowed him also to establish a limited vocabulary of Proto-Indonesian. He then subjected his construction to a test by a further comparison using three more related languages—Malay, Ngadju-Dajak of Borneo, and Hova of Madagascar—exactly as he had used the first languages and as a result was able to expand his proto-language vocabulary, elevate many of his tentative findings to the status of certainties, and correct his errors. He then compared his proto-Indonesian reconstruction with the Melanesian languages of Fiji and Malaita (Solomon Islands). He found that these two languages shared certain definite systematic phonetic innovations from the proto-Indonesian phonetic system and checked his findings by consulting sources from a large number of additional Melanesian languages. The Melanesian languages could now definitely be related to Indonesian, and Dempwolff believed that the differences in the two languages were the result of a long-past separation from the Malayo-Polynesian stock and subsequent divergence, dating from the period before the Indonesian languages had separated. Finally, Dempwolff attacked the Polynesian languages, to bring them into the framework of relationships that he was gradually erecting. Using Tongan, Samoan, and Futunan as his specimen languages, Dempwolff again analyzed the sound systems, grammatical structure, and vocabulary and found that these languages shared all the Melanesian sound-system changes from proto-Indonesian.

Such a wide range of commonly shared, basic innovations is far too great to be ascribed to chance and is undoubtedly the result of a common origin. Dempwolff, satisfied that he had established a relationship, did not attempt a classification, but his work was of prodigious significance without any systematic taxonomy. Since his time further research has shown certain insufficiencies in his sampling and weighting, and other workers, such as Dyen of Yale, have contributed to his monumental effort by adducing evidence for certain points in his theses that had been insufficiently documented.

In 1942, Paul Benedict, an American linguist, was working on the languages of Thailand in an attempt to determine whether or not these languages could actually be said to belong to the Chinese-Tibetan family.[3] Large numbers of Thai words were very similar to Chinese words and had led others to see a relationship to Chinese. Benedict found that in the fundamental or "core" vocabulary of Thai—that is, the vocabulary including basic, highly important everyday words such as "man," "fire," "water," etc.—the resemblances were all to the Malayo-Polynesian languages. He concluded that the Chinese words in Thai were the result of extensive culture contact with Chinese and that the Thai, Kadai, and Li languages of Formosa were non-Chinese, were interrelated, and had a relationship as a unit to the Malayo-Polynesian language. Therefore by 1942 the relationship of the Polynesian languages to those of Melanesia, Indonesia, and Southeast Asia had been scientifically charted in broad terms while Polynesian was seen as the farthest eastward extension of a language family rivaling our own Indo-European language stock in its extension on the surface of the globe.

Since World War II further studies have given us a far clearer picture of the way in which the Polynesian languages differentiated from each other as they spread through the island world of the Polynesian triangle.[4] Comparisons in detail of the languages of Western Polynesia show that there were probably two original dialects of Polynesian in use by the first settlers of these islands and that the speech communities of these dialects were separated early, allowing a fairly long period of time for the languages to develop different traits. Under such conditions linguistic changes occur in the sound systems, the grammar, and the vocabulary of languages in isolation, producing small changes at a slow rate. In this manner the modern Romance languages differentiated from their original Latin mother stock and have now become mutually unintelligible. The two original Polynesian groups each ultimately divided as colonization of the various islands in the Polynesian triangle began, and each island or island group began to develop its own distinctive dialect. As the Polynesians spread eastward, however, their language underwent a rather retrogressive change. The sound systems of the eastern languages, such as Hawaiian, Tahitian, and Marquesan, differ from those of the west, such as Samoa and Tonga, in that they have discarded many of the proto-Polynesian sounds and in other cases fused pairs of similar sounds, which have been kept discrete in the western languages. The grammatical structure of eastern Polynesian also is simpler than those of the western tongues; for example, Samoan ways of expressing tense of verbs are more numerous than those found in Marquesan. Also, there is in Samoan a complete series of honorifics used in speaking to persons of rank, not found anywhere in the eastern dialects.

Attempts have been made to date the separation of the various Polynesian dialects, using a technique known by the impressive names of "glottochronology" or "lexicostatistics." [5] This technique was developed by American linguists studying North American Indian languages. It was found that the words for certain key basic objects and concepts in American Indian languages tended to be impervious to borrowings from unrelated languages. As mentioned above, these items and concepts are things such as "sun," "knife," "woman," and low numerals, etc. A list of these terms and concepts was compiled, and study showed that the rate of change in the "core" vocabulary of any given language was relatively constant, occurring at the rate of about 20 per cent per 1,000 years. This presented a good opportunity to date the separations of various dialects of Indian language stocks, and such dating has been attempted with some success in North America and has also been applied to Indo-European languages. The technique works best on languages separated for periods of 4,000 to 5,000 years, however, and one must be able to record the *modern native speaker's* versions for each of the items and concepts on the list.

Attempts to apply this technique in Polynesia have met with varying success, mainly because the separations of the eastern and some of the western dialects took place in the last 1,000 years and change is not marked enough to show clearly. Also, native speakers were not always available and dictionaries were resorted to. The results give the date for separation of Polynesian and Melanesian languages as between 3,400 and 3,800 years ago.[6] The eastern-western division in Polynesia is seen as taking place between 1,800 and 2,250 years ago. Within Eastern Polynesia[7] the earliest date obtainable is for the separation of the Marquesan and Easter Island languages from the eastern mother stock, which occurred sometime before A.D. 500. At a later date, about A.D. 1000, old Tahitian seems to be the source of the Hawaiian, Maori, Tuamotu, and Rarotongan languages. A most recent development in Polynesian linguistics has been a family-tree grouping based on quantitatively determined degrees of relationship, a thing heretofore unattempted. Dempwolff, it will be recalled, contented himself with proving that the relationship between the members of the Malayo-Polynesian family existed, but did not spell out the finer relationships. Dr. George Grace[8] has recently contributed an outstanding analysis of familial relationships in the eastern Malayo-Polynesian languages (including all Micronesian languages, Polynesian, Melanesian, and eastern New Guinea coastal languages). He has found that the Polynesian languages in totality are members, with Fijian, Rotuman, and northern New Hebridean, of a subgroup of the New Hebrides–Banks Island supergroup. This finding reduces the Polynesian languages from their once lofty status, equivalent as a unit to all Melanesian and Indonesian languages, to a more subordinate position, giving us the true perspective of their actual moment based on objective linguistic grounds, with considerations of race and culture excluded.

An important advance which occurred in Polynesian linguistics recently is that made by Dr. Thomas Barthel of the University of Tübingen, who succeeded in unraveling the famous Easter Island *rongorongo* script, of which more will be said later in a separate chapter dealing with Easter Island specifically.[9] That which is of most importance linguistically is the fact that the script is not a haphazard conglomeration of signs, but is a structured system, the grammatical rules of which were derived by Barthel's analysis. Barthel believes that the script is *not* a unique development on Easter Island, but is a part of an original Polynesian heritage, lost elsewhere in Eastern Polynesia. There are scattered cryptic references to such a script's existing in the Marquesas and also in Tahiti,[10] and the late J. Frank Stimson, a student of Polynesian philology for over fifty years, claimed to have obtained evidence of such a script in the Austral Islands (Raivavae, Tubuai, Rapa Iti). This indicates that writing was probably once part of the Polynesian cultural heritage everywhere, although its use was restricted, of course, to the priestly and upper classes for ceremonial purposes only. The reason for the apparent abandonment of the script throughout Polynesia is difficult to explain at our present state of knowledge, and we have proof that it did not continue in use until the arrival of the Europeans. As a closely guarded secret of the powerful priests, the script may have escaped notice until its custodians took its secret to their graves. Although produced in wood on Easter Island, it was evidently written on highly perishable bark cloth in Tahiti, and on leaves in the Australs.

To sum up, we see that the Polynesian languages are members of the Thai-Kadai-Malayo-Polynesian language stock, with their roots on the coast of South Asia. This relationship is established on a firm body of data comprising phonological, grammatical, and vocabulary items. There is evidence that a form of script may have been part of the Polynesian cultural heritage and may also trace its descent to Asian writing systems. Further, Polynesian is actually a subgroup of a broad Melanesian family. The Polynesian-Melanesian separation may have occurred as long as 3,800 years ago. Sometime after this separation, the Polynesian languages divided into two major dialects, which developed and gave rise to the present dialectic diversity in the islands. The separation of these two languages may have occurred some 2,250 years ago. Linguistic division in the western group began at that time and before A.D. 500 it had begun in Eastern Polynesia. As the Polynesians moved eastward a process of phonetic and grammatical simplification seems to have occurred, increasing in intensity and emphasizing the east-west language differences.

5

The Door to the Past

The Europeans who first explored Polynesia were sailors, and as such they were quite naturally interested in the fact that the Polynesians had managed to settle their island world without aid of "modern" navigating instruments, in vessels much smaller and more crudely equipped than European warships of the period. Natural curiosity led them to question the Polynesians about their past: Where had they come from? How long ago did they arrive? Whence the pigs and dogs? And a host of other questions. They found that the Polynesians could answer these questions and more besides, as it soon became apparent that the Polynesians possessed a great fund of oral literature, both sacred and profane. The history of their people and of their various families of consequence was contained in this treasury of folklore as well as the entire story of the creation of the universe and the gods of the Polynesian pantheon. The Europeans were struck by the emphasis that the Polynesians placed on family trees and their custom of dating all occurrences in terms of a number of generations ago, apparently quite a precise system. Moreover, the tribal priests and historians, who held this vast store of knowledge mainly by rote memory, were highly trained in special schools for their sacred profession, and recitation of the genealogies, prayers, or legends was hedged with numerous sanctions reminding the tribal bards of the ghastly supernatural results accruing from a mispronounced or (perish the thought!) an omitted name. Tampering with the traditions was, of course, completely unheard of, for the fate visited by the gods on those attempting this would surpass comprehension.

The Europeans were quite impressed with the history of the Polynesians as they heard it; and through the years, from Captain Cook onward, a very firm belief arose in the minds of many Europeans that the legends so readily told them by the amiable Polynesians were the gospel truth and contained all that there was to know about Polynesia. It was impossible at that time to carry on any archaeological excavations in the islands, because the Polynesians understandably took a dim view of breaking the *tapu* on their old temple sites or taking a chance of disturbing many dead haphazardly buried around village sites and thus incurring their wrath. Why, however, should anyone want to excavate to recover the Polynesian past when it was available by word of mouth for the asking? Furthermore, Polynesian artifacts were not aesthetically appealing and certainly not as desirable as the loot being uncovered in archaeological excavations in the Near East during the nineteenth century.

For these reasons, justified or not, the study of Polynesian prehistory grew to rely almost completely on legends and by consequence during the course of the late nineteenth and early twentieth centuries a number of compilations were made and subsequently published, setting forth in "entirety" the history of the Polynesian people. William Ellis, a missionary in Hawaii, inclined toward the belief that the Polynesians had come from Asia.[1] Abraham Fornander,[2] who had worked in the Hawaiian Islands as a judge, believed he had found conclusive proof that the Polynesians were a Cushitic people of Aryan stock who had originated in northwest India and Persia and migrated into the Indonesian archipelago, finding the latter islands already inhabited by a Papuan race. Fornander used a comparative methodology, building up his case on evidence obtained from several island groups, also utilizing linguistic comparisons between the Polynesian and Semitic languages.

C. Percy Smith,[3] a New Zealander, was convinced that the Polynesian path indicated by Fornander was substantially correct, but differed in his somewhat more detailed presentation and his more sophisticated view of the relations of the Polynesians with the Indonesians and Melanesians. He believed that the homeland of the Polynesians was in Asia in the land of *Atia te varinga nui,* in 450 B.C., where a mighty stone temple-palace had been reared and the King *Tu te rangi marama* reigned. . . . Quarrels caused a migration to Java (in 65 B.C.), then known as *Avaiki,* where the Polynesians remained three or four centuries until driven out by the invading Indonesians, fleeing into Melanesia, whence they populated Polynesia in three migrations. The theory of E. Tregear,[4] another New Zealander, is much the same as that of his compatriot Smith.

In the 1920's and 30's, the American ethnologist E. S. C. Handy, field worker for the Bernice Bishop Museum in Honolulu, collected a large amount of legendary evidence, backed by some analysis of material culture, which led him to postulate the existence of two separate migrations into Polynesia, each of which had characteristic religious practices, social organization, and technological features.[5] The latest migration, he believed, on the basis of similarities between the names of a Chinese river people and a Polynesian high god, originated in China.

By this time, however, certain other trends had begun in the study of Polynesian prehistory. Rather than rely so heavily on tradition, many field workers were beginning to concentrate their efforts on studies of the distributions of various kinds of tools and technological traits throughout Polynesia, while the first archaeology was beginning in the form of surface surveys of the multitudinous stone structures found throughout Polynesia.

We will interrupt our historical narrative at this point, however, to digress a bit and discuss the validity of those Polynesian legends that played such a role in the early studies of Polynesian prehistory. Certainly the reader must have felt a little uncomfortable about some of the rather definite pronouncements made by Messrs. Fornander, Smith, and Tregear and would perhaps like some clarification of the validity of such claims, especially since, as we shall later see, certain circles in present-day New Zealand archaeology still place great faith in legends not only for history but for the dating of archaeological periods.

"The Truth About Legends," as a sensational magazine might entitle this chapter, is a mixture of the all-too-human tendencies to exaggerate and give quick credence, the humor of the Polynesians, and the misfortune of many anthropologists. It would be foolish, I must emphasize, to discount legends as completely valueless. They have definite utility, but as the only basis for a theory they are very inferior. Cross checks with other types of data are needed to protect one against the errors to be detailed below.

First, let us look at the way in which the data were collected. Naturally, only a few trained and consecrated people in the upper ranks of Polynesian societies were qualified to give the Europeans such information. This seldom troubled the collectors of legends, who obtained their material from mission students or anyone willing to co-operate rather than attempt to seek out the few informed individuals. Indiscriminacy of this sort was especially dangerous in light of the fact that there were apparently two versions of many important legends and chants in most Polynesian societies: one version, simplified and watered down for the laity, and an esoteric version containing the actual "truth" as only the priests knew it, with all the highly dangerous words invested with supernatural power ready to turn on the unwary user.

The tragicomic results of this policy can be illustrated by some examples demonstrating the implicit faith in sources, once all too common, and still by no means a thing of the past. Fornander could not visit all the island groups of Polynesia to gather data, and so he wrote to Europeans in the various islands asking them to collect texts for him. One of his correspondents was an indigent Englishman who resided in Tahauku on the island of Hiva Oa in the Marquesas. Among the material that Fornander obtained from this source was a very entertaining text called *Te Vanana 'o Tana'oa* or "The Chant of Tana 'oa" (the Polynesian sea god). This purported to be an authentic Marquesan version of the Biblical deluge with Tana 'oa starring as Noah. The tale followed the Biblical version quite closely, thus pleasing Fornander, who was seeking to prove a relationship between the Biblical peoples and the Polynesians. He never submitted the text to a Marquesan for approval, although many Marquesans were in Hawaii at the time. This was a fatal mistake, for the text is written in abominable sailor-Marquesan pidgin and its entire style and idiom is so obviously European as to leave no doubt that the good judge was taken for a surf ride by his Hiva Oa correspondent, who very possibly authored it himself.

Another factor often overlooked by the traditionalists in their collection was actual techniques of eliciting information. For this they are certainly not culpable, since even today many of our modern anthropologists will unintentionally lead a native informant in desired fashion by making the purpose of their inquiry so obvious as to be unmistakable even to the native. Quite often the native informant will comply merely to silence the inquirer and be rid of him in order to get down to the more pressing business of work and play. The New Zealanders were made quite aware of the effects of leading questions when they set about to determine whether or not the ostrichlike moa had been a contemporary of the Polynesians in that country.[6] The moa were unheard of for some time after the British occupied New Zealand, and for all intents and purposes they had never existed. Finally, naturalists discovered some large semifossilized bones, some as large as beef bones, and immediately recognized them as the remains of struthious birds. Questions put to the Maori living near the areas where finds were made elicited some rather fantastic answers, indicating only the vaguest knowledge of these birds. In a series of legends collected in North Island in the 1840's and 50's only five vague and oblique references to the moa were found. The current opinion was that the Maori had only heard of the bird vaguely from earlier Polynesian inhabitants of New Zealand who occupied the island previous to the coming of the Maori.

A new element was injected into the situation by the appearance of human tools in association with cooked moa remains, indicating definitely that men had hunted the moa on New Zealand soil. This touched off a tremendous controversy between those who claimed that the Maori had seen the moa and those claiming that the Maori had not. To document their argument, which was poorly supported by legends, as we have noted, the "Had Seen" group trotted into the field and began buttonholing (or rather cloak-holing) Maori and asking them about the moa. When done in the past the responses had been negative or very vague. Now, however, the Maori were beginning to learn how to handle inquisitive white men and all kinds of information rewarded the searchers. The moa was described in great detail as to its height, head and beak shape, eyelids, color and qualities of feathers, wingspread (unfortunately, the moa was wingless), size of nest, number of eggs, ad infinitum. The Europeans went home quite satisfied with their "data," probably having pressed a few shillings into the calloused brown palms of their *raconteurs* in more than one instance, and so both sides were happy. Perhaps the Maori was happiest, having had somewhat of a laugh on the *pakea* (Maori for "white man") who had taken his land but had never managed to get him to sign a peace treaty or even decisively defeat him in war. One needs only to ask himself how he would like his country to be overrun by Martians, let us say, who immediately tried to change everything and then spent their time going about asking silly questions to determine what the original situation was before they changed it.

A second case, dating from the present, of the same sort of Polynesian "one-up-manship" vis-à-vis the paleface, is one which I obtained in the Marquesas in 1956. A certain well-known "explorer" arrived in Nuku Hiva to do "the first archaeology ever done in these islands." From the dock I watched him arrive *à la* white hunter in pith helmet and bush jacket. He had come to "discover" a group of statues in Taipivai, well known since 1896 by the excellent photos of the German ethnographer von den Steinen. Arriving at the statues, he proceeded to ask the chief of the valley about the statues, their names, their purpose, etc. (I had also visited the site some weeks previously and had been unable to elicit any information of this type, but I was not giving "baksheesh" either, as our explorer friend was doing.) Money has a way of loosening Polynesian tongues and lubricating imaginative mechanisms; within a short time our explorer had learned the names of all the statues and the purpose of the site. He had also inquired about one statue that was broken in half at the waist. The chief standing nearby volunteered his services: "There is an old legend about this statue," he said as the pencil began to fly over the note page, "which relates that this idol was once invited to a party for idols in Fatu Hiva [another island in the Marquesan group]. While there, he was consumed with passion for a female idol, who unfortunately was married. The spouse of this female idol became angry at the intruder and they fought. This idol was broken in half, and naturally he lost and was returned here." It was strictly by accident that I first overheard my workmen (talking among themselves in Marquesan) laughing about the highly original and on-the-spot creation of Manuera, chief of Taipivai, and he laughed with them as they described the rapt attention with which it was ingested by the intrepid discoverer. (My workmen's statements on this particular incident are recorded in Marquesan, as I heard them in Taipivai valley in 1957, and are to be found in the archives of the Department of

Anthropology, American Museum of Natural History, New York.)

Obviously, in collecting legends one has to be aware of the fact that people may be prone to fabrication or may simply be ashamed to admit ignorance. Also there may be several versions of the same legend, each differing substantially from the other, all enjoying currency at one time. It is only by a judicious collection of a range of the variations that one can establish the content of the true legend.[7] The old traditionalists did none of this, believing that one legend would be sufficient for their purposes.

Finally, there is the problem of genealogical dating, a technique which as previously stated has played a large part in Polynesian prehistory and which still colors it today. The students of traditional Polynesian prehistory possessed what seemed to be a powerful tool in the genealogies collected throughout the islands, as many events of great historical importance apparently could be dated by them. There were several problems, however, which should have prompted a reconsideration of the possibilities of great inaccuracies in the system. First was the fact that the genealogies of Eastern and Western Polynesia were considerably divergent in length; the east, settled in relatively more recent times, possessed the longest genealogies in all of Polynesia,[8] running back to 2870 B.C., while the western islands, long settled and *source* of the eastern population, could display genealogies only penetrating about 500 years into the past with any certainty and 700 years at a maximum.[9] Also there was little similarity between the names in the genealogies despite the claims by earlier traditionalists that such existed. Therefore there was no way to establish any succession of historical datum points moving from east and most recent to west and oldest. In addition the east-west incongruence pointed definitely to a real lack of reliable dating standards.

As if these hard realities were insufficient, there remained one more problem, that of ascertaining how many years to assign to a generation, a figure that no one had ever obtained from a Polynesian. Arbitrarily twenty, twenty-five, or thirty years were used; finally a compromise was formed at twenty-five years. How reliable is this? An excellent example is at hand: in 1812 the American Navy visited Nuku Hiva[10] and had extensive dealing with the Taiohae chief, Keatanui, who died in 1831.[11] Some sixty years later Christian[12] collected the genealogy of the reigning Marquesan queen, Vaekehu, who numbered the deceased Keatanui among her direct ancestors, but by the 1890's *eight* generations had elapsed since his death, which on the accepted value of twenty-five years per generation would date Keatanui as living one and a half centuries before his actual time. One of the reasons for anomalies of this sort is that the Polynesians recorded many legends, chants, or natural personifications in genealogical forms and attached or inserted them in their own genealogies. Another cause of inaccurate genealogies is the frequent custom of a victorious chief's usurping the family tree of a beaten adversary. Also, all sorts of "adjusting" was done by individuals attempting to rise to positions of importance by rearranging their genealogies to bring them in closer to royalty.

It is therefore quite clear that genealogical dating is futile because of (1) ignorance of the varying number of years per generation and (2) inconsistencies and errors in the genealogical sequences themselves, caused by extraneous insertions, omissions, and other tampering. However, as noted above and as we shall see later in the course of the book, legends in many instances can prove most valuable, but they must have been collected with the proper care and they must have support in the form of archaeological, ethnological, or physical anthropological evidence before they can be accepted as valid.

We have gone rather deeply into the traditionalist approach and the use of legends from the earliest students, such as Fornander, into the 1920's, and have shown the pitfalls in such an approach and the high standards necessary for collection and use of such data. We can now pick up the chain of development of Polynesian prehistoric studies where we left it in the 1920's, with Handy's attempt at Tahitian prehistory reconstruction based on both traditions and a study of material culture. Actually, in studying the distribution of various items of material culture in conjunction with religious or sociopolitical concepts, Handy was carrying on a type of study which was becoming popular in Europe owing to the work of the famed Kulturkreise School of Vienna.[13] In these distribution studies, the occurrence of various selected cultural traits was charted geographically, and attempts were made to find clusters of traits that always or nearly always appeared together. These trait clusters were taken to represent the culture of a distinct ethnic unit generally, often believed to be both racially distinct and possessed of a distinct language.

A basic uninventiveness of mankind was generally presupposed, and all appearances of a given cluster of traits, or often of a single trait, were felt to be the result of a "migration." The assumptions underlying this approach make as much of a mental exercise as a study. We now know that the processes of culture, such as invention, convergence, stimulus diffusion, obsolescence, and so on, are quite complex, and we cannot accept the premise that migration alone is a source of cultural change.

Throughout the 1920's and 30's such studies were popular in Polynesia, generally drawing some support from legends and physical anthropology. Linton's[14] study of Marquesan material culture concludes with a reconstruction of Marquesan prehistory in this style. Burrows,[15] in 1938, published a study of various traits found in complementary distribution between Eastern and Western Polynesia. He did not, however, use a rigid migration mechanism for interpretations but pleaded for some recognition of other culture processes, as mentioned above, declaring that not all differences between the groups could be ascribed to migrations reaching or failing to reach various islands.

Simultaneously with increased interest in distributional studies, archaeology was begun in Polynesia, concentrating mainly on the numerous stone and earth monuments, such as temples, images, house platforms, council platforms, and forts found throughout the Tongan, Society, Hawaiian, Tuamotu, Marquesan, New Zealand, and Austral islands, as well as on far-off Easter Island. The results were primarily descriptive in nature, yielding classifications of various types of stone and earth structures as well as of stone, bone, or shell artifacts collected on the surface. Little excavation was accomplished during this period, and when done it did not often meet standards currently acceptable in other areas of the archaeological community.

Owing to the lack of stratigraphic excavation, it was almost impossible to establish any archaeological sequences of artifacts or culture phases, which is usually the first goal of the archaeologist. Only in New Zealand were extensive excavations carried out and the beginning of a sequence of cultures established. This was due largely to the fact that Polynesian artifacts, found in association with extinct moa bones, had acted as a decided stimulus to excavation.

In truth, the almost universal concentration on observing and recording surface architectural remains in Polynesia had steered attention away from the usual dream of the archaeologist—a site with a deep accumulation of cultural debris well repaying the effort of excavation by the number and variety of finds. Therefore, it was common in the not distant past to hear many anthropologists maintain that there was no stratigraphy in Polynesia, which was mainly because no one had ever looked for any.

Since World War II, however, the techniques of modern archaeology have appeared in the Pacific. Shortly after the cessation of hostilities, E. W. Gifford, of the University of California at Berkeley, carried out an archaeological survey in Fiji, at the back door of Polynesia, excavating several deep sites and using standard modern techniques. Later, Gifford, accompanied by Dick Shutler of the Nevada State Museum, tested the archaeological resources of New Caledonia in the same way. Emory, of Bernice Bishop Museum at Honolulu, long an outstanding contributor to all phases of Polynesian anthropology, began stratigraphic excavations in Hawaii that have yielded results of the greatest importance, both factual and theoretical. Since then archaeological work in Polynesia has been increasing by leaps and bounds. In 1955–56, the Norwegian Expedition visited Easter Island; and in 1956–58, I carried on my own work in the Marquesas. Golson, of the University of Auckland, has recently been pushing ahead into many problem areas of Maori archaeology, in addition to excavating in Samoa and Tonga. Well outside of the Polynesian area but still related to it, as we shall see, Spoehr's work has illuminated the age and certain aspects of the development of the Mariana Islands culture, with excavations on Guam, Saipan, and Tinian.

At this time, as this is being written, Emory is working on an extremely promising site on Kauai in the Hawaiian group, and Oliver and Green of Harvard are beginning work in the Society Islands and Mangareva.

In summary, the Polynesian emphasis on oral literature and their supernatural sanctions against violation of sacred precincts led to a great interest among Europeans in Polynesian traditional history and a neglect of "dirt" archaeology, which continued well into the twentieth century. At that time, a tendency away from a completely traditional methodology manifested itself in an interest in trait-distribution studies while interest in archaeology began to grow. Although the archaeology was primarily devoted to surface structures at first, after World War II stratigraphic excavation became *la mode*. Today one may say that Polynesian archaeology has finally reached its majority.

6

Out from Asia

In the past chapters we have reviewed the evidence of Polynesian language, racial affiliations, and floral and faunal connections to provide a background for the reader and indicate that the probable origin of the Polynesian race is to be found on the mainland of southern coastal China and Indochina.

Now, to obtain archaeological evidence of Polynesian origins we must survey this land of fairy-tale mountains, jungled valleys, and mighty rivers yellowing the greenish, island-dotted coastal shallows with their burdens of silt carried many miles from the rugged interior. Our search will also lead us to the seat of the ancient Chinese empire in the level, monotonous flood plains of the Yellow River, far to the north where a civilization blossomed 2,000 years before Christ. Man's antiquity in Asia is as ancient as anywhere else in the world, beginning in a limestone cave on a hill near what would someday be Peking, where *Sinanthropus Pekinensis* lived amid a noisome litter of broken tools, filth, and the remains of his human and animal meals. We do not wish to concern ourselves at present with the Old Stone Age in China, however, but shall direct our attention to the Neolithic or New Stone Age, the period in which domestication of plants and animals was achieved, village life began, and pottery and ground and polished stone tools were produced. The Neolithic is a tremendously important period in human evolution, for the development of our arts and sciences and our entire modern economy finds its source there. By learning the art of plant and animal domestication, man finally placed himself in a position to produce more than he could use for himself and his family. The surplus could be stored, or it could be used to support a craftsman specializing in some service not directly related to food production. In the Old Stone Age this had been impossible generally, and men had to spend their time in the food quest. They had no time to spend or waste on the study of nature that would lead to pottery, metallurgy, or the wheel, and so on.

The archaeological landscape of China during the Neolithic was quite interesting and diversified. In the north, in the Huang Ho plain, there appeared between 3500 and 2000 B.C. what archaeologists call the Yang Shao Culture.[1] This was a typical small village culture with houses of pounded earth. Possible storage pits are also reported, conical in shape with a narrow opening at the mouth and a base sometimes three meters wide. Pits of this size may just as well have been used for houses. The economy of the village was based on rice (kernels of which were found in excavation), livestock (pigs, sheep, goats), dogs, fresh-water fish, and mollusks. Dwelling on the river, the ancient Yang Shao inhabitants naturally utilized the food resources available in this stream, and there is evidence that fishing and boating were well developed.

The Yang Shao people used a large range of stone tools, including hoes, arrow points, axes, knives, and adzes. The adzes are remarkably like the Polynesian adzes of three millennia later. Although Yang Shao was certainly not the home base of the Polynesians, as we shall see, the Yang Shao culture apparently participated to a large extent in a general milieu of which these tools were a part. Their source is probably to the south in Indochina and the South China coast.

The pottery of Yang Shao was a beautiful red ware with geometric designs painted in black. Fragments of gray-and-black pottery and red cord-impressed pottery were also found. Pottery vessels were ordinary bowls, three-legged cooking vessels, and some pointed-base storage jars.

Other tools found in the Yang Shao village site were bone ornaments and various types of piercing tools, including projectile points. Shells were used for ornaments and cutting implements.

Finally, the racial affiliation of the Yang Shao dwellers

was definitely Mongoloid, substantially resembling the modern dwellers of North China today.

This culture is found at many other sites in the western part of the Huang Ho plain, while on the eastern side, closer to the coast, appears the Lung Shan or "Black Pottery" Culture. As far as stone tools are concerned, this is much the same as Yang Shao with the exception of the characteristic black pottery which has given the culture its name. The most famous and best-excavated of the sites of this culture is the site of Ch'eng-tzu-yai in Shantung,[2] where a large village existed in the Neolithic period. This site is interesting because it possesses a tamped earth wall encircling the settlement, apparently erected in Neolithic times. The wall, nine meters wide and six high, is an imposing structure and seems to indicate the presence of a rather powerful central authority in Neolithic Ch'eng-tzu-yai. Obviously, a group of simple farmers could hardly erect a wall of this size, encircling a 450-by-390 meter area, and tend their crops at the same time. A central authority was surely present to collect the surplus produce of the farmers and use it to free some of them from their crop labors to work full time in erecting and later repairing the wall. The central authority, whether chief, king, or elder, would also give the necessary directions and initiate and terminate the task.

Evidence of a definite riverine orientation of Ch'eng-tzu-yai economy was also found in the form of fish bones and mollusks. The evidence from Yang Shao and Black Pottery sites together indicates a fairly well-developed river-going technology with boats, nets, fishing tackle, and so on.

In the northern Chinese Neolithic of 3500–2000 B.C. there existed a broad regionally variant village culture with a mixed agricultural–stock raising and riverine economy, probably possessing, at least in some larger villages, a centralized government, already undertaking various forms of public works. Certain implements in the total inventory of this culture indicate a sharing of parts of the substratum from which the Polynesians branched.

Turning now to South China, we find a somewhat different picture. At the same time that North China seemed to be heading for bigger and better things in the sociopolitical and economic field, South China still was in a barbaric state to a large extent.

Our knowledge of the archaeology of this area is derived

from excavations on Formosa,[3] in the Hong Kong and Lamma Island district of Kwangtung[4] and surface collections in the Hoifeng district north of Hong Kong.[5] A great amount of archaeological work has been done since 1949 in this area under the auspices of the Communists, who are stirring the bonfires of nationalism with an archaeological spade, so to speak, creating interest in their country's past. Much of this work is apparently quite substandard and no dramatically different material has been recovered in South China. Moreover, for non-Chinese speakers the work published to date is inaccessible, as publications are almost exclusively in the national language without English summaries, which were thoughtfully included under the old regime.[6]

Our present data suffer from certain deficiencies, however, in that the Formosan sequence is the only one of those mentioned above that has been established by stratigraphic excavation. While Finn's Hong Kong collections were excavated, they were in a nonstratified deposit, and Maglioni's Hoifeng collections were made without any excavation. The unfortunate circumstances that did not permit stratigraphic excavations in Hong Kong and Hoifeng are offset by the quantity of the artifacts recovered. Such large numbers allow us to be reasonably certain that various artifact types and cultural assemblages appearing in the collections are not just one-in-a-million chance occurrences, but are actually representative of the actual state of affairs in prehistoric South China.

Throughout the South China coast and adjoining islands, the earliest-known Neolithic cultures resemble each other quite strongly and apparently were all regional manifestations of a single cultural unit. The characteristics of this earliest culture are: cord-impressed reddish pottery, often poorly fired, soft and sandy; lentoid, rectanguloid adzes; and a distinctive kind of adze known as the Hoabinh adze, first found in Indochina in the region of the same name. Stone beaters for bark cloth (tapa) are also found with this cultural assemblage on Formosa. In Hoifeng, other types of pottery are found with the cord-impressed ware; these often bear some incised decorations. This cultural manifestation has been called the Cord-Impressed Culture in Formosa, the HSY Culture on Hong Kong and Lamma Island, and the SOV and possibly SAK Cultures in Hoifeng. (HSY, SOV, and SAK are handy abbreviations of longer Chinese names; such abbreviations were used exclusively by both Finn and

Maglioni.) This early stage of the Neolithic was probably contemporary with the early Yang Shao culture of the North China plain. Although a radiocarbon age determination for the SOV Culture has been made, it gives an age of about 1200 B.C., which is probably much too recent. In the absence of definite data on the method in which the sample was collected, we must not make any premature judgments. However, the possibilities of obtaining valid age determinations from archaeological charcoal exposed on the ground surface are very poor indeed. Weathering and any number of natural phenomena may affect the carbon-14 content of the sample.

The Cord-Impressed Pottery Culture of the Neolithic persisted in many areas for some time and was succeeded gradually by a late Neolothic culture, similar to Yuan Shan of Formosa and the PAT of Hoifeng. At this time the Huang Ho cultures of North China had begun to manifest themselves by the appearance in South China of the black, gray, and brown pottery of the northern plain as well as painted pottery decorations. Most interesting for us, however, are the stone adzes found in sites of this general cultural manifestation. These are by no means of North Chinese derivation, but apparently originated on the South China coast or somewhere in the interior of South China. These adzes are fitted with narrow tangs extending from the rear of the blade, which have been produced by cutting away at the bottom and/or sides of the adze, producing a stepped effect on the bottom or a pair of lateral shoulders at the point where the blade abruptly tapers into the tang. Such adzes are *distinctly Polynesian in type and do not appear elsewhere in Asia.* Though the lentoid, rectanguloid adzes of the earlier Neolithic cultures are quite similar to Polynesian forms, they are also found elsewhere throughout the entirety of Asia and into the New World. The stepped and shouldered adzes, on the other hand, are purely Polynesian.

Recent research by Chinese Communist archaeologists has shown that the stepped and shouldered adzes are quite common throughout South China; therefore they are no longer to be considered unusual.[7] Upon further examination of the Late Neolithic cultures, more Polynesian traits appear. Most prominent of these is the so-called *patu,* a flat-bladed chopping club found in varied form throughout all of Polynesia and developed to artistic perfection by the New Zealand Maori. Stone *patu* are particularly characteristic of the Formosan Yuan Shan Culture.[8] Also found in the Formosan Late Neolithic sites are stone bladelike implements used for awls or files which have exact formal-functional counterparts in the Polynesian coral and stone files.[9] Other Polynesian artifact types are the stone flake-cleavers, shell beads, and polished stone jewelry.[10]

The Late Neolithic people of South China had a maritime orientation, fish and shellfish forming a large part of their diet. Archaeological evidence indicates further that they were probably horticulturists and kept domestic animals.[11] The distribution of Late Neolithic (PAT Culture) sites in Hoifeng indicated to Maglioni that these people had come from the coast and moved inland. The majority of Late Neolithic Formosan cultures are on the west coast facing China, and one must conclude that they are "cultural reflections" of what was transpiring on the China coast. It is probable therefore that this was a coastal culture with navigatory capabilities sufficient at least to allow them to cross the Formosa Strait.

To the south, in Indochina, the earliest Neolithic cultures [12] show a definite resemblance to those of south coastal China. In this area, however, certain regional variant adze forms, called the Bacsonian and Hoabinhian (after the regions of Bacson and Hoabinh in which they were found), are predominant, which is not the case in South China. These forms are quite similar to each other, both being ovoid adzes, often flaked on one side only and scarcely ground to sharpen the cutting edge. Crude pottery of cord-or mat-impressed type occurs with these tools also. The sites of this cultural manifestation are generally rock shelters, usually of rather small dimensions, which would seem to indicate that wandering, possibly nonagricultural groups had inhabited them, again contrasting with China's south coast, where the earliest known Neolithic cultures apparently are both horticultural and stock-raising. There is evidence that some of these people had general Melanesoid physical traits.

Despite a lack of technique in the French excavations and a confusing *rapportage* in the literature, the similarities to the South China coast sequence are very evident. In sites of both the Bacsonian and Hoabinhian sequences, stepped and shouldered adzes, as well as rectanguloid forms, appear side by side with the local forms. These Polynesian types are also found at the shell midden site of Somrong Sen, which fits into the Neolithic sequence in Indochina at the level of late Bacsonian.[13] In the later Neolithic stages of Indochina (late

Bacsonian and Somrong Sen) the pottery associated with the stone tools takes on a decided resemblance to the Chinese wares with incised geometric decorations and variegated techniques of impressed or stamped decoration.

The Indochinese archaeological sequences resemble those of the surrounding areas to a certain extent, similar tools and complexes being found in Burma, Siam, and Malaya.

To summarize the picture for Indochina, we see that the Neolithic cultures there were probably less well developed in their subsistence economy than those of the South China coast. The numerous Polynesian adze types found in South China occur also in Indochina in association with those of the Bacson-Hoabinh type found early on the coast of China but gradually phased out by the development of the more advanced Polynesian types.

The Late Neolithic of China and Southeast Asia presents a somewhat complex picture with a well-developed village economy flourishing in the Huang Ho plain, showing definite signs of strong political organization, as well as high productivity and advanced technology. There is little cause to suppose, from the relatively voluminous archaeological material published on the Yang Shao and Cheng-tzu-yai Cultures, that these were directly linked to the Polynesian migrations. On the coast of South China, however, the upper Neolithic cultures were not as advanced as their North China cousins in the area of subsistence and technology. Although possessing a village economy also, the South China Neolithic settlements were small and not protected, probably shifting frequently. A greater reliance was placed on fishing and shellfish gathering than in the north. The culture of the Late Neolithic in the south displays, as we have seen, marked resemblances to that of the Polynesians of a much later date. These resemblances to Polynesian forms are shared by Neolithic Indochina, which was on a much more marginal subsistence level evidently. The strong similarities between the Neolithic of the South China coast–Indochina area and the cultures of Polynesia leave little doubt that this rugged sea coast is the Hawaiki of the Polynesian legends, the ancient homeland in the setting sun, whence began the great trek across *Te Moana* (The Sea), the only ocean that the Polynesians knew.

Similarities have been indicated between Asian and Polynesian archaeological finds in the diverse forms of adzes, weapons, and even such mundane implements as scrapers and files. In addition, we have noted that the South Asia coastal dwellers were seamen of some ability and that their economy—fishing, shellfish gathering, horticulture, and stock raising—was like that of the early Polynesians. Further resemblances probably would have been found if the Chinese investigators had been informed of the wide range of shell tools used by the Polynesians, as many of these may have been overlooked in publication as unimportant beside the very beautiful polished-stone implements.

It must also be borne in mind that some 1,500 years of cultural evolution separates these Asian cultures from the earliest known Polynesian cultures, and during this period a considerable amount of change was forced upon the Polynesians owing to the restrictions of their environment. It is therefore all the more surprising that such basic tool types have survived.

On the present evidence we have indicated that the home of the Polynesians was in South Asia, in the South China–Indochina coastal area. The next question immediately rising to mind is why did the Polynesians leave? The answer is to be found in terminal Neolithic and Bronze Age developments in the North China plain. It was noted that the Huang Ho Neolithic Cultures had exercised some influence on the South China Late Neolithic, especially in the field of ceramics. The presence of this influence indicates that the economic relations of the Huang Ho Cultures were expanding, and one may infer that the population also was growing in the villages of North China. The tendency toward strong government, so evident in the Cheng-tzu-yai fortification walls, would have been accentuated out of the necessity of controlling larger populations and greater food surpluses.

About 1600 B.C. the climbing growth curves of the North China Neolithic produced one of the most fascinating cultures the world has ever seen, the Shang Bronze Age [14] with its weirdly beautiful cast-bronze vessels bearing the first examples of a Chinese script and the strange dragonlike *t'ao t'ieh* masks. This was an urban culture in which village size and population had greatly increased. Large buildings are known and burial customs were extremely elaborate. Religion was well organized and pervaded all aspects of life; as a matter of fact, the bronze vessels of this period are actually intended for ritualistic uses. Writing appeared, and the modern equivalents of the Shang characters often resemble their 3,600-year-old antecedents enough for the similarity to be obvious even to one who does not read Chinese. The earlier political development of Cheng-tzu-yai had been consolidated, and monarchy appeared first in this period, manifested in extremely elaborate tombs with offerings and slave burial. At first the monarchs may have been only rulers of large city-states, similar to the Greek *polis,* but later they were all subject to a single ruler. The hierarchy of later Chinese royalty apparently began to develop here. Warfare was also increased as witnessed by the appearance of horse-drawn chariots, helmets, swords, battle-axes, and evidently bows and arrows. Art was flourishing in the form of beautiful jade, marble, and limestone sculpture, as well as the exquisite cast bronzes which are the hallmark of the culture.

With the events of the terminal Neolithic and the establishment of the Shang dynasty in the Huang Ho and surrounding regions, the foundation of the Chinese empire was laid and marked expansion to the north and south began. It is this expansion between 2000 and 1600 B.C. that was the catalyst in the South China region producing the Polynesian "migrations." (When speaking of ancestral Polynesian migrations I do not imply that the Polynesians left the coast of Asia as an integrated unit, but rather I use the term to indicate the broad ethnic group from which the Polynesians later branched.) As the Chinese empire expanded, the backward marginal ethnic groups were gradually driven to the wall and forced either to amalgamate with the sophisticated northerners or flee if they wished to survive. The disturbances produced in this manner spread outward from the Huang Ho plain like ripples from a pebble dropped into a placid pool, setting off a chain reaction in which more powerful groups were forced to move and in turn evicted less powerful groups who consequently had to seek a home for themselves on the lands of still weaker peoples. In this turmoil the groups from which the Polynesians would ultimately arise began their movements outward into the Pacific, probably around 1700 B.C. or somewhat earlier. These were not large-scale one-way voyages moving quickly across large spans of ocean and skipping many island groups—few primitive migrations may be said truly to be of that type. Rather, the ancestors of the Polynesians left the coast of Asia gradually over a period of several centuries in a large number of short movements, island hopping and "coasting," selecting the proper seasons for movement. Probably many voyagers returned to Asia only to depart again. Some doubtless remained behind, for we know that dark-skinned peoples with marked maritime abilities dwelt on the shore of South China even as late as A.D. 600 in the T'ang Dynasty.[15] It is further probable that regional physical variations existed among the various groups departing from South Asia, as well as differences in dialect and culture. Some groups may have resembled the modern Polynesians reasonably well; others may have been more Negroid in appearance; and still others, who had been in closer contact with the Huang Ho invaders, were more Mongoloid. Unfortunately, the data on the human skeletal remains in South Asia Neolithic sites are very meager and therefore no help in pinpointing Polynesian racial origins more precisely.

After the ancestral Polynesians had substantially departed the South Asian area, the archaeological record gives us further clues to their itinerary through the main archipelagoes of the western Pacific—Melanesia, New Guinea, the Philippines, and Indonesia—although a precise tracing of their exact movements is impossible at present. Every place where the ancestors of the Polynesians touched and settled they left their mark in the archaeological record in the form of the characteristic adze types: shouldered and stepped, tanged quadrangular adzes, and the lentoid or cylindrical adzes. In addition to these prime index fossils, other evidence is found in the form of stone tapa beaters, pig and chicken bones, fish hooks, and pottery recovered in archaeological middens in the western Pacific.

In general, the evidence indicates that these emigrants touched the Philippines first and then filtered south through that archipelago into Melanesia and Papua, and possibly Indonesia. It is, however, quite possible that Malayo-Polynesians reached Indonesia by simply voyaging southward and eastward along the Asian coast, forming a separate arm of migration that may or may not have ultimately contributed directly to the occupation of Polynesia.

In the Philippines[16] there is a wealth of archaeological material available for study, although, strangely enough, few reports of individual excavations have ever been published. The picture here seems to be fairly clear, despite the absense of stratified sites and a tendency to rely on a more logical than empirical cultural division. The first classification arrived at by Beyer[17] consisted of a four-stage division of the Neolithic, adhering to that proposed by Heine-Geldern.[18]

The first stage of the sequence was the proto-Neolithic,

characterized by the Bacson-Hoabinh adzes found in Indochina and South China. The Early "true" Neolithic was characterized by adzes with cylindrical or lentoid cross sections (termed "Walzenbeile" by Heine-Geldern). The Middle Neolithic is characterized by the shouldered adze, the ridged adze (a variety of the stepped adze), the Polynesian tanged adze, and a transitional type between the oval or rectangular shouldered and ridged types. Beyer characterizes the Late Neolithic in terms of the rectangular-section adze and an increase in jade jewelry, also tapa beaters and advanced, neatly polished stepped adzes.

On the basis of the coastal Chinese data, however, it appears that Beyer's work should be revised somewhat and the Middle and Late Neolithic Periods combined. The rectangular adze can no longer be said to be a late feature in the Philippines, for it occurs in association with the early cord-impressed pottery on Formosa. There were no reports until recently of pottery being associated with stone tools, but some stone adzes have recently been found in very early Christian-era jar-burial sites [19] and it is a certainty that much earlier antecedents of this pottery will be found.

The ancestors of the Polynesians probably arrived in the Philippines in the first half of the second millennium before Christ and brought with them the culture represented in Beyer's Middle and Late Neolithic divisions. Aside from the adzes and tapa beaters already mentioned, these people brought the pig and dog and were probably excellent woodcarvers, as is indicated by the number of small adzes suitable for fine carving work. Jade working was quite pronounced, as in the PAT Culture of Hoifeng, and the techniques employed were quite like those later used by the Maori of New Zealand.

The Malayo-Polynesians were not the first people into the Philippines. The islands had evidently been long inhabited at least by Negrito groups, who are still found in inaccessible regions of Bataan and Western Luzon. There is a definite possibility that the islands were inhabited from Paleolithic times onward,[20] as some scattered finds of generalized Asian Paleolithic tool types have been found in the Rizal district.

Farther east, both the Marianas and Palau were settled by migrations from the Philippine Islands. The Marianas were probably occupied around 2000 B.C. according to Spoehr [21]; the earliest radiocarbon date, run on a sample from near the top of a rather deep deposit, is 1500 B.C. Spoehr believes that another five centuries would account for the deposits beneath the level of the dated sample. The pottery of this earliest Marianas culture is quite like the red-slipped ware found in the Philippines as late as the beginning of the Christian era.[22] Palau was settled somewhat later, possibly, about the start of the Christian era or a little before. The pottery is again like Philippine Iron Age material,[23] and there are further corroborations for a relatively late date for Palauan settlement in the form of several types of beads, the earliest of which may be from Han dynasty China (206 B.C.–A.D. 220). Osborne believes that the old Palauan culture is essentially a Philippine Iron Age offshoot with a later Melanesian influence.

Moving south now, away from the Philippines, we must consider Indonesia. Unfortunately, little work has been done in the Neolithic sites of this region, more attention being devoted to the spectacular Metal Age tombs, monuments, and temple structures of the proto-historic and historic periods. There are, however, a large number of isolated Neolithic type of surface finds, and a few sites of that period have been excavated, but so few that no consistent picture can be constructed. The most recent summarization of Indonesian archaeology,[24] however, indicates that the stone-adze types that we have associated with the Malayo-Polynesians (shouldered, stepped, rectangular, lentoid, etc.) are all present. Hoabinhian affinities are also evident in the stone adzes. In addition highly decorative "rouletted" pottery similar to that found in the Lapita site in New Caledonia appears in several places[25] (see below). Heekeren himself equates the rectanguloid adzes (including the "roof-shaped" and shouldered varieties under this rubric) with Austronesians or Malayo-Polynesians, who distributed the artifacts in question from Indonesia to Madagascar on one side and Easter Island on the other.[26]

In Melanesia, our knowledge of prehistory is still somewhat limited, as the area is quite large and relatively little stratigraphic archaeology has been done. What has been done in Fiji and New Caledonia, however, is of excellent caliber[27] and gives us a good basis for tracing the movements of peoples leading to the population of Polynesia. The radiocarbon time clock indicates that New Caledonia was inhabited by at least 800 B.C. and Fiji was probably occupied contemporaneously, although the radiocarbon dates from there have a somewhat shorter span, 2000 B.C. ± 500.[28] There is some reason to believe that the Malayo-Polynesian groups moving into Melanesia found some of the islands already occupied by Negrito pygmy or other Negroid groups speaking completely foreign languages with much simpler material cultures. Occasionally artifacts are found in Melanesia that are extremely primitive in nature, such as a group of tools resembling Paleolithic hand axes which I examined in the Fiji Museum at Suva in 1958. There is, however, no stratigraphic evidence of such an occupation as yet, but the archaeological work to date has not been extensive enough to negate completely the possibility of such finds.

The burden of the similarities existing between Melanesia and South Asia is in the field of ceramics; stone adzes can only be of secondary importance, since few were found

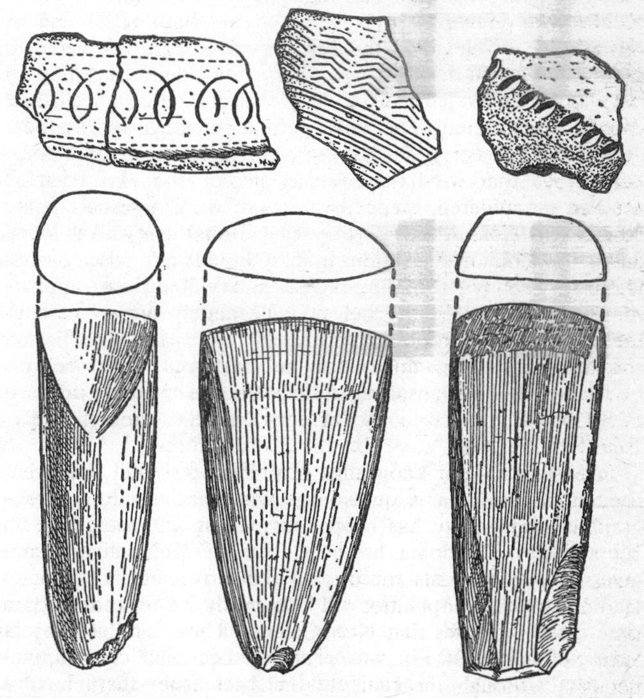

Fig. 4. Potsherds and stone adzes from Fiji (after Gifford, 1953)

in the excavations. In Fiji, two major periods were outlined by Gifford's excavations of Site 17 at Navatu, Viti Levu, a rock shelter with an eleven-foot-deep fan of cultural debris in front of it. The Early Period was characterized by potsherds showing impressions producing an effect of zigzag or criss-crossing relief lines. The reconstructions showed the total vessel shapes to have been globular with constricted necks and flaring rims, which often bore pie-crust decoration and grooving. Other sherds appearing in this horizon showed cord-impressing. Most of the relief pottery of the Fijian Early Period resembles that of the impressed pottery of Southern China.

The Late Period pottery found in the upper level of Site 17 is characterized by an abundance of incised sherds bearing designs roughly similar to the comb-incised pottery of the South China Neolithic and that of North China.

In the excavations in New Caledonia both relief and incised pottery related to the Fiji materials were recovered, in addition to quantities of plain, very crude utilitarian pottery. It was impossible, however, to establish stratigraphic superpositions of any pottery types on one site such as was found at Navatu on Viti Levu. Nevertheless, at Lapita, near Koné, a site was located and subsequently dated as having been occupied at about 800 B.C. At this site some unusual pottery was excavated, differing from that found elsewhere in the New Caledonian excavations in its stamped and incised decorations.[29] This pottery appeared in small quantities on unexcavated sites in Fiji [30] and may ultimately attain increased archaeological importance. Although appearing elsewhere in the western Pacific, this pottery is not found on the coast of Asia and is an Oceanian original trait. The stone adzes of both New Caledonia and Fiji are much like those found on the South Asian coast in the Cord-Impressed Culture of Formosa and the SOV Culture of Hoifeng: the Melanesian adzes are lenticular or ovoid in section and short, but differ in their high degree of polish, which is an original Melanesian trait. There are other features of Melanesian archaeology which do not necessarily bear resemblances to the cultures of South Asia but will later be shown to be antecedent to certain Polynesian culture traits. These are rectangular earth and stone house platforms found in Fiji,[31] knives made of perforated snail shells found in both Fiji and New Caledonia [32] in early sites, octopus lures found in New Caledonia,[33] and a large number of various crude New

Caledonian stone scraping and chopping tools and shellfish hooks of Polynesian style.[34] Further antecedents of Polynesian developments are the megalithic monuments—uprights, tables, slab enclosures, alignments and mounds—found throughout Melanesia.[35] In New Caledonia a remarkable series of petroglyphs have been recorded [36] whose motifs are much like those found throughout Eastern Polynesia, one common mask-like motif often duplicating the Easter Island *makemake* mask.

Although practically nothing is known archaeologically of the New Hebrides, as no excavations have been done there, pottery still being made there by the aborigines resembles that of New Caledonia and Fiji in many respects, which could be anticipated on the basis of linguistic and other cultural connections between Fiji, New Caledonia, and the New Hebrides.

In New Guinea, where Malayo-Polynesian speaking groups have spread along the north coast, there has only been one

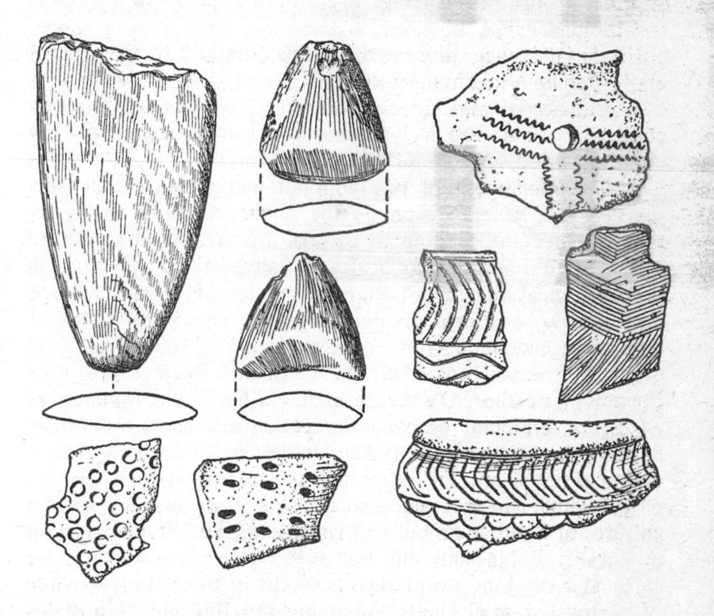

Fig. 5. Potsherds and stone adzes from New Caledonia (after Gifford and Shutler, 1956)

archaeological excavation so far reported.[37] This excavation, along with a few scattered surface finds, indicates that substantial similarities exist between archaeological and recent Melanesian pottery. Also, the presence of an unknown cultural unit, producing beautifully incised pots, has been detected.[38] At present, excavations are beginning in inland New Guinea in the Wahgi Plateau, where unusual finds of suspiciously Polynesian-looking artifacts have been made by white farmers, but it will be some time before the results of this work become available.

This survey of Melanesian archaeology then indicates that by approximately 1000 B.C. the islands of Melanesia on the border of Polynesia had been settled by Malayo-Polynesian speakers who brought with them a tool kit of South Asian origin. The archaic character of the pottery and adze types found in the earliest Melanesian sites indicate that the settlers of this particular group of islands may have left Asia somewhat earlier than other groups or that they were a somewhat retarded group on the fringe areas of the major South Asian development.

In the evidence presented in this chapter there are six major points to be emphasized:

1. Archaeological evidence shows that the basic population pool from which the Polynesians diverged developed on the coast of South Asia.

2. The movement of this population into the Pacific was sparked by the expansion of the advanced cultures of the Huang Ho plain, leading to the rise of the Chinese empire.

3. This movement can be traced across the Pacific in the archaeological records of the Philippines, Melanesia, Papua, and Indonesia, using certain characteristic artifact types as cultural indices.

4. The evidence at hand indicates that by approximately 1000 B.C., at least, the fringe areas of Polynesia (i.e., Melanesia) were already occupied by Malayo-Polynesian speakers bearing the antecedents of Polynesian culture. These people had also settled in the Philippines and in coastal New Guinea.

5. Other groups were also moving through the western Pacific, occupying Palau and the Marianas, for example, in a general push eastward.

6. To conclude: the stage was therefore set in the first millennium B.C. for the final population movement into the Polynesian triangle from the islands of the Fijian group and other areas of Melanesia.

7

Sails and Stars

To reach the western fringe of the Polynesian triangle by the second millennium B.C., the ancestral Polynesians had to traverse a wide expanse of ocean. Many islands were scattered along the way; parts of the passage may have been merely a matter of island hopping between the high, easily visible volcanic islands of Indonesia, the Philippines, and Melanesia-Papua. Other legs of the journey to the Polynesian fringes were not so easily franchised, such as the initial phases between China and the Philippines or the gap between the New Hebrides and Fiji. These involved crossing several hundred miles of open sea in each case, with no stops between and without foreknowledge of even the existence of a destination in the direction of voyage. Once native exploration had begun in the Polynesian triangle itself, the magnitude of distances covered in settling the islands of New Zealand, Hawaii, and Easter Island, to mention the most outstanding cases, represents genuine feats of navigation and survival of the highest rank.

Considering the Polynesian geography, the Polynesians appear to stand among the greatest mariners of all human history, their accomplishments in this field making the Vikings, Romans, and Phoenicians look rather insignificant by comparison, especially considering that the voyaging was made against the prevailing winds and currents for the largest part. We cannot invoke "land bridges" that conveniently appear and disappear to explain any part of this population dispersion, as there is simply no post-Pleistocene geological evidence of any such thing existing in the Polynesian triangle. When the probabilities of the success of such a population movement are considered, the objective achievements of the Polynesians and their ancestors seem incredible, and one is prompted to demand "How?" In answer to such queries there is fortunately some evidence at hand with which we can partially reconstruct the state of Polynesian shipping and navigation both as it was in the days of European contact and in the dim past when the Polynesians first entered their present home. We stand indebted to the first European explorers for much of what we know of Polynesian naval science. Ethnographies give considerable data also, especially on smaller types of canoes that are still seen in use. Unfortunately, the actual navigation techniques are little known although much speculation has been expended on them.

There were apparently two main types of craft in use by the Polynesians when the Europeans first appeared; these were canoes and rafts. Of the two the former was far and away the more important. These two types can generally be further subdivided, since several broad varieties of canoes and rafts can be identified aside from the native typologies and regional differences in design found throughout Polynesia.

The canoe was the most important of the Polynesian seacraft, and its production was often a matter of no small gravity. In many Polynesian islands canoes were made by specially trained craftsmen working under numerous ritual restrictions. In the Marquesas,[1] for instance, the tree from which the hull was to be made was felled to the tune of the creation chant, an extremely sacred element of the liturgy. The tree was hewn where it fell, a sacred building being constructed over it to protect it and shelter the workmen. These men slept on the spot, as they were consecrated for the duration of the task. The "patron," for whom the canoe was being built, fed the entire work group, which often numbered into the hundreds. Women and strangers could not approach the sacred precincts. The finishing of a canoe and the removal of the ceremonial restrictions imposed during its construction were the occasion for a feast of great size. A chant recorded by Handy in the Marquesas lists in detail the step-by-step procedure followed in the building of the canoe of the mythical hero Motuhaiki, who had to catch the sun to gain time to finish his work. All parts of the Marquesan canoes were named for persons or legendary characters. The launching of a new canoe usually was soon followed by a raid on an enemy tribe to get victims whose *mana* or supernatural power would be transferred to the canoe, thus validating its existence completely. The Hawaiian native historian Malo [2] has given a very complete account of the Hawaiian ceremonies involved in canoe construction, which generally seems to coincide with Handy's Marquesan data. The Hawaiian *Kahuna,* or canoe-building expert, was present at all stages of the production from the selection of the proper tree to the launching of the finished canoe. No progress could be made without his participation at each and every step, with the proper prayers and charms to insure success. As a result of this, Malo observed, "The building of a canoe was an affair of religion." [3]

The canoes of the Polynesian islands can generally be divided into three major classes: the small dugout outrigger canoe; the larger planked outrigger canoe; and the double-hull canoe. Of course the natives in each island group had, and often retain to this day, their own local types and terminology as well as slight design differences, but these are minor and need not be of great concern at present.

The dugout canoe is the simplest type known, its hull consisting of a shaped and hollowed log with gunwale strips sometimes attached and the usual outrigger complex of booms, connecting struts, and outrigger floats. In the Marquesas, Porter [4] saw small dugout canoes that were nothing but the keels of the larger plank canoes with the strakes and all superstructure removed.

The plank canoe consisted generally of a long dugout base to which the strakes and gunwales were lashed with coconut fiber. The joints between the planks were often provided with tongues and grooves, while the spaces between the planks and in the lashing holes were calked with vegetable fibers and gums. In some cases seams were also covered with strips to keep in the calking compounds.

The Tuamotu islanders, as an exception, built a somewhat different type of plank canoe, using a technique that resembled our own technique for plank construction, in which a keel and framework with vertical ribs were first constructed and then covered with planks lashed in the usual manner.[5]

The bows and sterns of the planked canoes were often highly decorated; those of the Maori were carved to a degree unequaled elsewhere with the distinctive Maori spiral and tiki motifs. The Marquesan canoes [6] had bird-head prows, and small tikis or human skulls were fixed on the upturned stern, facing the bow as though to invoke supernatural guidance in all enterprises undertaken in the canoe.

The Hawaiians [7] had small, upturned, spatulate canoe prows which were known also as "birds" (*manu*), but actually could only be said to represent possible abstractions thereof.

The bows and sterns of the Polynesian planked outriggers were usually covered a short distance toward the center of the ship with lashed plankings. Seats were placed across the open midships area of the canoe. The outrigger attachments were the same on these larger craft as on the small dugouts. Masts for sailing were stepped in holes in the seats and keel sockets. Such masts were most often of an inverted leg-of-mutton or lateen type, made of fine mats. The steering was done by large oars at the stern and often at the bow, so that coming about could be effected merely by reversing the sail, raising the stern steering oar as the stern became the bow, and dropping the idle bow steering oar into service.

The size range of outrigger canoes of this type was tremendous and depended on function rather than on the whim of the builders. Porter reports that the Marquesan war canoes of 1813 were 50 feet long and 2 feet wide,[8] which is corroborated by statements of Marquesan natives almost a century later [9] who claimed that war canoes were 60 feet long. I had the opportunity to see a miserable remnant of the last surviving native war canoe in the Marquesas, despoiled by souvenir-hunting members of an earlier "expedition" who hacked off the carved bows and stern. In its pristine state it may easily have been 60 feet long.

Finally, there are the double canoes made of two canoe hulls lashed together athwartships without any exterior outriggers, the double hulls giving ample stability. On the booms that connected the two hulls amidships, a platform was erected and often one or more small huts were built to house the crew. Masts were stepped on one hull usually and could be manipulated as in the plank canoes to change direction without actually coming about, while steering oars were placed at bow and stern to facilitate such "end changing." The Fijian *ndrua* double canoes [10] were equipped with steering oars as much as 45 feet in length, a pair of which are still to be seen in the Fiji Museum at Suva. These tremendous vessels were completely decked over for their entire length, and the hulls could be entered only by hatches at the plat-

form amidships. All living was done on this plat
a house or shelter stood.

The double canoes were the biggest vessel
nesians possessed, often running over 100 feet in length with depths and widths of 6 feet or more.[11] A legend collected by Handy in the Marquesas records a voyage of the greatest double canoe ever known to the Marquesans.[12] This canoe, named *Ka'a hua,* was built in the valley of Puama'u on Hiva Oa and was so deep that the bailers had to climb the sides to throw out the bilge water. This canoe was provisioned with a great amount of breadfruit paste and sailed from Hiva Oa to Nuku Hiva, thence to the east to a land called *Te Fiti* (Peru?), after which it returned to its home port. This, of course, may well be exaggeration, but the observations of early European explorers substantiate the fact that many Polynesian canoes came close to this size.

The double canoes were used for the most exacting of all tasks, long, deep-water voyages and exploration for new lands. Owing to their immensity the carrying capacity of such vessels was quite high and their seaworthiness was unequaled. With their platform huts and deep storage space they could accommodate provisions that would well provide for extended trips. Such a ship would not quickly fall prey to the vibration and torsion which it was subjected to on the high seas. The lashings that held it together permitted a good measure of play in every joint in a situation where rigidity would have been disastrous. The double hull gave the craft many of the qualities of a catamaran as far as speed and maneuverability were concerned, thus adding to its praiseworthiness.

Aside from the outrigger canoes, the Polynesians also made some use of rafts. These were manufactured from bamboo or logs of other types but were not in great vogue. In many island groups rafts saw service only in emergencies. The Moriori of the Chatham Islands constructed peculiar rafts called *Whaka pahi'i,* composed of cratelike frames in which were placed bundles of a local reed, *Phormium tenax,* along with large quantities of kelp. The reed bundles were lashed to the inside of the frame, forming a crude boat-shaped structure with a flat-bottomed rectangular section. These rafts reputedly carried sixty people or so, but this sounds like Maori humor again, and it would seem more likely that they could carry no more than five or ten. They did not have sails but were paddled.[13]

On the island of Mangareva[14] the outrigger canoe was evidently phased out gradually and the islanders traveled to points within the atoll ring on rafts made of tree trunks. These were used in daily work and were propelled by pole, paddle, or sail. The rise in popularity of these rafts in Mangareva is difficult to explain but may have been occasioned by a serious shortage of suitable canoe wood.

Bamboo rafts were well known in the Marquesas if one can judge from their frequency of appearance in legends. One large specimen was supposedly made in five tiers, three above the water and two below, and conveyed He-pea-Taipi, a mythological character of Hiva Oa, to Havaiki and back.[15] Others have been described as 12 by 10 yards in size, with mat sails and a capacity of from forty to eighty people, which for a surface area of that size taxes credulity. My own Marquesan informants mentioned bamboo rafts in recounting legends to me but were quite positive that although of large size they had no sails and were carried at the mercy of the currents. With the exception of He-pea-Taipi's raft, all other rafts mentioned in Marquesan legends were used by beaten tribes to escape in extreme emergencies when the wrath of the victors was to be feared.

Because of the distribution of rafts throughout Polynesia, it is fairly certain that this type of craft was part of the original culture of the Polynesians and was brought from Asia, where indeed rafts are common.[16] The word for raft on the South China coast closely resembles the Polynesian equivalent, *paepae*. Rafts are mentioned early in Chinese annals as having been used by illustrious individuals.

Records of the double canoe in Chinese historical documents date back as far as the eighth to fifth centuries B.C.

There is no question that the outrigger and double canoes were the forms used by the Polynesians in their population movements, The nonhydrodynamic rafts would scarcely have survived voyages of this type; furthermore, they were extremely unmaneuverable, while the outriggers were fast, could lay very close to a wind, and could sail rings around European ships because of their novel method of end changing rather than turning, a system which is striking in its simplicity. Finally, in all the legends of island settlement throughout Polynesia, it is invariably outriggers or double canoes that are mentioned, never the rafts.

The techniques of navigation used by the Polynesians are unfortunately not known to us in any detail, and this has led some "theorists" to hypothesize that precise methods never existed—which is a rather willful assumption at best. No systematic interrogation of any Polynesian was ever carried out at the time the Europeans moved into Polynesia; therefore no detailed information was bequeathed to us. All that we have are rather circumstantial accounts, composed of statements of early explorers, gleanings from legends, and recent ethnographical information. Nearly all agree on one point: stars were used for course setting and bearings. The Polynesians had a detailed practical knowledge of astronomy which has mostly perished through lack of use in recent times. They knew by long experience the season of changes of the sky and the portions of the horizon and relative times at which the various stars made their appearances. The Samoans used three-star alignments for positioning.[17] They took bearings on various stars as soon as they appeared on the horizon, and their course was kept true by a man lying on the canoe bottom lining up course stars in the vault of the heavens. An old Samoan once kept an ethnographer awake all night rattling off stars and their purposes, soon completely exhausting the ability of the European to identify the stars of which he spoke.

The French missionary Laval, arriving in the Tuamotu island group in 1849, was forced to travel exclusively by native transportation and logged much time in the double canoes of the Tuamotuans. He reported that the stars were the navigators' guideposts, with series of stars indicating the location of all the islands known to the natives. As the stars moved across the heavens away from the horizon, they were replaced by new ones just appearing.

Today, Marquesans fishing off their rocky coastline, or traversing the 120 miles between northern and southern islands of the archipelago, orient themselves by the stars. Significantly, there have been no cases of boats being blown out to sea, in recent times at least.

Other aids to navigation that the Polynesian utilized were the winds and their seasonal cycles. If voyages to the east were contemplated, the annual period was awaited in which the southeast trade winds reversed themselves, and when the northwest wind began the big stone anchors were lifted. This use of seasonal wind changes is no trick of the Polynesians alone but was used by the Alexandrian Greeks, and later the Romans, in striking directly across the Indian Ocean from the mouth of the Red Sea to the tip of India.[18] The Chinese also used winds in their voyages in the Chinese coastal regions and out to the Philippines, as well as in their contacts with the coast of East Africa. The Polynesians had an extensive terminology built up for winds, with various terms denoting the direction, the strength, and often the effect of the wind on the water, and their observations would obviously have been of aid in navigation.

Beside winds, knowledge of current directions could be of great help in orientation when clouds obscured the sun and stars usually relied on for bearings. The regular South Pacific current flow, as well as many of the baffling currents in the straits between islands or island groups, were all well mastered by the Polynesians. Water color was often a way of detecting currents, as it was of determining water depth. Birds and other natural phenomena, such as driftwood bearing marks of human workmanship, etc., were also clues. In dangerous waters in coral atoll groups or near reefs, the sound of the breakers could be used, as could the smell of land, a thing difficult for the untrained Occidental nose to distinguish. Many other phenomena were used at various times to determine the presence of land. I have often noticed that landfalls are made by Polynesians on the basis of the clouds above the land, before the land itself is visible. In this connection, the white-bottomed shallow lagoon of the famous island of Ana'a in the Tuamotus casts such a reflection on the clouds above it that steersmen can set their courses by it in the daytime.

To conclude this discussion of navigation techniques, brief as it must be, I would like to give a testimony on my conversion to a firm belief in Polynesian navigational ability. In 1958, we returned from the Marquesas to Tahiti aboard the *Tiare Taporo,* a Tahitian copra schooner captained by Louis Tapoto, also Tahitian and one of the most able captains in all of Polynesia. We ran into a cyclonic storm shortly after the Marquesas had slipped over the horizon, and stayed in the middle of that perturbation for three days, during which time the wind boxed the compass roughly every four hours and neither sun nor stars could be seen to take a "fix" of our location. We were running straight for the northeastern side of the treacherous Tuamotu Islands, which have never been satisfactorily mapped even to this day, and I frankly admit that by the third day I had visions of our ending up on a lonely atoll reef, spilling our overload of copra and passengers onto the rough coral. With only the compass and his own knowledge, Captain Louis sailed onward, however, and spent a couple of hours in the cabin the night before we were to make landfall, calculating and thinking. He emerged and said without fanfare, "Seven o'clock tomorrow morning we'll be at the pass at Takaroa."

At ten minutes to seven Takaroa was not to be seen, although a lookout was in the crow's-nest. At seven o'clock, still no Takaroa, but plenty of fog. At ten after seven, *"Era te fenua O Takaroa pa'i!"* ("There's the land, it's Takaroa!"), sang out the lookout, and there we were a mile offshore. The surf crashing on the reef was just visible as a thin, writhing white line above which vague, dark, low shapes flitted in the fog—the coconut palm stands of Takaroa. The skill that Louis Tapoto had acquired in forty years of sailing was carried in his head. It was not obtainable in a book but by instruction from masters and by personal experience. And so it was with the ancient Polynesians also. Although they were taught their basic navigational skills by tribal experts, a great majority of their knowledge was derived from constant practice, producing the kind of skill that is often very difficult to defeat, analogous to the 25,000-hour airline pilots of today's air age, who know their planes and their medium better than anything else and have acquired an indefinable sixth sense in addition to their purely mechanical skills.

Aside from the above incident, my life has often been in Polynesian hands in the bosom of the sea—in outriggers, whaleboats, copra schooners, or twenty feet beneath the surface of a Marquesan bay. As the reader can see, my trust was justified, and I attribute this to the marine aptitude which is an integral part of the Polynesian way of life, part of a tradition beginning on the coast of Asia, passed on from many mouths into many ears across a span of three millennia and 8,000 miles, and still continuing today.

The survival problems aboard a Polynesian vessel bear discussion. The myriad marine creatures provided an ample source of protein for voyagers, and all that had to be carried was vegetable food and water, in the case of the short voyages. The popular staple, fermented paste made of pounded taro or breadfruit, was ideal for this use, as having once begun fermentation it would not readily spoil. It could be carried in large leaf packages slung inside the hull or the deckhouse, or in a surface silo on the deck. Water could be obtained from rain and the fluid in fish flesh, but additional supplies would be carried in large bottle gourds fitted with stoppers of wood.

For long voyages of exploration or, possibly, migration when the seeding of a new colony was imminent, however, all the possible food and useful plants were stored in the canoes so that they could be planted upon arrival. Thus the new colony would begin its career with the full complement of agricultural possibilities that the mother group had possessed. This posed some problems, for such plants as yams, taro, sweet potatoes, and others are very perishable and must be carefully packed in earth to preserve their viability. Coconuts must also be handled with care. Besides the plants, dogs, chickens, and pigs were included in the passenger list, and rats and lizards usually came uninvited. The dogs and pigs aboard such an expedition probably lived off human feces in part and were victimized in their turn when food supplies ran low. There were numerous indications in the legends of Polynesia that voyages of exploration and settlement were provisioned in this way, and archaeological evidence is now at hand to support the legends. The Hawaiian Islands were settled by a fairly sizable and well-provisioned expedition [19] that carried with it all the necessities of life. Likewise, in excavating an extremely ancient village site in the Marquesas, a site probably inhabited by some of the actual Marquesan "first families," I found definite evidence in the form of food-preparation tools that the Marquesans had *arrived* with coconuts, root crops, and breadfruit, as well as with the pig and the dog.

With all of our discussion of Polynesian vessels, navigation techniques, and survival practices, we have still not touched directly upon a very important topic. How effective was all this maritime knowledge in enabling the Polynesians to get about from island to island, making long round-trip voyages? A mere glance at the isolation of many of the Polynesian islands, such as the Marquesas, Easter Island, Hawaii, and Rapa, would lead one to a rather favorable impression of the navigational prowess of the Polynesians. The picture is not all so simple, however, for there is much evidence that would contradict that point of view. Such evidence was recently summarized in the book *Ancient Voyagers in the South Pacific*, by Andrew Sharp,[20] presenting an essentially negative appraisal of Polynesian voyaging. In brief, Sharp's thesis is that navigation techniques did not permit accuracy over long distances. Therefore, intentional voyaging was restricted; consequently, the majority of settlements in Polynesia came about because of accidental voyages of ships blown off course while fishing, and so on. These accidental voyages, according to Sharp, occurred in both directions, against and with the prevailing winds, with Eastern Polynesia being settled first by accidental voyages from Western Polynesia, and then the intervening islands being settled by accidental voyages from the east back to the west. Sharp insists that settlement voyages were not purposeful but accidental, food and domestic animals arriving piecemeal by later accidental voyages. Sharp believes that extensive voyaging took place in these areas only: [21] the Rotuma and Ellice Islands; Fiji, Tonga, and Samoa; Tahiti and the Tuamotus; and Rarotonga and Atiu, none of which involved any distance of over 300 miles.

This unusual thesis is based on selected historical and anthropological data that in the main support Sharp, definitely showing there is some reason to doubt that at the European contact period the Polynesians were doing a great deal of long voyaging. Sharp's data, however, are by no means an adequate summary of the literature available; and as Katherine Luomala has said,[22] the entire presentation of the thesis has more of the aspect of a pet notion than that of a scientifically developed theory. It is beyond the scope of this chapter to deal with Sharp's book in detail, but in all fairness and objectivity after criticizing Sharp, I must present a basis for my own views or else accept the same strictures just applied to him. Briefly, there are several points concerning *Ancient Voyagers* that bear illumination:

1. Sharp has in many cases overlooked nonsupporting evidence. He states that "there are no records of deliberate voyages to and from the Marquesas by native craft . . . so far as a diligent search of the published literature can establish." [23] Such records are numerous in chants of Tahiti and Hawaii, and legends of Mangareva, as well as of the Marquesas.[24] Again, he makes much of the statements of a Tahitian priest who accompanied Captain Cook from Tahiti. This priest, Tupaia,[25] had sailed much in native craft and had visited and heard of many islands. His statements indicated that long voyages were generally made only with difficulty. Sharp neglects to mention, however, that when Cook reached Indonesia, thousands of miles away, the same Tupaia could give the exact course setting for Tahiti merely by reference to

the stars. Unfortunately, Tupaia died in Java, and all too little is recorded of him in Cook's journals.

2. Sharp's accidental-voyage mechanism for the population of Polynesia is used to argue in both directions, using accidental voyages to bring Polynesians far to the east against most of the winds, then invoking accidental voyages to send them back westward again. In cases such as Easter Island and the Marquesas, to the east of which no islands exist, Sharp begs the question, as there is no source from which these islands could be settled. Sharp never discloses why the Polynesians were not "accidentally" carried to Asia again by the largely southeast winds. Obviously, "accidental voyages" is a handy panacea for all the ills of Polynesian migration theory and could be applied to any area of the world with equal facility.

3. Finally, even if one grants the thesis that Polynesians of the eighteenth century were somewhat restricted in their voyaging, this does not mean that they always were so in the past. The Polynesians once had pottery but subsequently lost the art, as we shall see later. We have already noted the probability of a native script's being lost also. In the eighteenth century, when all of Polynesia had been settled, why is it so difficult to suppose that the practice of long voyages was dying out?

Other factors, of which Sharp could not be cognizant when composing his work, were the archaeological data from Hawaii and the Marquesas indicating that both were settled by well-equipped expeditions. In the case of the Marquesas at least, the settlers came from a long distance. Recent evidence from the earliest Polynesian camps in New Zealand indicates that sweet potatoes or other crops were brought by the Polynesian discoverers of those islands.[26] The settlement legends of Easter Island[27] and the recently partially translated Easter Island tablets also speak of deliberate settlement voyages carrying all necessary food plants and animals to begin a new colony. Such evidence is definitely against Sharp's refusal to admit any purposeful settlement by equipped expeditions.

The present status of our knowledge of the Polynesian navigational arts can be summarized as follows:

1. The Polynesians had a well-developed technology, producing extremely seaworthy vessels of a wide size range.

2. Empirical navigation techniques were numerous, and their value, even today, cannot be arbitrarily dismissed. A

dearth of scientifically recorded information, however, does not allow us to state their value objectively.

3. Definite archaeological evidence exists proving that well-provisioned expeditions occupied both Hawaii and the Marquesas. This accords with legendary evidence from all over Polynesia that not all settlements were made by chance, although some may have been.

4. Although there is evidence of a curtailment of voyaging in historic times, this has no bearing whatsoever on the state of navigation 2,000 years previous.

5. The "accidental voyage" thesis explains nothing, being applicable to any situation in the world owing to its lack of specificity. Although such voyages undoubtedly often occurred, they seldom would have resulted in permanent settlement.

In conclusion, we have very definite evidence, both from archaeological and documentary sources, of Polynesian ability in navigational matters. The actual sequence in which the islands of Polynesia were settled can only be determined by archaeology, however, as no amount of theorizing can substitute for hard facts. When the archaeological sequences of all the major island groups of Polynesia are well established we will be better able to make statements about the navigational ability of the Polynesians. Only then can we trace inter-island contacts in the forms of artifacts of stone and shell, and only then will we finally attain a more certain grasp of the ultimate truth.

8

Hawaiki

On the western border of the Polynesian triangle lie the islands of the Samoan group, with rugged crests rising from the brilliant aquamarine of their reef borders. To the north and west of the Samoan group is the tiny kingdom of the Tongan Islands, some of which are of the flat makatea type, others of volcanic origin. The population of both groups is flourishing, and life in Samoa and Tonga represents a very ideal blend between the old native culture and the irreversible march of Western civilization, in which the native language, form of government, social organization, and literary background are retained while plantation systems, copra crops, and a cash economy are also accepted.

This evidence of a continuing future for the Western Polynesians of Samoa and Tonga is matched by omnipresent witnesses of a hoary past in the form of many house ruins, tombs, and fortifications scattered through the uncleared brush around the modern villages and in the remote areas of the interior. In Samoa there is practically no place, except of course in modern towns, where some archaeological monuments do not confront the observer. A drive along any of the roads from Apia will carry one past many fields, coconut plantations, or thickets in which the low, weed-covered mounds of ancient house platforms are to be seen. Without leaving the auto it is also possible to see the earthworks of fortified villages and the stone cairns covering the graves of long-dead chiefs. In Tonga antiquities of a similar nature also greet the visitor, chief among which is the incomparable "trilithon," a great stone arch made of two huge uprights capped by an equally imposing lintel.

It is these islands, with their impressive past (and present), which were the "Hawaiki" or dispersal point through which the Polynesians passed in their movement to the far reaches of the eastern Pacific. Actually, the Hawaiki of Polynesian legends probably does not refer to any one island or island group in particular, but to several. Each time the giant double canoes moved eastward, another homeland or Hawaiki disappeared in their wakes and a new Hawaiki was located which would ultimately become the source for more migrations. Let us say then that the Samoa-Tonga area was the Hawaiki for the entirety of the Polynesian triangle, the source to which all island settlements must ultimately be traced.

Previously, we have seen that Fiji and New Caledonia and probably the New Hebrides were inhabited as early as 1000 B.C. by Malayo-Polynesian speakers bearing a culture similar to that found in Western Polynesia. Other islands, such as the Philippines, closer to Asia but yet within reach of Western Polynesia, had been inhabited even earlier by the brown voyagers, but culturally, linguistically, and geograph-

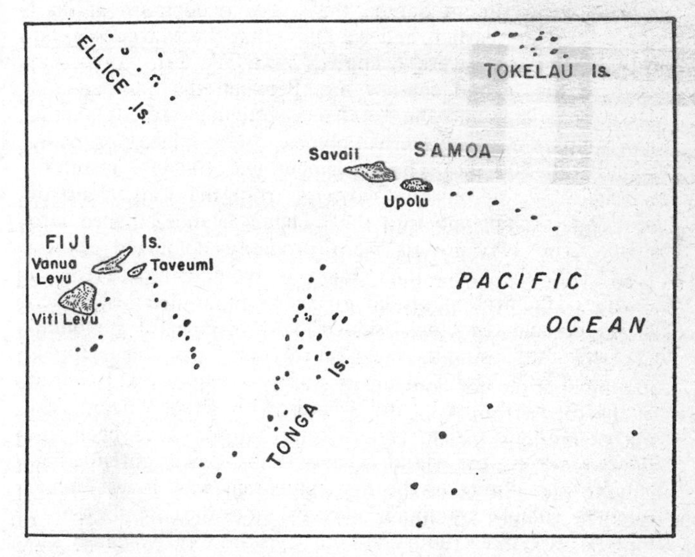

Fig. 6. The Western Polynesian islands

ically the Melanesian islands seem to be most favored for the source of Western Polynesian culture in the current state of our knowledge. True, there is a difference in physical type between the extremes of human variation in the two populations, but there is also a large overlap with many individuals being in an intermediate position between the extremes. The differentiation of the population extremes may be a result of microevolution caused by the relative isolation of the two groups. The large intermediate population group, which also is geographically intermediate, may be a remnant of the older basic population from which the two diverged, and not, as many have thought, the exclusive result of late miscegenation with Polynesian groups. Furthermore, we know nothing archaeologically of the earlier Melanesian population, and there is a possibility that these populations may have differed considerably in their make-up from the present-day groups, on which we must base our theories.

The movement into Western Polynesia probably began during the first half of the first millennium B.C., and continued for some time. We have no definite dates for this occupation as yet, as archaeology has been unfortunately limited in the area, but we do have radiocarbon dates from an early archaeological site in Samoa that show occupation at least by A.D. 1, if not earlier, and we know that the Marquesas, far away to the east, were occupied by a Western Polynesian group in the second century B.C. Between the Samoan and Marquesan dates and the 1000 B.C. settlement of Melanesia, the occupation of Western Polynesia took place, probably around 750–500 B.C. The settlement was likely a result of reconnaissance and fishing voyages from the Lau group of the Fijian archipelago into the Tongan Islands, thence into Samoa. The two groups were probably colonized at approximately the same time, but one would suppose that a heavier concentration settled on the Samoan Islands, which are large, volcanic "high islands" with wonderful surrounding reefs and desirable tracts of relatively flat coastal lands with good soil. The Tongan group, by comparison, is flatter and consists of raised coral islands with some volcanic examples of smaller size, and therefore would have been less attractive from the standpoint of subsistence potentialities than Samoa. Wherever the first settlement was, it was surely followed rapidly by more colonies, and the population of Western Polynesia flourished at a rather early date. The

Tongan and Samoan islands were fairly close and maintained some contact with each other throughout this period, as there are many basic cultural similarities between these two main ethnic groups. Differences obviously also arose in material culture and sociopolitical organization while the dialects of the groups diverged, but the basic similarities are still overriding.

Our knowledge of Samoan archaeology is derived from a few short articles of descriptive nature and some very capable stratigraphic excavations done recently by Mr. J. Golson of the University of Auckland, New Zealand.[1] In Tonga, an extensive survey with excavation was conducted in the late 1920's by a well-known American Indian archaeologist, J. W. McKern.[2] The publication of this work, however, was incomplete: no detailed analysis was ever published of the ample collections. Golson was able to survey Tonga also in 1956, during the same field season in which the Samoan work was done. Consequently, the archaeological resources of Tonga have also received a more recent appraisal.

Beside the results of these excavations, we can reconstruct much of the early Western Polynesian culture by a study of the distribution of various artifacts in Eastern Polynesia. If a certain type of tool, for instance, appears universally in early archaeological sites in Eastern and Marginal Polynesia, we know that it was part of the original main stream of culture from which the Eastern and Marginal societies branched, and not a result of independent invention in each and every island group. Distribution studies give us reason to believe that various kinds of artifacts were once used in Western Polynesia, despite the fact that they are at present unknown there. Future archaeology of more extensive nature will undoubtedly recover evidence of these artifacts hidden in the depths of ancient sites. Beside distribution studies, we have stratigraphic evidence from the Marquesas Islands, which were apparently settled by a group of Western Polynesian migrants in the second century B.C. One of the first villages which these migrants established has been extensively excavated. As a result we know a great deal about the culture that Western Polynesians brought to the eastern border of the Polynesian triangle, and therefore, by extension, can make some valid statements about the Western Polynesian culture that was the source of the Marquesan discoverers.

With this background, we can discuss the history of

Samoan and Tongan society from the archaeological deep past to the historical and ethnological present.

The early cultures of Samoa and Tonga were undoubtedly much the same, as the effects of isolation had not yet produced any local cultural idiosyncrasies to distinguish the two. Although no Tongan sites have as yet been positively identified as representing the early period, the site of Vailele near Apia in Samoa represents a later stage of that period. This site attracted the attention of Golson during his survey of Samoa because of the large number of earthworks and house platforms in the area signaling the existence in former times of a large settlement which dated to about A.D. 1650, according to native traditions. Excavations on this site, however, demonstrated that this seventeenth-century village had been constructed on the ruins of an earlier village of a different nature, for beneath the surface structures, but distinct from them, ran a stratum of black earth in which a large amount of rather crude pottery and some stone adzes were recovered. There was considerable evidence of construction in this black stratum in the form of postholes and pits dug into the undisturbed subsoil. Carbon samples from the pits gave an age of 1950 ± 120 years ago, indicating, therefore, that the site habitation represented by the black stratum took place sometime between 111 B.C. and A.D. 129. The Polynesians who occupied Vailele then were evidently living in pole and thatch houses built directly on the earth. These differed considerably from the houses built by their descendants on elaborate earth mounds when they reoccupied the site some 1,500 years later.

The most astonishing find at Vailele was the large number of potsherds in the black layer, as pottery had heretofore been unknown in Samoa. The pottery resembled Melanesian and Tongan material, as would have been expected, and is one more proof of the Western Pacific–Asian derivation of Polynesian culture. Pottery was found in Tonga in quantity both by McKern (1929) and Golson (1957) at Mu'a, Mangaia, and Ha'ateiho, but the dates of these sites are still uncertain as assays of radiocarbon samples are presently incomplete.

The stone adzes of the early culture of Western Polynesia were probably quadrangular or truncated triangular in cross section. Some had shoulders and steps chipped into the butts so that they could be fixed to a wooden handle in such a way that the coconut-fiber lashings would not get in the way when the adze was used. Triangular and cylindrical cross-section adzes were probably also used, and some of these may have been obtained by trade from Melanesia long after the settlement of Western Polynesia.

Although no fishhooks were found by Golson in his survey, we can be sure that the earliest inhabitants of Western Polynesia brought with them both the one-piece bait hook (made of mother-of-pearl, tortoise shell, or wood) and the composite trolling hook formed of a shell shank to which a bone, shell, or tortoise-shell point was lashed. A tuft of big bristle tied at the upper end of the shank topped off the ensemble, and added to the rather powerful attraction this type of hook had for the tuna and bonito for which it was intended.

The early Western Polynesians had a large variety of shell scrapers and knives, using shells often scarcely altered from their natural state. Most noteworthy of these is the knife made from a marine snail shell. A hole was drilled or punched through the snail shell near the mouth, and the edges of the hole were ground sharp. When these sharp edges were scraped across a taro root or breadfruit, they removed a strip of skin, which issued from the mouth of the shell. The knife functioned like a modern cabbage grater. This knife is particularly interesting as it is found in Melanesia almost exclusively [3] but occurs only rarely in Western Polynesia [4] and in the earliest culture of the Marquesas. This type of knife is apparently a good index or hallmark of the early culture of Western Polynesia and an indication of its Melanesian relationships.

No animal bones were uncovered in Samoa or Tonga, but we know from the excavations in Melanesia [5] that the pig, dog, and jungle fowl had been brought into that area by 1000 B.C. We can presume that they were included in the passenger lists of the vessels that first penetrated Western Polynesia, as they were transmitted from there to the Marquesas by the second century B.C. In Tongan and Samoan excavations no evidence exists to indicate what vegetable foods were utilized in the diet, but again Melanesian and Marquesan evidence indicates that the standard Polynesia root-crop starches (such as taro, yams, and sweet potatoes) and tree crops (breadfruit and coconuts) were in vogue. The sea, as always, provided an abundance of protein to experienced fishermen and was exploited in every way possible.

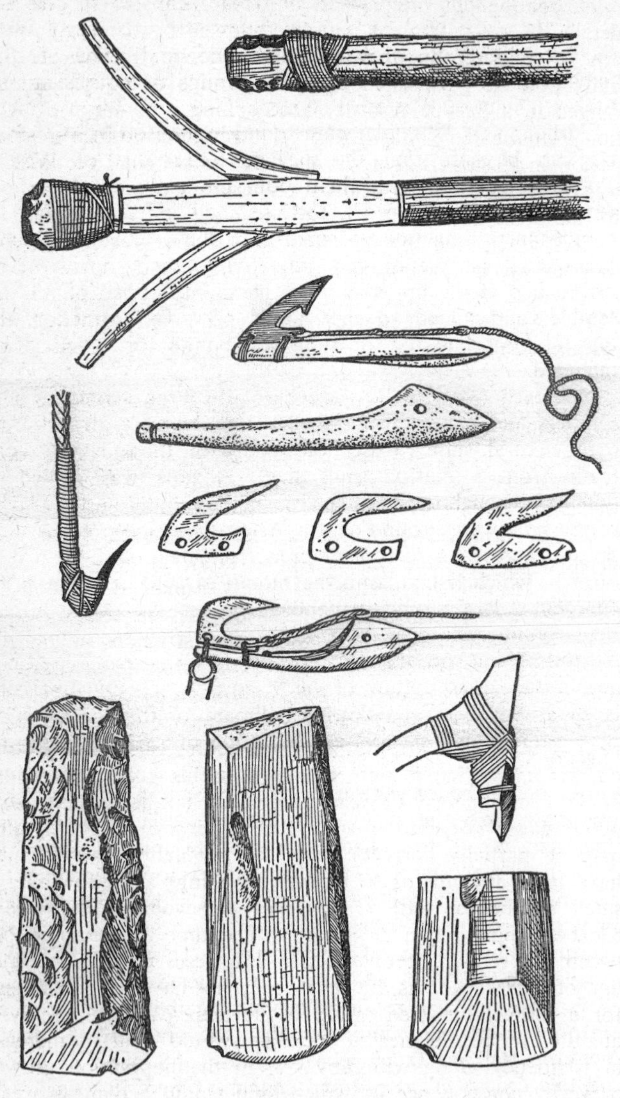

Fig. 7. Samoan artifacts: stone blades, bonito hooks and stone adzes (after Buck, 1930)

Not enough of the Vailele site was excavated to give any details of the settlement pattern followed by the early Western Polynesians, but there is much evidence to indicate that habitation sites consisted of small groups of houses not arranged in a particular order and lacking a common orientation. This pattern was followed throughout the prehistoric period in Eastern Polynesia also, but as we shall see later, it was abandoned in Western Polynesia in the Christian era for a more orderly configuration.

This, then, was the early culture of the Western Polynesians as we can reconstruct it from the present state of our knowledge:

1. A society composed of small groups living in scattered clusters of simple houses of poles and thatch, each cluster composed of several houses.
2. The subsistence pattern was based on root and tree horticulture, fishing, and domesticated animals.
3. The artifacts—pottery, stone adzes, and shell knives—demonstrate the relationships of this culture to Melanesia as well as to the Malayo-Polynesian cultures farther to the west.
4. No large monuments of stone or earth were constructed at this time as far as we know at present.

The Western Polynesians evidently remained in their islands for some time without venturing too far afield. As yet we have no evidence in the archaeological record of any exploring activity on their part until the Marquesas colonization in the second century B.C. Future archaeological work, however, may demonstrate the presence of Western Polynesians in the eastern islands even before this date, so that our reconstruction is only tentative at this point. The cause of the continuance of eastward expansion is frankly anyone's guess. We can offer several hypotheses, all of which may be partially correct. First, the population density may have been an impetus to further voyaging. The growth of a small number of settlers in a new, benevolent environment can be astounding in its rapidity. The time that elapsed between the settlement of Western Polynesia and the occupation of the Marquesas, however, may not have been sufficient for a respectable-sized group to develop. Warfare, a given quantity in all Polynesian societies, would tend to increase in frequency along with any rise in the population growth curve by consequence of which land would become scarcer. Groups defeated in warfare may have fled to the sea, departing in search of more genial surroundings. Another explanation for groups "budding off" from Western Polynesian centers is the absolutely intangible motivation to move which defies scientific explanation. Why does the Eskimo travel such distances in winter or the Australian aborigine go on his "walkabout"? Such psycho-cultural phenomena are seldom explicable; consequently they are in themselves poor explanations for other phenomena, but are nevertheless real factors in culture history.

Finally, we may admit the possibility that some settlements *may* have occurred as a result of accidental voyaging. This is certainly not the prime mechanism, however, by which Polynesian population movements occurred, as we have indicated previously.

In the first 1,000 years after the birth of Christ, the cultures of Tonga and Samoa developed and probably began to diverge, evolving local differences in various items of material culture which were elaborated along distinct lines. Linguistic divergence also developed, ultimately resulting in the mutually unintelligible dialects of modern Tonga and Samoa. Many of the concrete manifestations in the archaeological record, such as tombs, house mounds, fortifications, and villages, also bespeak changes in the sociopolitical organization, as we shall indicate below.

By the end of the first millennium of the Christian era the divergences between Samoa and Tonga had become rather marked, and it is here that we shall pick up the thread of Western Polynesian prehistory once again.

The Samoan culture of A.D. 1000 and later was quite different from the culture of the earliest settlers in those islands. The house forms had changed and a rectangular form of domicile was developed, raised on a stone-faced earthen platform (*paepae*). These houses were no longer scattered in small clusters but were organized into neatly planned villages with intersecting sunken paths or roads, located near the sea. The villages were generally fortified with walls of stone or earth and ditches. The subsistence pattern of the Samoans may have also been slowly shifting to an emphasis on taro and other root crops, with a trend away from sweet potatoes and breadfruit. The one-piece shell hooks of the early culture had begun to disappear, and the composite hooks for bonito or tuna were developed in elaborate form and exaggerated in size. The absence of the one-piece "bait" hooks was undoubtedly compensated for partially by development of net techniques.

Whatever the changes in subsistence pattern, they obviously had no deleterious effects on the Samoan culture, if the village sites described above are any indication. Planned fortified settlements are only possible when large supplies of surplus food are available to support the labor involved in their construction. Likewise, a strong central authority must be present to organize production, collect the surplus, and redistribute it in initiating and supporting large-scale public projects of this type. The developmental changes in Samoan subsistence patterns evidently brought increased productivity rather than scarcity.

It would seem that strong chieftainships, in relatively self-sufficient district villages, were forming at this time, evolving from the earlier political organization which was probably a looser decentralized community spread over a relatively large geographical area with less temporal power vested in the hands of the chief.

Besides fortified villages, fortifications were constructed separately at vantage points throughout the islands, some even occurring deep in the interior. These forts were often similar in nature to village defenses, which utilized stone walls, ditches, and earthworks. On narrow, steep-sided ridges, transverse trenches were often all that was needed for adequate protection, for an enemy attacking along the ridge crest would have to descend into the trenches to reach the strong point and in climbing down would be helpless against the missiles of the defenders. Other forts used wooden palisades [6] of irregular tree trunks with inner supporting timbers. Towers on the palisade protected the entrances. The construction of such forts gives additional weight to the hypothesis that strong chieftaincies evolved at this time, as such undertakings are obviously tasks of great magnitude necessitated by the presence of strong enemy groups to whom lesser defenses would present no appreciable obstacle.

Samoa, then, at this time was probably well divided into a number of small territorial units, each with its main village and possibly satellite villages, ruled by a powerful chief. Each of these units may have been involved in tenuous and often openly belligerent relationships with the adjoining territorial groups.

In the area of material culture further changes were occurring. Pottery apparently was becoming less common and may have disappeared altogether by this time, as it had completely disappeared by the time of white contact and was not even to be found in ancient legends. The stone adze types of the early Samoan culture probably included a wide range of variation, but the quadrangular cross-section adze was developed to a high degree, while many of the earlier triangular and circular types began to disappear. The majority of adzes from Samoa today are of the quadrangular cross-section variety, which has been designated as the Western Polynesian type par excellence.[7]

The Tongan culture was no less tardy in development than that of Samoa, presenting something of an anomaly, for *makatea* islands of this type seldom possess a high agricultural potential. Yet, Tongan society had a sound economic basis as far as can be judged from the impressive archaeological records of their accomplishments in the field of architecture. In the eleventh century[8] the Tongans began to enter into a phase of building activity, constructing large mounds for tombs and for pigeon-hunting positions, as well as rectangular dwelling platforms (*paepae*). Many of the tombs of the type called *langi,* built for royal burials, are particularly impressive. These are rectangular stepped structures faced with tremendous limestone slabs, 10 feet by 6 feet by 1 foot in size, cut from solidified coral reef deposits. These slabs were first outlined in the quarry face by cutting deep grooves around them. The groove would then be deepened on all four sides until a natural bedding plane was reached, allowing the quarry men to lift the slab without undercutting. Dragged to the *langi* and set in place, the rough slabs would then be dressed on their exposed faces and edges to present a good external finish and to fit the neighboring slabs. Other tombs for chiefly personages were mounds of inverted-saucer or truncated-conical shape, often concealing stone slab vaults at their centers. McKern traces the development of tombs and other mound structures through a series of four stages. First, ordinary unfaced mounds of earth were constructed. Second, mounds were faced with unworked stones. Third, cut-stone slab facings were used on mounds. This stage represented a climax of Tongan megalithic architecture, of which the *langi* mentioned above are a good example. Finally, a decadence in architecture began to manifest itself and a return to unfaced earth mounds apparently occurred about the sixteenth century as a result of several debilitating dynastic wars among ruling families.[9]

There were apparently no specific standard types of mounds similar to the Samoan house platforms built to support houses. Tongan houses were evidently not always elevated, but even when placed on mounds the mounds were merely rectanguloid, slab-faced earth platforms with no obvious characteristics identifying them positively as house foundations. Tongan houses were not grouped into compact, fortified villages as in Samoa but were scattered in small clusters of several houses each. Despite the lack of village fortification, however, the Tongans were not be outdone in defense and constructed well-planned forts.[10] These were built on well-selected sites that would provide good defensive possibilities. The works consisted of a moat external to a large wall of stone and/or earth which was further surmounted by a fence of heavy timber uprights. The gaps between timbers were filled with reed bundles tied by vines and bark cord. Secondary walls were constructed to back up the exterior fortifications, especially around the gates. Lookout platforms were erected in the enclosure and around the walls, while access to the fort was possible only by narrow ramps over the moat that were well protected by towers. Within the fort, deadfalls were placed to trap the unwary enemy if he should be fortunate enough to penetrate the outer walls.

The most spectacular feat of Tongan megalithic architecture is the huge "trilithon," the *Ha'amonga 'a Mau'i.* This monument consists of two enormous coral stone uprights set in the ground and capped with an equally enormous lintel, set in sockets in the uprights. The stones, weighing between thirty and forty tons each, were erected in pits dug in the coral stone "bedrock" and propped in place by debris.[11] According to informants, the stones were shaped at the quarry and dragged to the site. There they were pushed up an inclined plane of earth and wattles and upended into position from the peak of the plane. The lintel was then moved into place in the same manner, after which the inclined plane was removed, leaving the *Ha'amonga 'a Mau'i* standing free.

Little is known about the subsistence pattern of Tonga archaeologically, but we may surmise that it was equal in productivity to that of Samoa despite a less favorable environment. It probably depended on root crops, such as taro, yams, and sweet potatoes, somewhat more than on breadfruit, which is frequently more favored in Eastern Polynesia.

The monumental stone and earth structures of Tonga, like those of Samoa, can be interpreted as evidence of strong central authority and large surplus food productivity. However, the absence of planned villages indicates that there may have been a qualitative difference between the type of political organization found after A.D. 1000 in Tonga and that of Samoa. That a difference actually existed is adequately attested by the historical documents of Western Polynesia as well as by ethnographies. Dr. Marshall Sahlins of the University of Michigan [12] has pointed out that this difference in political organization is primarily due to a difference in the clustering of vital resources in the environments of the two groups. In Tonga the resources are scattered, and hence one finds familial specialization in particular aspects of production. As a consequence of this, families disperse, each to be near the area in which its particular specialties are most easily produced. In Samoa, on the other hand, the more lush environment brings about a situation in which all vital food resources are found in close proximity. Therefore, there was no need to travel long distances for foodstuffs, and as a consequence centralized villages developed in which all would have equal access to the fruits of the surrounding countryside.

Tongan fishing tackle followed the Samoan developmental trends, one-piece bait hooks being discarded for the large composite bonito and tuna hooks, while net fishing probably increased its contribution to the food supply.

The distinctive quadrangular adzes of Samoa are paralleled in Tonga by a regional variation that is somewhat smaller and more highly polished, with rounded lateral edges. Golson believes that these quadrangular types may have evolved from the trianguloid cross-section types which we have seen were present in the culture of the earliest settlers of Western Polynesia. (See Fig. 7.)

Unlike the Samoans, the Tongans did not allow their pottery to become obsolete but were still producing it in quantity when Captain Cook arrived in the late eighteenth century. The diminished frequency of potsherds on Tongan archaeological sites known to have been occupied in the eighteenth century, however, indicates that a decline in popularity may have begun which might have ultimately phased out pottery in favor of wooden vessels.

Throughout the entirety of their prehistory the Tongans maintained some contact with the Fijians by numerous voyages on the part of both groups. McKern sees a possibility of Fijian influence in the megalithic stone structures and mounds [13] as well as in the fortifications which the Tongans so capably erected.[14] He has further pointed out the similarities between Fijian and Tongan pottery [15] and is supported in this by the later work of Gifford and Shutler,[16] as was indicated above. In later times a great deal of Tonga-Fiji intercourse took place as a result of the preference of Fijian chiefs for Tongan "mercenary" warriors. The Tongans may have been the toughest adversaries of the Pacific, and the Fijian wars served as an admirable training school for Tongan warriors. The pay for such services rendered was often in the form of large Fijian canoes, for which the Tongans apparently had an affinity despite their inferiority to the Tongan type. Other items traded to Fiji were red feathers and the exquisitely woven fine mats for which the Tongans are justly famous. Fijian exports were usually pots and whale ivory.

The Tongans and Samoans also maintained some contact, which had the effect of keeping regional cultural variations from becoming greater than they were by the mutual exchange of any innovations. According to tradition, in the thirteenth century the Tongans occupied Samoa, driving many of the tribes into the interior of the islands. The scope of this occupation and its effects have yet to be archaeologically assessed, however; and until more excavations have been made we cannot attempt to evaluate the effect of this influence, if it may actually be so designated.

The voyages of the Western Polynesians certainly were not restricted to the circumscribed Fiji-Tonga-Samoa area. Although, at present, we have no further concrete evidence of Western Polynesian settlements in Eastern Polynesia, besides the Marquesan occupation, historical traditions from various outlying smaller islands indicate that the Western Polynesians were still colonizing uninhabited islands in the middle regions of the Polynesian triangle until a relatively late date. Among these are: Pukapuka, a small coral atoll on the northern rim of the Cook Island group, reputedly colonized from Tonga in A.D. 1300; Tokelau, a group of atolls north of Samoa, supposedly settled by Samoans (possibly also by a Rarotongan element); Uvea, in the French-held Wallis Islands west of Samoa, possibly settled by Tongans; and Tikopia, one of the best-known Polynesian outlyers, which was evidently contacted by Tongans.[17] Such legendary statements stand in need of concrete documentation, however.

Having sketched the prehistory of Western Polynesia from its settlement in the first millennium B.C., all that is needed to round out the picture is a brief description of the cultures of Tonga and Samoa as they were at the time of first contact with Europeans. This is not difficult, for we possess ample data of excellent quality in the form of historical records [18] and ethnological reports.[19] Further, both of the societies in question may still be observed as functioning entities to this day, although years of colonization and concessions to the Western industrial economy have certainly altered much of the milieu.

Tongan society was of a rather complex semidespotic nature in its native state. The various islands of Tonga were ruled by three paramount chiefs, the highest of which, the *Tui Tonga,* exercised a tremendous authority by virtue of which he could appropriate goods and chattels, land, or even human lives at a whim for very minor offenses. Tongan social organization was of the branching lineage or "ramage" type [20] in which the society was divided into a number of lineages tracing their descent from a common ancestor. These groups were ranked as follows: at the head of the highest-ranking lineage was the living Tui Tonga; below this the other groups branched off from the lineage of the Tui Tonga through less important relatives, as inheritance was passed from first-born son to first-born son, and secondary offspring were grouped in lower-ranking lineages. Each branch from the main line was further divided into sub-branches and a person's rank in the society as a whole was a function of his genealogical distance from the main line of the Tui Tonga lineage. There were three classes in Tongan society: royalty and chiefs, chiefs' attendants, and commoners. Land was doled out in tracts to minor chiefs who would return quantities of produce to those of highest rank at yearly ceremonies. It was indicated above that Tongan resources were scattered, and therefore chiefs had to supervise and coordinate the various types of production going on simultaneously in their districts. The lineage organization served as a very efficient device for the collection of the widely scattered food surpluses and utilization by redistribution during the financing of chiefly projects, such as tombs and house platforms. Thus it appears that Tongan society was closely integrated to its environment in a mutually reinforcing relationship, the origin of which is lost in the mist of time.

The Samoan sociopolitical organization was different from that of Tonga, as has already been shown. Rather than a system of branching lineages, the Samoan social unit was a group of people tracing common descent through male ancestors. [21] (This group is known as a "descent line" in the literature.) Each descent line was vested with a series of titles and positions in the village council, or *fono,* and several descent lines might occupy one village. There was no main line of reference from which one could measure the genealogical rank of the various sub-lines, as in Tonga, for the titles alone were significant to the Samoans. The titles gave titleholders positions in the village council, which might contribute members to a super-council made up of representatives from several villages. Rank was established through the titles, as each title could be traced back to the gods irrespective of the actual genealogy of the titleholder in sociobiological terms. The chiefs, through the councils, controlled agriculture as well as other tasks involving community labor. The highest chiefs (i.e., those holding highest *fono* titles) were accorded a great deal of respect and deferential treatment in the form of special salutations and euphemisms in address, specially elaborated life-crisis ceremonies, and harshly sanctioned *tabu* on the chiefly frame and belongings.

The village orientation of Samoan prehistoric culture is evident here in the *fono* system of village councils which integrate easily into super-village units of ascending size. The self-sufficiency imparted by the environment is reflected in the political self-sufficiency of the village, which is a microcosm of all larger units.

In summary, the prehistory of Western Polynesia began in the early half of the first millennium B.C. when the main islands of Tonga and Samoa were occupied from nearby Melanesia. The settlers of Western Polynesia retained contact with each other and direct or indirect contact with Melanesia, which is reflected in material culture traits, such as pottery, house types, forts, etc. The development of marked regional variation was somewhat retarded by this cultural intercourse. By the second century B.C. Western Polynesian migrants had already penetrated to the far border of Eastern Polynesia. Subsequent voyages may have resulted in the population of Western and Central Polynesian small atolls. At approximately A.D. 1000 stone construction began in both Tonga and Samoa. The distinctive political organization of each group is seen as a result of the relationship between the culture and the environment.

In conclusion, the islands of Western Polynesia were the earliest occupied of all the Polynesian triangle and the source of all subsequent settlements in Polynesia.

9

Search in the Dawn

To the east of the Samoan and Tongan Islands lies a lonely expanse of open sea in which only a few tiny atolls can be found popping up their palm-crowned coral islets from the blue wastes. Beyond this no-man's land, islands appear again, however, in increasingly larger numbers as one pushes eastward from Western Polynesia. First encountered are the Cook Island group of atoll and volcanic islands, lying astride the Tropic of Capricorn, arranged roughly in two lines running toward the southeast. If one were to sail along these island lines, orienting the ship by the northernmost of the pair, and continue to sail on that heading, within two days a landfall would be made in the Austral Islands of French Polynesia, which appear to be an attenuation of the axis of the Cook group, lying farther to the south between twenty and thirty degrees south latitude. The Australs are cooler and damper, and considerably less hospitable, than the islands closer to the equator.

Northeast of the Cooks is situated the large Society Island group of which Tahiti, perhaps the most famous member, is the current administrative and commercial center for all of French Polynesia. The Society group is composed of several large volcanic islands, Tahiti, Raïatéa, Huahiné, Bora Bora, and Mooréa, and a few more diminutive, less important volcanic islands and atolls. It is the large volcanic islands, especially Tahiti, Moréa, and Raïatéa, which present the most favorable conditions for human habitations with wide fringing reefs, coastal flats, and deeply dissected

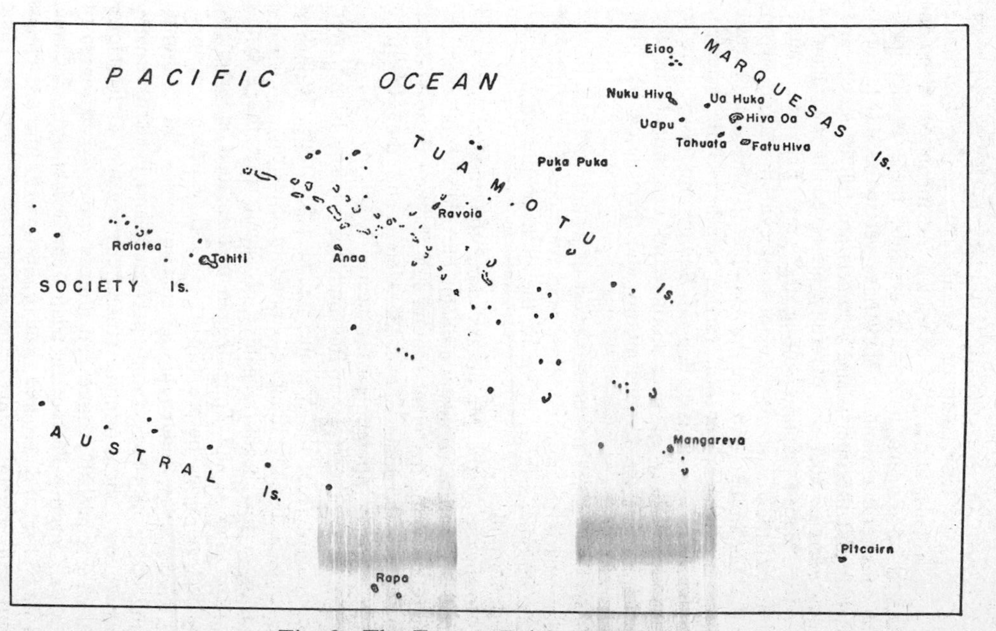

Fig. 8. The Eastern Polynesian islands

verdant valleys in which clear streams run from the jagged, almost lunar mountains into the sea.

East of the Society Islands a swarm of coral atolls is scattered on the waves along a roughly northwest-southeast axis. This is the Tuamotu Archipelago, numbering some seventy islands, about half of which are inhabited. Even in this era of modern navigation systems, these islands present considerable danger. They have yet to be satisfactorily charted, and the inter-island channels are full of shoals and tricky currents that are carefully preserved in the memory of every native captain sailing the area, but have never yet found their way into a pilot book. Off the southern tip of the Tuamotu group are the Gambier Islands, Mangareva being the best-known. Still farther south is little Pitcairn, the home of the tragedy-dogged *Bounty* mutineers, now a flourishing colony of over a thousand descendants of the participants of the famous mutiny and their native Tahitian wives.

Some 800 miles to the northeast of Tahiti and east of the Tuamotus is the remote Marquesan Archipelago, a group of eight volcanic islands lying in the path of the cool Humboldt Current.

Northwest of the Marquesas along the equator are scattered a few tiny, almost uninhabitable islands and then an empty sea until the giant Mauna Loa, home of the goddess Pele, rears its dome above the clouds and the Hawaiian chain appears, stretching over nearly 1,000 miles.

Last, but not least, far to the southeast is Easter Island, over 2,000 miles from the Marquesas and 1,500 miles from the nearest aboriginally inhabited island of Pitcairn.

It is to this beautiful galaxy of islands that the Polynesians of Samoa and Tonga began to turn their attention in the last centuries before Christ. How they became advised of its existence, hidden in the sunrise behind the 500-mile corridor of open sea separating Western and Eastern Polynesia, is moot, but before the second century B.C. at least one group and probably more had already crossed into the eastern half of the Polynesian triangle to establish themselves in new island homes, and they began to write the last chapters of the brilliant history of their race.

In the past, students of Polynesian prehistory had generally tended to accept the hypothesis that the Society Islands had been settled by a migration from Western Polynesia quite early in the Christian era, after which secondary migrations departing from Tahiti or Raïatéa had dispersed the Polynesians to the limits of their present distribution, resulting in the occupation of all of the islands of Eastern Polynesia including Hawaii and New Zealand. The central position of the Society group was one reason for crediting it with the dynamic role in the occupation of Eastern Polynesia. Another reason was the evidence of traditional Polynesian history, according to which migrants from Tahiti had discovered and settled the Hawaiian Islands, while other Tahitians had sailed off to the southwest to colonize New Zealand. Other islands closer to the Society group than those mentioned above presented many cultural features similar to the aboriginal culture of Tahiti, and consequently the conclusion was drawn that the marginal islands of Eastern Polynesia had been colonized mainly by expeditions emanating from the larger islands of the Society group, of which Tahiti and Raïatéa were the most important.

Recently, however, new evidence has appeared, requiring a modification of this view of Eastern Polynesian occupation. The evidence referred to is that obtained as a result of excavations in the Marquesas Islands, where a Western Polynesian group had already established themselves in the second century B.C. The tools and ornaments brought by this group to their new home leave little doubt that the migration from the west was direct with little or no stopping en route and was accomplished by a well-planned and outfitted expedition.

Recent archaeological work in Easter Island by members of the Norwegian Expedition and Dr. Thomas Barthel of the University of Tübingen demonstrates a possibility that Easter Island may have been originally settled by a migrant group of Marquesans.[1] Likewise, researches by Dr. Bengt Danielsson on the island of Raroia on the northeastern edge of the Tuamotu Archipelago indicate that this island as well as others near it may have been settled by Marquesan migrants seeking refuge from an intertribal war in the fourteenth century.[2] Therefore, it appears that the Marquesas archipelago was settled quite early and functioned as a second main population dispersal point in Eastern Polynesia in addition to the Society group.

We have had occasion to discuss in a previous chapter the techniques of navigation and the sailing craft that were at the disposal of the Polynesians for these last steps of their great exodus from the coasts of Asia. In that chapter a discussion was included of the Sharp theory of "accidental voyages" according to which the settlement of the entirety of Polynesia is attributed to sheer chance. The present facts, it will be recalled, give the Polynesians credit for a greater ability than Sharp is willing to concede, an ability which would allow them to penetrate the Eastern Polynesian islands without too much difficulty.

According to our interpretations the discovery of the islands of Eastern Polynesia probably began as a series of purposeful voyages in that direction undertaken with a view to exploration. These voyages may have made use of the equatorial countercurrent flowing to the east, or they may have utilized the annual reversal of the trade winds and ridden the wind as far to the east as they could go, after which they tried to find land and then possibly returned with the resumption of the trades. The remains of Polynesian occupation have been found on tiny equatorial islands,[3] proving that at least a few of the double canoes ventured that way and even stayed for a time.

Whatever the fate of the majority of these voyages, some were successful and resulted in the discovery of the larger islands of Eastern Polynesia—particularly the Marquesas and Society group. These islands are high (Tahiti is over 6,000 feet; the highest of the Marquesan group is about 4,500 feet) and consequently are visible from quite a distance at sea, whereas the lower coral atolls and *makatea* islands would only be visible for a few miles from the gunwales of a low-lying sailing canoe. It is obvious, however, that chance would often favor the discovery of some lower volcanic island, such as Rarotonga, before the larger high islands could be approached. Therefore, evidences of early habitation may ultimately be found on a few of the less significant islands. The main settlements, however, were made first on the high islands of the Society and Marquesas groups. In time a complex series of voyages began from these two dispersion points. Some may have been undertaken for pure exploratory purposes, others by reason of necessity after a defeat in war. Still others may have been accidental, in Sharp's usage of the term, as the probability cannot be excluded that fishermen or travelers were caught in storms and blown off course. To use such a probability as the sole mechanism for the population of such a wide area as Eastern Polynesia, however, is unrealistic.

Once landfalls were made in any of the major island clusters, such as the Tuamotus, the Cooks, or Australs, it would be only a matter of a few years before other neighboring islands would be discovered. The large Tuamotu Archipelago covers a wide area, but the islands of which it is composed are relatively close and it is possible to navigate long distances within the archipelago keeping land constantly in sight.

The discovery and settlement of the Gambiers and Pitcairn probably resulted from native Polynesian exploration among the Tuamotu Islands. It should not be thought that "exploration" means that the Polynesians had an urge to conquer the vastness of the sea simply because it existed. Often specific resources were being investigated, and in the case of the Tuamotu Islands these were probably pearl shell and sea-bird feathers. In later times we have some evidence that both Tahiti and the Marquesas carried on a trade with islands of the Tuamotu group to obtain highly prized mother-of-pearl for fish hooks and ornaments.[4] Thus, by obtaining footholds in various island groups and following up with reconnaissance that resulted in further landfalls, the Polynesians ultimately occupied all habitable islands of Eastern Polynesia and visited most of the others, if not all, in their extensive travels. There is an excellent probability that they also managed to see the snowy heights of the Andes rise out of the dawn and ground their heels in the cool waters of the South American coast, but the evidence for this will be discussed in another chapter at more length.

The important points concerning the Polynesian occupation of the eastern islands are as follows:

1. The occupation began before the Christian era and was under way by at least 200 B.C.

2. Purposeful voyages of exploration apparently accounted for many of the island occupations.

3. The Society Islands and the Marquesas were settled early and were the two main dispersion points from which subsequent colonizations of the more peripheral islands were effected. Other smaller volcanic islands, such as Rarotonga, may also have had a part in dispersing the Polynesians, but the role was quite probably secondary to that of the Society and Marquesas groups.

4. Owing to the "clotting" of Eastern Polynesian islands, one landfall in an archipelago could easily be exploited in many cases by observation from mountains gaining visual bearings for further discovery. Point-to-point visual naviga-

tion was sometimes possible for good distances, as in the case of the Tuamotu Islands.

5. By a combination of mainly purposeful exploration, forced refuge flights, and accidental discoveries, the settlement of Eastern Polynesia was complete to the limits of human habitability before the advent of the Europeans in the sixteenth century.

With the above as an orientation, we will now describe the various cultures of Eastern Polynesia, as they are known from the archaeological record and from ethnological documents, to show in more detail the dynamics of the occupation of that area.

10

The Land of Men

The fantastically rugged Marquesas Islands of French Polynesia lie along a northwest-southeast axis some 400 miles northeast of the Tuamotu Archipelago in French Polynesia. There are two main groups of islands, the northwestern consisting of the largest island of Nuku Hiva and the adjacent islands of Ua Pou and Ua Huka, with a pair of small uninhabited islands—Eïao and Hatutu—situated fifty miles north of Nuku Hiva. In the southeastern group the largest island is Hiva Oa, with two small islands—Tahuata and Mohotane—close by. The southernmost of the Marquesas group, Fatu Hiva, is fifty miles south of Hiva Oa. The islands are exclusively of volcanic origin and their rock-bound cliff coasts rise black-brown and jagged out of the incessantly beating waves. Above these walls of layered volcanic outpourings the grassy uplands rise steeply, broken by jutting knife-edge ridges, like refugees from a lunar landscape, sculptured into fantastic forms by the work of wind and rain over the million years since the islands were born in the fury of a volcanic explosion. High above the crenelated ridges, peaks like turrets on a medieval battlement tower to heights of 4,000 feet and more, their sides covered with gray-green lichens and aerophytic plants. The forbidding coast is broken at points by narrow entrances of deeply indented bays opening from narrow high-walled valleys often penetrating far into the central plateaus of the island interior. Streams cascade down the faces of the steep valley walls from the plateau, bringing water that is conveyed along the uneven, rock-strewn valley floors in numerous routes and then seeps out into the sea. As a result of this supply of water, the soil of the valley bottoms is fertile and vegetation grows in verdant profusion. The blessing of water does not fall everywhere on the islands of the Marquesas, however; the southeastern sides of the islands receive the lion's share of the precipitation from the moisture-bringing trade winds that are caught by the mountain and ridge complexes and release much of the burden on those areas. Hence very little rain reaches the leeward sides of any Marquesan island which are consequently arid and bare, covered with only coarse grasses and scrubby vegetation.

The sea floor drops away rapidly off the Marquesas, allowing the waves, unrestrained by any fringing reef, to crash with full force on the rock-bound coasts. The sea's coolness and the abrasive erosion debris suspended in the coastal and bay waters have inhibited the development of a fringing coral reef like that of Tahiti. Coral polyps cannot exist in such an environment. The lack of reefs does not help the Marquesans in their quest for food, for many of the edible reef fish simply are not found. Other deep-water fish, such as tuna, bonito, and wahoo, are plentiful, however. Less innocuous marine life—sharks of all kinds, manta, and sting rays—come into the bays with impunity, often being seen near the beaches and sometimes, in the case of sharks, washed ashore by unexpectedly forceful waves.

These are the Marquesas Islands. All that is needed to complete the picture are gray clouds floating low around crest and crag, the sun's rays striking feebly through on the red, clayey soil and dark, glistening green of the palms, and one has captured the *élan vital* of these islands—a rugged, almost masculine sense of strength shrouded in an aura of foreboding and tragedy.

To its inhabitants this is *te henua 'enana,* the land of men. Its name is derived from the fact that the Marquesans do not refer to themselves as "inhabitants of such and such an island," as do the Tahitians, but, rather, call themselves generically *te tau 'enana,* "the men."

The anthropology of the Marquesas is fairly well known through ethnological monographs by von den Steinen, the Handys, and Linton,[1] and a number of shorter papers by a variety of authors, as well as historic documents in the form of ship captains' journals and missionary diaries.[2] These have imparted a good working knowledge of the native culture in broad terms, but little was known until recently about the prehistory of the Marquesas, as only one short descriptive monograph had been consecrated to a study of the ancient Marquesan stone temples, dance plazas, and house platforms.[3] No attempts had ever been made at excavation, for it had been decided *a priori* that nothing would be found, and consequently, in a fashion highly characteristic of archaeology in Polynesia in the past, research stopped there.

In 1956, I was fortunate to participate in the Crane Marquesas Expedition under the leadership of Dr. H. L. Shapiro of the Department of Anthropology, American Museum of Natural History. My duties were to survey the archaeological resources of the islands before the arrival of the main part of the expedition. The possibilities for archaeological excavation were quite rich, and our first short season was productive beyond our expectations. I returned to the islands in 1957 with my wife for a year's sojourn, sponsored again by the American Museum, and the work begun in 1956 was resumed. Fourteen sites were excavated and numerous others surveyed. In the course of the excavations a very large collection of stratigraphically documented artifacts and human skeletons was recovered, being supplemented by additional collections of artifacts and skeletal material made on the surface. After a year spent in careful analysis, the outlines of the prehistoric sequence in the Marquesas became clear. My scientific report of this work will be published by the American Museum of Natural History.

The prehistory of the Marquesas has been divided into a series of periods on the basis of the analyses of the evidence of excavation. Each of the periods is characterized by a complex of distinctive artifacts, such as house types, stone adzes, or megalithic architecture, settlement and subsistence patterns, and inferred sociopolitical traits, to be described in more detail below.

The dating of the various periods is based on a combination of radiocarbon dating with a technique known to archaeologists as artifact seriation, in which sites are placed relative to one another by the fluctuation in frequencies of various key artifact types relative to one another.[4]

SETTLEMENT PERIOD, 150 B.C.–A.D. 100

In any discussion of the culture of a particular Polynesian island or archipelago, the first question usually heard is "Where did they come from?" We have already had occasion to mention the fact that the Marquesans were probably of Western Polynesian origin and arrived in the Marquesas about 150 B.C.,[5] but that statement must now be substantiated by a description of the distinctive features of the culture of the earliest Marquesan settlers.

Most of what is known of the culture of this period of Marquesan prehistory is derived from our excavations in the beautiful deserted valley of Ha'atuatua on the northeast coast of Nuku Hiva. There a tidal wave had exposed evidence of an extensive archaeological deposit on the sand hills behind the beach. Hearing from the natives of large quantities of "pig bones" exposed on the beach, I visited the valley (in 1956) and found to my happy surprise that the "pig bones" were actually human, representing a sizable burial area around which were traces of ancient dwellings and the broken tools and other debris of a relatively heavy occupation, all well preserved in the sand. Excavations in 1956 were followed by more in 1957, and radiocarbon dates prove now that the site was inhabited at approximately 120 B.C. (2080 ± 120 years before present). The cultural remains on the site were rich, permitting a reconstruction of this early culture in detail, surpassing our knowledge of some of the later periods.

The Polynesians who first set foot on the beach of Ha'atuatua in the second century B.C. probably comprised a part of the expedition that discovered the islands. A few artifacts found in the site are of materials not found in the Marquesas or anywhere in Eastern Polynesia and must be considered to have been imported from the Western Polynesian home of the first Marquesans.

The main group probably split up to reconnoiter their new island home, after which the small detachments, each possibly representing the occupants of one or two canoes, settled down here and there on the verdant east coasts of the islands to take up life anew. There is no evidence at present to indicate which island in the archipelago was settled first; as a matter of fact, colonies were probably established on the main islands of Nuku Hiva, Ua Pou, Ua Huka, Hiva Oa, and Fatu Hiva almost simultaneously. Other islands, however, such as Eïao and Mohotane, were not settled until later.

On arriving at Ha'atuatua the settlers built a group of small, low, boat-shaped thatch houses near the mouth of a stream at the north end of the beach. The houses were built directly on the sandy surface with no paved floor, mats probably serving in place of a pavement. South of the little house cluster, at a considerable distance, a small temple was built, consisting of an oblong enclosure of small stones a few inches high, within which stood a pair of columnar basalt uprights. This was an *ahu* or altar to which the gods would descend when properly invoked, entering and animating the solid basalt uprights. Around the altar the dead of the little colony were buried, in due time, leaving a legacy that two millennia later would allow us to state positively that these people are Polynesians and members of no other race. The various traits that distinguish the Polynesian skeleton from all other races are very definitely present in these earlier burials.

A study of the burials affirms the existence of cannibalism, probably of a ceremonial nature, even in the early days of Marquesan occupation. An ancestral cult featuring preservation of male skulls is also in evidence. There is a conspicuous lack of grave furniture placed with the dead, indicating a lack of pronounced status differences.

In excavating the area where the village had stood we found evidence that the houses had often been rebuilt, probably as a result of natural decay, and moved slightly in the process. The patterns left by the decayed house posts of successive houses overlapped each other in a confusing manner. Around the house clusters were traces of small fires and scattered remains of the shellfish that the ancient dwellers in Ha'atuatua had eaten. Many tools used for food preparation were uncovered in the house ruins and these, together with the food remains, permit us to reconstruct the economy of the early Marquesans. The settlers had brought the pig and dog with them intentionally and the rat had tagged along uninvited; the remains of all three were found in the excavations. Bird bones were recovered but they have not yet been positively identified. Therefore it is impossible to say definitely that the jungle cock was also brought by the settlers, although this is practically a certainty, for it was definitely present by A.D. 1100. Vegetable foods brought in the big double canoes included coconuts (inferred from the presence of numerous coconut-grating tools of mother-of-pearl), root crops such as taro and yams, and breadfruit (inferred from the presence of rind-peeling knives of Tonna shells). Naturally, as seafarers, the Polynesians depended to a large extent on the food resources of the ocean, and fish bones of all sizes and shapes littered the site along with the broken shells of edible shellfish.

Many of the artifacts recovered were directly related to fishing. Most interesting of these were the beautiful mother-of-pearl one-piece hooks, some circular in shape, others with recurved points, still others with straight, unelaborated points ranging from a half inch to six inches in length. These had been rough-cut from mother-of-pearl valves with sharp basalt flakes, which were found by the thousands on the site, and shaped carefully with bladelike files made of polished coral. Another common hook type was the familiar composite bonito hook described in connection with Samoa and Tongan archaeology. Basalt adzes of several varieties were found, the most frequent being the untanged type with rectangular cross section, characteristic of Western Polynesia. Tanged varieties were also recovered but in small quantity. Most interesting are the examples of the long, narrow, triangular cross-section adzes, also found in Western Polynesia, and two remarkably Melanesian adze types: a highly polished ovoid or cylindrical section variety and another type with a plano-convex section and tapering cutting edge. Both of these latter adze types are quite similar to Fijian adzes, and the ovoid variety also occurs in Western Polynesia. It will be recalled that all of the above-mentioned adze varieties are found also along the path of Polynesian migrations all the way from Asia.

Surprisingly enough, small potsherds were found, marking the first discovery of pottery in Eastern Polynesia and thus indicating that the Marquesan settlers had brought the art of pottery making with them from Western Polynesia, where it was known to be flourishing at that period and long after. The small size and number of the pieces do not allow a detailed description of the vessels, but a few facts are deducible. The vessels were red, unpainted, and probably narrow-necked with flaring mouths. The technique of manufacture was rather uneven, some sherds being of well-fired hard clay, others of poor, crumbly quality. The one rim sherd that was recovered shows a typical Melanesian lip treatment, a wiped, flattened lip with a groove running along it.

Ornaments of mother-of-pearl were found, of which one type is especially significant. This is a disc, varying between 2½ and 4 inches in width, with notched edges and a pair of drilled holes through the center. Small, button-sized replicas of the larger discs were also found. Together they represent the component parts of a handsome, typically Melanesian

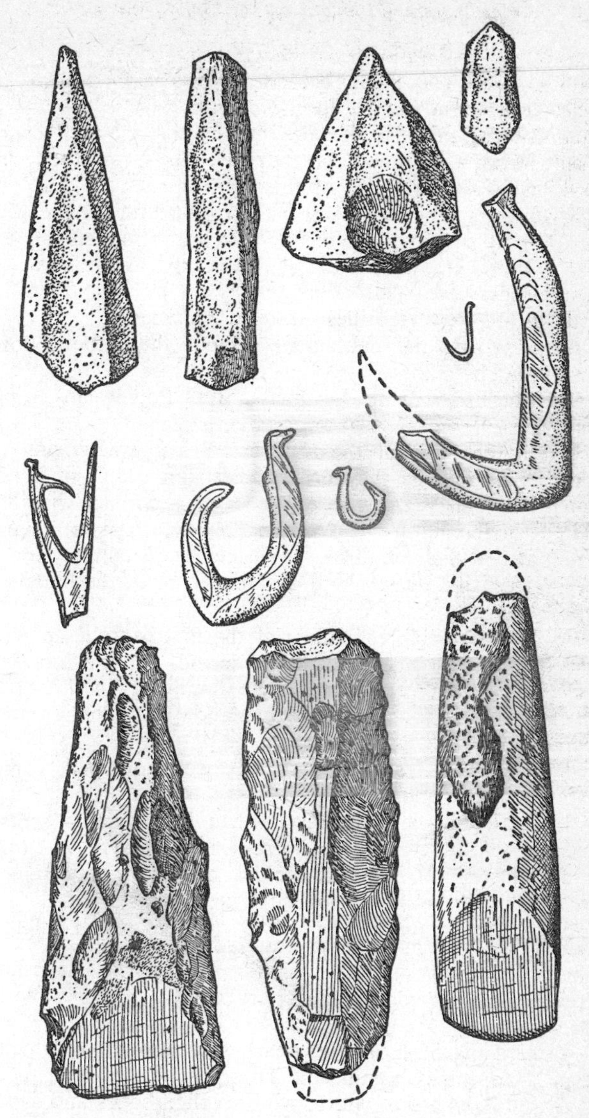

Fig. 9. Marquesan artifacts: coral files, fish hooks of pearl shell, stone adzes (after Suggs, 1959. Courtesy of the American Museum of Natural History, New York)

headdress that is known as the *kapkap,*[6] which consists of a shell disc with a finely carved tortoise-shell overlay fitted to it. It is worn on the forehead with a wide coconut-fiber band. In the sands of Ha'atuatua the tortoise-shell carvings disappeared with time, but the shell discs remained to inform us of the presence of this trait at such an early date. *Kapkap* ornaments were still used by the Marquesans as late as 1890. It is highly significant that this ornament appeared in the Marquesas alone, of all the islands in Polynesia. The next closest place that it appears is on the island of Santa Cruz in the New Hebrides group of Melanesia.

Summarizing the Settlement Period, then, the following points may be made:

1. The settlers of the Marquesas were Polynesians in physical type.
2. On the basis of the artifact types characterizing their cultural assemblage they originated in an island of Western Polynesia. This island was either in close contact with Melanesians or the culture of Western Polynesia had not been differentiated sufficiently from the Melanesian culture, for pottery, adzes, rind peelers, and ornaments are of the Melanesian type.
3. The original island home of the first Marquesan settlers was furthermore a high, volcanic island, for the tool kit of these settlers indicates a complete familiarity with the type of environment found on a high island (i.e., adept stone-tool manufacture).
4. The voyage of discovery was well equipped, carrying domestic plants and animals.
5. Small colonies were established in favorable spots on most of the main islands. The settlement pattern was one of small clusters of ovoid thatched houses with ceremonial areas apart from the living sites.
6. Burials demonstrate a lack of marked status difference, the presence of an ancestor cult, and cannibalism.

DEVELOPMENTAL PERIOD, A.D. 100–1100

After the Western Polynesian groups had settled down and begun adjusting to their new homeland, gradual changes began to take place in the budding Marquesan culture. Some of these may have been due to minor peculiarities of the environment of the Marquesas, as almost all volcanic islands differ in some respects from each other while retaining large basic areas of underlying environmental similarity. The changes that occurred were intended to integrate the culture and the environment more closely, as one would expect, and perhaps the most basic of these was the orientation of the subsistence pattern toward a heavier reliance on breadfruit than is seen in many other Polynesian islands. Breadfruit grows extremely well in the Marquesas, a fact that must have been obvious to the early Marquesans. Excavations in a site of the late Developmental Period in the valley of Ho'oumi uncovered numerous breadfruit-scraping knives made of cowries differing from the Tonna peelers found in the Settlement Period, but exactly like the scrapers used by the Marquesans today.

Further changes can be noted in the house structure. The small thatched houses that must have resembled overturned canoes in shape were no longer built exclusively on the ground surface, nor were they so small. Pavements of a single stone in thickness were placed beneath these houses, attaining at least forty feet in length. Settlement patterns remained the same, but new types of ceremonial structures were built.

The Ha'atuatua site was still occupied during the early part of the Developmental Period, during which time the small temple structure there was gradually elaborated and enlarged into a much bigger complex. The altar itself was covered by sand fill and a stone pavement, and a large area was marked off on the inland side of the stone pavement by the addition of a rectangular gravel-surfaced tract, enclosed on its long side by simple sunshade structures similar to lean-tos. The *ahu* type of altar disappeared completely after this period in the Marquesas, being replaced by temples in the form of dwelling houses. There is a possibility, however, of a somewhat later survival in the southern islands of the *ahu*.

The population in this period was still centered in the valleys on the hospitable east coasts of the islands. No movement into the arid western regions had as yet taken place. We may safely hypothesize an upswing in population growth during this period, as a result of the increased productivity in breadfruit. In the succeeding period there is ample evidence to show that such a population increase actually took place in the Developmental Period.

Many of the Melanesian type of implements that had been found earlier began to disappear. Although pottery still remained in use, its manufacture had degenerated and the ware was of a course, crude nature, scarcely fired and soft. It probably failed to survive the end of the Developmental Period. The Melanesian type of stone adzes had also been abandoned, and a few varieties of the beautiful one-piece pearl-shell hooks had become obsolete. Among these was the almost circular variety, called the "rotating hook" by Polynesian anthropologists because it rotates in the mouth of a hooked fish, rendering it impossible for the fish to escape by slipping off. This hook type as well as others probably became obsolete, because the fish which they had originally been designed to catch in the Western Polynesian home of the Marquesan settlers were simply not available in the Marquesas or failed to bite on the hooks. New varieties were gradually developed, however, to replace the old types.

During this period, approximately A.D. 400, a group of Marquesans probably decided to migrate in search of new lands in the face of the rising sun. Perhaps to those who stood on the stony narrow beaches and shouted their *Ka'oha* as the sleek double canoes pulled away into the unknown sea, this event was merely a repetition of a rather familiar occurrence and little thought was devoted to the matter besides the longing for absent friends, relatives, or lovers who would probably never be seen again. This embarkation was to be of some significance to the anthropologists of the late nineteenth and twentieth centuries, however, because it led to the discovery of that isolated bit of volcanic rock called Easter Island, where flowered a most unique and fascinating Polynesian culture.

According to Dr. Alfred Métraux,[7] who conducted an exhaustive study of the Easter Island culture in 1934, a consideration of other Polynesian cultures resembling most closely that of Easter Island indicates the Marquesas as the source of the Easter Island colonization, rather than Mangareva or New Zealand, the next best candidates.

"The Easter Islanders were a part of the migratory waves that headed eastward occupying the Marquesas, the Gambiers and the Tuamotu Islands. After staying in the Marquesas for several generations, one or two tribes which constituted that ancient population detached themselves to discover new islands in the east. Chance carried them to Easter Island where they became established."

In a later chapter devoted to the interesting archaeological problems of Easter Island, the cultural similarities between Easter and the Marquesas will be more precisely discussed. For the present, it will suffice to designate this period as that in which the Easter Island migration probably took place.

In summary, during the Developmental Period the Marquesans extended and solidified the economic basis of their society, relying on the abundant breadfruit more than in the past. Settlements were still limited to the most fertile valleys on the east coasts of the islands. The characteristic strong valley tribal organization of later times was probably jelling at this time. Population was increasing, probably at a geometric rate. The culture brought to the Marquesas by the discoverers was undergoing some extensive changes: houses were getting larger and more complex; old varieties of stone adzes and shell hooks became obsolete and were replaced; native pottery was degenerating and probably was abandoned before A.D. 1100.

EXPANSION PERIOD, A.D. 1100–1400

The relatively peaceful, quiet development of Marquesan culture in the previous periods was suddenly interrupted about A.D. 1100 by a burst of activity. Population pressure seems to have reached a critical point in the fertile east coast valleys of the main islands, apparently resulting in an increase in internecine warfare. Small groups of inhabitants of the east coast centers broke away and established little settlements in the less favorable areas, such as the arid west coasts or tiny, inaccessible satellite valleys near some of the larger population centers. Dispersion to remote areas of the islands was not the only result of this population explosion; some groups apparently were forced to migrate by sea, for we have traditional evidence that the island of Raroia was occupied by a Marquesan chief and his people who fled there after a defeat in A.D. 1250.[8] Other islands in the region of Raroia may also have been occupied at this time by similar Marquesan refugee groups.

Possibly contemporaneous with these migrations was the settlement of the small islands of Eïao and Mohotane.

It was probably at the beginning of this period or during the final years of the Developmental Period that another group of Marquesans discovered the island of Mangareva far to the south at the tip of the Tuamotu Archipelago. According to the French missionary Laval, our source for the legendary history of Mangareva, the island was first visited sporadically by fishing groups[9] and ultimately settled after a long period of such transitory visits. A study of the remains of ancient temples and house platforms on Mangareva indicates that the source of the first settlers was probably the Marquesas.[10] The discovering groups may have sailed into the Mangarevan region in the course of exploration within the Tuamotu Archipelago. The temple structures of Mangareva are like those of the Settlement and Development Periods of the Marquesas, and the house floors with paved verandas and elevated sleeping platforms are quite like the Expansion Period house floors to be described below. The traditional date for Mangarevan settlement, A.D. 1275, may not be more than a century or two in error, as the Mangarevan structures tie in so well with the Marquesan houses and temples of approximately that date. Although legendary evidence indicates the possibility of other later arrivals at Mangareva from other Polynesian island groups, the original occupation was probably Marquesan.

It may be objected that this sudden period of migrations and settlement in the Marquesas, while possibly denoting population pressure, does not necessarily denote warfare. However, there is a great deal of evidence to show that warfare was becoming more violent at this time. Huge fortification complexes were built on the central plateau of the island of Nuku Hiva by the Te'i'i tribe of Taiohae Valley for defense against the dreaded warriors from the large and fertile Taipivai Valley. These forts, built at excellent observation points, consisted of systems of earthworks, wooden palisades, and ditches cut through the knife-edge Marquesan ridges. Within the fortifications small houses were constructed, and large storage pits had been dug for breadfruit paste, a Marquesan staple, and other foodstuffs against a day of siege. Walking over these grass-grown fortifications in 1956 with the clouds sailing by almost within arms' reach, I found many polished beach stones that had served as ammunition for the highly effective Marquesan *maka*. This war sling, made of coconut fiber, could propel a large stone at a rate of speed sufficient to inflict a serious injury if a reasonably direct hit was obtained. It is not only the fortifications that attest the bellicosity of the Expansion Period culture, but also the location of the marginal settlements themselves. They were invariably in caves or rock shelters rather than in the open, indicating a definite desire for security.

In the main valleys several interesting innovations occurred. The community settlement pattern of scattered house clusters and separate temples remained the same but there were definite changes in architecture. A new form of house appeared along with a new version of the old ceremonial structure.

The houses were rectangular in ground plan and their surfaces were divided into two sections longitudinally, a lower section or veranda and a slightly elevated section on which the house itself, used mostly for sleeping only, was constructed. The first houses of this type in the Expansion Period were built on mere pavements, but later a new practice began of elevating the house and veranda on an earth-filled terrace-platform with a retaining wall of large stones on three sides.

The new ceremonial center was an outgrowth and elaboration of the earlier temple and plaza complex in Ha'atua-tua. The elaborations consisted of: (1) an increase in size of the rectangular plaza, which sometimes reached a length of 500 feet; (2) construction of low step-terraces along one or both sides; (3) construction of houses along the edges of the lateral terraces; (4) in the late Expansion Period the plazas were elevated on large artificial terraces, rather than built on a roughly leveled ground surface. Around the periphery of these artificial terraces earth was piled and leveled to construct the low, steplike terraces described above, upon which the spectators sat.

These ceremonial plazas, known as *tohua,* were the sites of all important ceremonies for the tribes and subtribes of each valley. According to the statements of early European visitors, missionaries, and ethnographers,[11] the *tohua* were constructed by subtribal groups as a community project, serving as a focal point for the pride of the entire community. In war, one of the most drastic insults a victor could inflict was to raze the *tohua* of the enemy, a deed tantamount to the desecration of a cathedral. We may therefore suppose that the construction of the *tohua* of the Expansion Period was also the work of a subtribal group, directed by a chief who could issue the commands necessary for the construction as well as provide the food to feed the workmen thus employed, who were of necessity away from their own taro patches and sweet-potato hills to participate in the chief's project. Indeed, the *tohua* themselves appear to be an index of the growing prestige of the chiefs and the priesthood.

Much is known about the material culture of the Expansion Period as a result of our excavations in two very unusual neighboring dry-rock shelters in Uea Valley on the west coast of Nuka Hiva. These shelters had escaped the humidity of the tropic climate because of large quantities of guano deposited within them by birds. The guano covered and protected the debris scattered so long ago by the Marquesans around their rock-shelter homes, preserving not only the bone and shell implements found in open sites but also the vegetable fiber and wooden implements that have normally long disappeared from any archaeological site where moisture has unimpeded access to the trash accumulation. The picture of Marquesan home life imparted by our excavations in these shelters is likely to be a little shocking to romanticists of the "noble savage" school. The living floors were covered by a litter of basalt flakes, shell fragments, leaves, wood chips, pieces of broken wooden tools, unnumbered scraps of braided coconut fiber, fecal matter, broken water gourds, animal and fish bones, dead insects, fragments of desiccated lizards, scraps of old discarded tapa loincloths, charcoal, and ashes. Along the wall of one of the shelters was a dirty heap of shredded banyan fiber upon which the inhabitants slept. In the other shelter, close by, an oven contained the remains of a young child who had been cooked and partially eaten. The skull and hand bones had been scattered over the cave floor during the feast, but the torso had been dumped back into the oven, after which life had gone on as usual, as signalized by an accumulation of several inches of undisturbed trash over the surface of the oven and its pathetic contents.

The tools recovered in excavations in these and other sites show that changes had occurred in Marquesan technology. A new hook was invented by the Marquesans at this time, differing completely from any found elsewhere in the Pacific. In plan it looks like any ordinary one-piece pearl-shell hook. The unusual feature, however, is a neatly tailored piece of pearl shell, exactly duplicating the shank of the hook, which is attached against the shank and lashed to it along its entire length. This extra shank component and its lashing impart extra strength as well as flexibility to what would otherwise be a rigid hook. It is impossible to say what fish this was used for, but one can conjecture that it was large and highly spirited.

In the sites of the Expansion Period are found the first traces of the stone pestles used by the natives to make poi. These early pestles were short and conical with transverse bar or knob grips at their apexes. Some, however, were carved into humorous little anthropomorphic faces with rounded domes and pointed chins, with small button eyes peering at the examiner in wide astonishment. The little poi-pounder handle carvings represent the earliest attempt at artistic stone carving known so far in the Marquesas and differ considerably in style from the later elaborate poi pounders of the Historic Period, which have become a favorite of art collectors the world over.

The poi pounders with the bar grips merit further discussion. They may represent evidence of a contact with the Society Islands or some other islands within the Society sphere of influence, for they resemble the archaic Society Island poi pounders quite closely. It is possible that this contact was mediated through the Tuamotu Islands into which the Marquesans often voyaged, either fleeing from defeat or trading for pearl shell. Simultaneously, the Tahitians were carrying on similar trade with the Tuamotus from the western side of that group and Marquesan warriors or traders may have come across Tahitian artifacts in the Tuamotus and returned with them, without ever having had direct personal contact with a Tahitian sailor. Conversely, should Marquesan artifacts turn up in Tahiti, we might expect a similar mode of transmission to account for their appearance. Another possibility exists; namely, that the Marquesas Islands are the home of the poi pounders now thought to be of a characteristic Society Islands type. As the number of these exotic types in the Marquesas is small, however, and the type was rapidly eclipsed by the development of a unique Marquesan style in poi pounders, we can feel reasonably sure that the appearance of these implements in the Marquesas is a result of foreign contact, possibly of an indirect and definitely sporadic nature.

In sum, the Expansion Period saw a population increase in the eastern valleys reach a critical point, erupting with internal warfare that resulted in refugee groups streaming out into the marginal areas of the islands. Others put out to sea in search of other lands, settling small Marquesan islets or the northeastern Tuamotu atolls. In the midst of this warfare, the powers of subtribal chieftains and priests were growing stronger, as witnessed by the beginning of large community projects on the subtribal level, requiring effective organization of both labor and food resources under a central authority. Food resources were undoubtedly increasing although we have no direct evidence for it.

Some contact with Tahiti may have occurred at this period, resulting in the introduction of Tahitian poi pounders.

These articles apparently triggered a florescence of Marquesan stone carving, which at first was somewhat imitative of the Tahitian models but ultimately broke away in the formation of a unique Marquesan style.

CLASSIC PERIOD, A.D. 1400–1790

In this period the culture of the Marquesas flowered abruptly with rapid spectacular advances in the field of technology, especially in megalithic architecture, art, and subsistence production. There is evidence that many important sociopolitical developments took place simultaneously, which were closely related to these advances in technology.

The hallmark of the period was the astounding megalithic architecture that characterizes ordinary house platforms as well as the ceremonial sites and temples. The raised house platforms (*paepae*) of the Expansion Period set the general style for the Classic Period, but the resemblance ceases there, for the *paepae* of the Classic Period are constructed of huge stones, often weighing several tons, the largest being carefully selected for display in the front wall of the platform. The rear walls of the platforms were built of small stones, however, which were more easily handled but less stable. The reason behind the use of enormous stones in the platform façade undoubtedly involved the prestige of the owner of the structure, who could brag artfully that he had used tremendous quantities of food to feed the huge work crews necessary to carry such stones, thereby elevating himself in the eyes of his fellow men as a person of wealth who was willing to pay the additional fee to have a first-class homesite rather than be satisfied with mediocrity.

In the *tohua* of the Classic Period one has the most outstanding examples of megalithic architecture and construction on a grand scale in the entire archipelago and in most of Polynesia. The *tohua* Vahangeku'a in Taipivai was the biggest of such structures excavated during our year and a half of field work in the Marquesas. It consisted of a huge artificial terrace (600 feet by 80 feet) containing an estimated 240,000 cubic feet of hand-carried earth, which had been dug out of the hillside on which the site was located. The retaining wall on the downhill side of the plaza terrace was over ten feet high, constructed of boulders piled with a slight batter to allow the wall more stability. Around the borders of the terrace, low stadiumlike steps of earth and stone had been built to hold spectators for the sacred ceremonies that were to take place on the plaza. The stadium structures were broken by huge house platforms, one of which was eleven feet high with a façade composed of three-ton boulders. Such houses may have been permanently inhabited by the subtribal chiefs and priests. Other smaller, less elaborate structures were probably temple platforms and were inhabited only periodically. In excavations at Vahangeku'a we found that the huge plaza terrace concealed a succession of earlier terraces, stretching back several centuries into the Expansion Period, when the site was first inhabited. The house platforms around the plaza showed signs of frequent elaboration also in the form of numerous small superfluous additions made more or less randomly, with the result that many platforms supported large superstructural complexes of smaller platforms. Excavations in some of the main platforms showed that they contained the remains of smaller earlier structures that had served their purpose once and then were used as cores around which more ambitious buildings could be erected. On Vahangeku'a one of the characteristics of the Classic Period structures was a lavish use of slabs of cut red tufa, a soft, easily quarried volcanic stone that was regarded as sacred by the Marquesans. Slabs of the red tufa were often set on edge to serve as a retaining wall for special ceremonial structures or as a facing for the elevated section of the house platform surface.

On sites of this period, such as Vahangeku'a, we discovered a great proliferation of types previously unknown on earlier versions of the *tohua*. These are mainly various kinds of highly specialized platforms intended for some specific use, such as the display of sacrificial victims, the exposure of tribal offerings, and the elevation of tribal deities, to mention but a few. Also other large ceremonial buildings appeared at this time away from the *tohua;* these were called *me'ae* or temples and were built in the form of an ordinary dwelling house, but were intended for habitation by the deity to whom they were dedicated, and his servants. Although such god-houses were brought to the Marquesas by the original Polynesian settlers, they were probably always of a miniature form in the earlier periods and built of highly perishable materials. It is for the first time in the Classic Period that they appear full-size in enduring stone; indeed, it is often possible to distinguish them from an ordinary dwelling site only by excavation.

One may well ask, how could the Marquesans move large stones and great quantities of earth for these buildings? The answer is simple: by the brute strength of large masses of manpower, strong ropes, rollers, levers, and inclined planes. Stones were dragged long distances if too large to handle or, if smaller, were lashed to carrying frames. Earth ramps were built for rolling large stones over obstacles or into position in upper courses of walls. Many such ramps still survive on the old *tohua* sites. Where possible, effort was minimized by building near large supplies of suitable building rocks. Small pebbles were used to brace and wedge the larger stones in constructing walls, and every care was taken to obtain a good fit between the component stones of the platform façades.

In this development of megalithic architecture Nuku Hiva was the center from which influences slowly radiated out to the other islands of the Marquesas, with the result that the islands of the southern group remained somewhat behind the architectural pace set by Nuku Hiva. This cultural lag is very evident in the simple state of development of the *tohua* plazas and the less spectacular house platforms on the islands of Fatu Hiva and Hiva Oa.

Stone carving was more highly developed in the southern islands than in the northern group, especially carving of a monumental nature. There are several huge statues still standing on the *me'ae* of Te' I'ipona in Puama'u, Hiva Oa,[12] whose size or virtuosity has never been approached by any Nuku Hivan examples. These statues are also made of the soft red tufa used in architecture, representing the typical Marquesan *tiki,* a short squat figure with bent legs and hands clasped over the abdomen, turning the closed lids of huge goggle eyes to the onlooker. The mouth is opened and the tongue protrudes slightly. This figure resembles the pose of *tiki* from elsewhere in Polynesia, but the face is uniquely Marquesan in its execution and style, differing markedly from the stone carvings of the Expansion Period. Other forms of art work are well known from this period: a proliferation of bone carving of small *tiki* figures began, and we may hypothesize that the well-known historic woodcarving for which the Marquesas Islands are justifiably famous took its present form in this period.

Another famous art form of the Marquesas, tattooing, developed into its most complex form in the Classic Period. It is only at that time that the designs used in the tattooers' art are present in the archaeological record, in the form of petroglyphs carved on isolated boulders along warriors' trails or on the stones in house platforms.

Fig. 10. A selection of Marquesan petroglyph motifs (after Suggs, 1959)

What was the basis for this great development of Ma quesan culture after A.D. 1400? Three main factors can designated as contributing to this efflorescence, each ine tricably related to the other: (1) optimal productivity; (large population; (3) efficient political organization. T post-1400 Marquesas probably possessed a population w in excess of 100,000. This was attained through an exc lent utilization of the potentialities of the land for agricultu of the Polynesian type. Large groves of breadfruit trees a extensive systems of taro patches provided a tremendo amount of food by the Classic Period, an amount far in cess of what the Marquesans could immediately consun Surplus crops were funneled off by the powerful chi through their lineages, which were of the branching or ram type already noted in Tonga. The large surpluses th accumulated could then be used to finance the building such ambitious projects as the *tohua* of Vahangeku'a a many more like it, in each subtribal district of each vall The temples (*me'ae*) were built by priests who obtained th share of the surplus through redistribution from the chi or the tribal high priests. The proliferation of ceremor structures that we noted above may indicate a rise in prestige of the priesthood during this period, as we kn that the priests of the Historic Period were more powerfu sacred matters than the chiefs, who seem to have been l ited to affairs of a profane nature.[13] Thus we see that a la population was producing a sizable food surplus which appropriated by the upper classes of Marquesan society, chiefs and priests, and utilized in supporting the populat in large public works that of course also reflected the gl of the chiefs and priests, reinforcing their power.

In such a milieu, competition for good land was stro as further expansion into other ecological niches on the lands was impossible; all suitable land was occupied. T high population density could be relieved only by emig tion or annihilation, and war became more sanguine th ever. The first Europeans who visited the Marquesas in the periods speak of hilltops bristling with fortifications, fr quent raids, and a high cultural value placed on prowe in war.[14] Cannibalism was especially developed as larg numbers of captives were taken.

The Classic Period, then, represents a florescence of Ma quesan culture through a complex interrelationship of ec nomic and social factors, despite the deleterious effect of in ternal strife that occasioned much waste. Had Marquesa

. A Fijian man of Kanathea Island *Courtesy of American Museum of Natural History*

2. Samoan *taupo* girls. These specially selected girls play a prominent role in all village ceremonies. *Courtesy of American Museum of Natural History*

3. Clad in tapa cloth, a Samoan girl sits on a fine mat in stylized ceremonial posture. Tutuila, Samoa.

Taniha Taupotini, one of the few remaining full-blooded
arquesans, shown with his wife, Tehono'itemoana, who
umbers a European among her ancestors.

5. A gatherer of wild mountain bananas, Tahiti

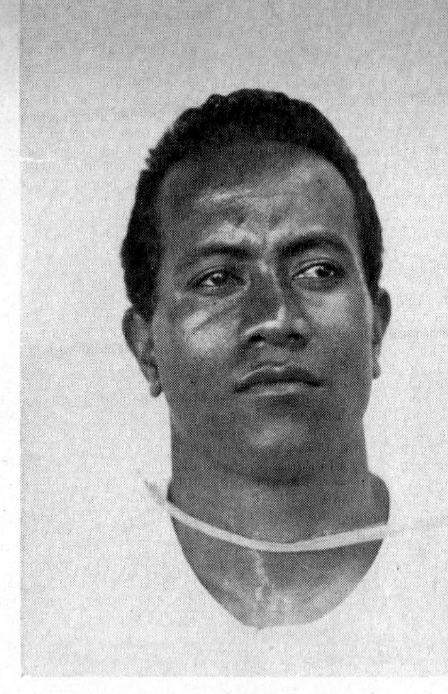

6. A young man of Tonga *Courtesy of Bernice P. Bishop Museum*

7. A typical Tongan woman *Courtesy of Bernice P. Bishop Museum*

8. Native women of New Guinea or Papua

9. A large Fijian double canoe. With such well-constructed water craft the Malayo-Polynesians occupied the islands of the Pacific. *Courtesy of American Museum of Natural History*

10. Maori men lined up for a *haka* dance before the impressively carved posts and gable of a meeting house at Whakarevareva, New Zealand. *Courtesy of American Museum of Natural History*

11. A large stone image at a temple site on the island of Raïvavaé in the Austral Islands, French Polynesia *Courtesy of American Museum of Natural History*

12. A desiccated Maori trophy head showing the intricate *moko* facial tattoo that was the pride of the Maori warrior. *Courtesy of American Museum of Natural History*

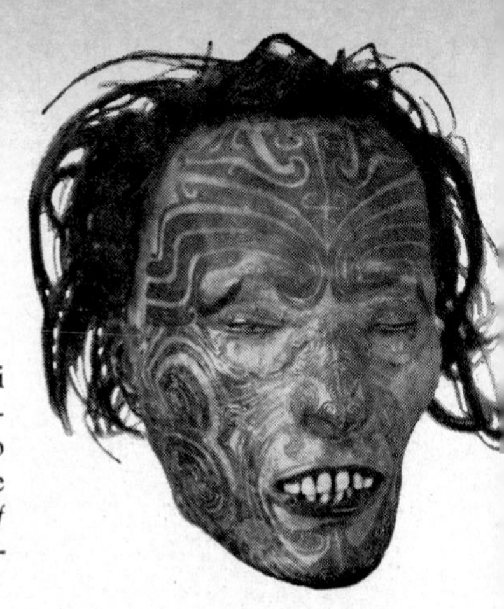

13. Pottery-making in Fiji. The boy in the center brings the prepared clay lumps, and the women shape the pots with the aid of wooden paddles. *Courtesy of American Museum of Natural History*

14. Pride of the Marquesan warrior: the head of a handsomely carved war club or *u'u*. Fashioned with carving implements of shell, animal teeth, stone, and bone, these masterpieces of primitive art were wielded with great dexterity in pre-European wars.

15. Carved Maori house posts display the complex art style that distinguishes the culture of New Zealand Polynesians. These posts, carved in realistic and highly stylized forms, represent ancestors and gods. They decorated the façades and interiors of Maori ceremonial houses.

16. One of the great stone images of Easter Island standing inside the crater of Rano Raraku *Courtesy of American Museum of Natural History*

17. An Easter Island ancestral figure—Moai Kavakava—exemplifying the culmination of artistic development on that island

18. The Tongan trilithon (Ha'amonga'a maui) traditionally built in the eleventh century *Courtesy of Bernice P. Bishop Museum*

19. Massive stones in the wall of the altar of *marae* Tai Nu'u, Te Vai Toa, Raïateá *Courtesy of Bernice P. Bishop Museum*

20. Excavations in the Marquesas. The field party of the American Museum Crane Expedition at work in Akipou rock shelter, Ue'a Valley, Nuku Hiva, August, 1956 *Courtesy of American Museum of Natural History*

21. Cliffs and peaks surround a narrow valley of a typical Polynesian volcanic island, Omoa Valley, Fatu Hiva, Marquesas.

22. Marquesan megalithic architecture. Wall of the great *paepae* on the ceremonial plaza of Vahangeku'a, Taipivai, Nuku Hiva. This platform supported the house of a chief or high priest. *Courtesy of Bernice P. Bishop Museum*

23. Polynesia in the age of discovery. Captain James Cook and his staff receive a pig offering before a temple in the Sandwich Islands. Drawn by John Webber, an eyewitness.

24. Polynesian regatta. Cook's artists capture the nobles of Tahiti embarking in full ceremonial attire during the *Endeavour's* sojourn at Opari.

25. A flat, coral shingle islet of a typical atoll of the Tuamotu Islands. Note the low gnarled scrub vegetation with coconut trees rising in the background. The great atoll extends beyond the lagoon horizon at the left.

cultural evolution been allowed to develop of itself, without the influence of European civilization, there is little doubt that the internal strife would have gradually succumbed to a more sound political organization which might have united entire islands or groups of islands, rather than an organization limited to subtribal or, at the most, tribal control, extending over a few valleys. Certainly the development of this culture was cut off before it was really well under way, and another few centuries might have produced advances more surprising than those which occurred in the last 400 years before white contact.

In 1596, however, the Spanish navigator Mendana discovered the southern group of the Marquesas on a voyage from Peru and named his discoveries collectively after the wife of his patron the Marquis de Mendonca, who was then viceroy of Peru. Mendana had few friendly contacts with the natives during his short stay, owing to his unswerving devotion to the gentle Spanish creed of convert or kill. It was fortunately not until 1767 that another white explorer visited the islands, this time in the person of the great Captain Cook, whose visit was also short and marred by unpleasantness with the natives. Within a decade and a half of Cook's voyage, the appearances of Europeans increased as whalers moved into the Pacific after 1790. In 1796 the northern Marquesas were sighted by Captain Ingraham of Boston, and in the next few years whaling visits were fairly common. A Russian expedition to the Marquesas in 1803 found two white sailors "on the beach" already, both refugees from the harsh life aboard whalers. In 1813 the American Navy, under Captain David Porter, established a base in Taiohae Bay, Nuku Hiva, and stayed for over a year. Supporting the nonproductive Americans during this prolonged occupation placed a great strain on the native economy, already weakened by a famine around 1810.

The Marquesans quickly became familiar with firearms and acquired a few of their own, with the result that intertribal rivalry took on a bloodier aspect than before. After the departure of the American Navy the arrival of whalers was more frequent, and for thirty years the riffraff of every land descended on the islands, bringing tuberculosis, smallpox, childhood communicable diseases, alcohol, and more and more firearms. Venereal disease, certainly established after the U.S. Navy's stay if it had not preceded the appearance of Porter and his men, began to have a profound effect on the birth rate.

Greater impositions were made on the native economy by the Europeans, who provisioned their ships constantly at the natives' expense, swapping old worthless flintlocks, iron fragments, and cheap trinkets for pigs and chickens that were far more important to the native economy.

In 1840, the French occupied the islands after a short period of "softening up" by a band of French missionaries. The fate of the native culture was sealed at this moment. The mission, backed by military force, succeeded in gradually weeding out recalcitrant chiefs, replacing them with hand-picked men often from the ranks of the malcontents. Clothing was required for the naked natives, but of European type, for the native dress was banned. Gradually, as resistance weakened, native dances, musical instruments, songs, and even tattooing were banned also, so that by 1890 the culture was well broken. The terrible effect of venereal diseases, tuberculosis, smallpox, and leprosy, combined with the stagnation resulting from the extinguishing of so much of the native culture, resulted in a simple loss of the will to live. The birth rate plummeted to the point where an anonymous French official reported, in the late nineteenth century, that thirty years would see the complete extinction of the race, barring any unforeseen natural catastrophes that might bring it about even sooner. The dire prophecy was almost fulfilled when the census counts of the 1920's showed a population of 1,500 for the entire archipelago.

The situation at present is considerably better, however, the population having risen over a period of thirty years to about 4,500. The ancient past is quite remote, unfortunately, and is largely a subject for archaeological study rather than technological inquiry. Elderly people can still be found who recall the last gasps of the old life, but they are growing fewer while a new generation is arising, lacking both a continuity with their own cultural background and a sense of belonging to the culture of France. The rootlessness of these new Marquesans may not be so bad as it might at first appear, however, for there are definite signs of a rebirth of spirit among "the men," and in the future their rugged little islands may well become the home of a hardy, self-reliant people once again. That day is, undoubtedly, rather distant, but one can only survey the wreckage of their colorful past and wish them success in the years to come in their attempts to rebuild what the Europeans, with or without good intentions, have so completely destroyed.

II

Tahiti Nui

A square-rigged European warship, tattered and beaten after an arduous voyage around the Horn, lumbered through the swells on the windward side of a large Pacific island.[1] Beyond the tumbling breakers marking the island's protecting reef was a placid lagoon, on whose shores small thatched huts were discernible here and there beneath the tall palms that covered the coastal flats. Behind the coconut groves on the beach rose steep grassy slopes, gashed here and there by great valleys penetrating deep into the island's interior. Garden plots could be seen on the hills, the red, overturned earth standing out sharply against its green surroundings. Climbing relentlessly upward, the slopes culminated in a jagged mass of towering peaks and crests.

As the jaded crew hung on the rails surveying their first landfall in months, the officers scanned the coastline with their glasses, watching the evidence of mounting human activity ashore. Lapses in the breeze brought the sound of booming drums from the shore and small figures could be seen hurrying to and fro beneath the trees.

Suddenly, amid the general tumult on shore, groups of people could be seen dragging long objects from low sheds, half hidden beneath the trees, down onto the beach. Once on the sand these groups erupted into great activity, milling around the long objects in their midst, lifting and laying down poles, flinging ropes, and generally keeping very busy. It became quite obvious to the watchers on the quarterdeck of the European ship that the long objects were boats of some type. More boats appeared in droves along the white beaches as the excitement ashore increased apace with the progress of the warship. Soon some of the canoes had been pushed into the shallows. Brown bodies splashed through the water, vaulting into place along the gunwales, and wide-bladed paddles began to dip in unison as the canoes moved gracefully and rapidly out from the shore toward the pass in the fringing reef.

The European crew waited with a feeling of apprehension. Suppose these people were openly hostile? Would this striking landfall become a cemetery for many of their number rather than a fulfillment of the promise of a rest from the hard routine of forecastle life? Their fears were soon allayed, however, for the first canoes to pass the reef, after clustering up for a while as if to take counsel, approached the warship warily. The native occupants could now be seen clearly; one was standing waving a long green leaf and shouting unintelligibly but with a friendly air. Finally one canoe moved forward from the pack closing with the large warship, and a young man grabbed the chain of the rear mast and climbed to the rail, where he scrutinized the whites through a pair of large, brown, awed eyes. Soon another native appeared, reinforcing the courage of the first boarder, and together they descended to the deck. As they exchanged curious stares with their hosts, a large ram (one of a number kept aboard the warship to provide meat for the officers) became interested in these new visitors. Deciding to challenge them, he ran full tilt at the unsuspecting natives and dealt one of them a sound thump in the derrière. In panic the victim and his friend hurtled over the side, casting terrified glances at the ungodly horned beast, and plunged into the sea to rejoin their comrades standing by in the canoe.

The warship aboard which this odd encounter took place was the H.M.S. *Dolphin,* commanded by Captain Samuel Wallis. Among its officers was a very promising lieutenant by the name of James Cook. The place was the northeast coast of Tahiti at Tai'arapu. The occasion was the discovery of Tahiti (and the Society group) on July 19, 1767.

This rather awkward incident heralding the first meeting between European and Tahitian served more as an "icebreaker" than anything else, for soon the ship was mobbed by Tahitians who were consumed by a burning curiosity to plumb the deepest secrets of this huge vessel. Native curiosity was quickly replaced to a large measure by acquisitiveness as objects that were not nailed down began rapidly to disappear into the Tahitian canoes alongside the *Dolphin*. The Tahitians' ability to gain the advantage in a new situation was certainly surprising.

Equally surprising to Wallis and his men was the culture of the Tahitians later discovered when explorations ashore were finally begun in the region of Matavai Bay. Here was a colorful society of brown robust giants ruled by a class of warrior chieftains and high priests to whom the mass of the populace granted utmost deference. Scattered along the coast, among the little native hamlets, were large temples with high, stepped altars upon which the gods of the Polynesian pantheon could descend. Around these sacred places were displayed the grisly remains of human sacrifices, among rotting piles of foodstuffs offered to the deities. The Tahitians did not suffer want, for the produce of the gardens and the sea was abundant and varied.

More interesting to the sailors, of course, were the Tahitian women, who were immensely attractive after such a prolonged sea voyage, cheerfully providing a way out of the abstinence of the reeking forecastle for the small price of an iron nail or so. The ships were full of nails and provided a seemingly limitless source of currency for this traffic—which was unfortunately cut short after sailors had been apprehended withdrawing nails from the ship's timbers!

The culture of Tahiti, as Wallis saw it in 1767, was found later in much the same form on the other islands of the Society group, although some minor variations existed between the "Windward" Society islands of Tahiti and Mooréa, and the "Leewards"—Huahiné and Bora Bora, etc. As a consequence the islands of this group may be regarded as constituting a single cultural unit. Owing to this general cultural similarity, we must assume that the prehistoric sequences of the various Society Islands were generally uniform and interrelated throughout. Therefore, in this chapter the discussion will include references to other islands of the Society group besides Tahiti, although the concentration will be on the latter.

Early European visitors to the Society Islands have left us a good record of the native culture as it existed in the early days of the historic period and during colonization.[2] There is, however, in all the various kinds of data collected through the years very little reliable information concerning the prehistory of the Society Island culture.

The earlier studies of Polynesian legends always included references to Tahiti, but they were mainly concerned with its role in the population of Hawaii and New Zealand, neglecting the problem of specifying Tahitian origins. Indeed, references to the genesis of Society Island culture in native legends are couched in terms which may be described as allegorical at best, if not completely mythical.[3]

In the 1920's members of the Bishop Museum staff carried on field research in the Society Islands, collecting native traditions and studying the remains of the aboriginal culture. The results of this study appeared in a monograph by E. S. C. Handy, constituting a first attempt at establishing the prehistory of Tahiti through an ethnographical methodology.[4]

Handy found both legendary and material culture evidence, which led him to believe that there had been two successive Polynesian migrations to the Societies. The earliest inhabitants of the islands, according to this view, were organized into clan groups, each ruled by a chief who combined in his person the attributes of war lord, priest, and temporal ruler. The religious concepts of this ethnic substratum revolved around the worship of Tane and Tu, great gods of Polynesian theology, involving, in addition, an ancestral cult on the family or clan level.

The early inhabitants of Tahiti lived in rectangular houses, raising taro, sweet potatoes, and coconuts. Their canoes were the simple dugout type. Later, around A.D. 600, according to Handy, a new Polynesian group arrived from the west, establishing themselves in the Leeward Islands first and then moving into Tahiti. This group was ruled by an aristocratic class called the *'ari'i,* who were considered to be charged with supernatural power. The conquerors drove the early inhabitants of the islands into the hills and marginal areas, appropriating the pleasant shore-line tracts for themselves. There they reared their imposing temples, dedicated to the worship of Tangaroa, the sea-god, and their deified heroes of the past. The function of priests among the *'ari'i* was no longer combined with that of temporal ruler in the person of the chief, but a separate organized priesthood had been formed.

A class of young *bon vivants* was included in the complex structure of the culture of the conquerors as well as a large number of groups of trained trade specialists. In the post-conquest period the houses of the *'ari'i* were oval in plan and their canoes were of the double-hulled type, called *pahi* by the Tahitians.

Since these studies, and especially in the last few years, more data on Polynesian prehistory have come to light, indicating that the theory constructed by Handy may require modification in several respects. The difference between the two "cultures," of which he believed to have found evidence, may not have been the result of two discrete migrations as supposed, but only the result of a steady evolution of culture. There is also reason to believe that the relative chronological position of some of the traits listed in Handy's constructs needs some revision. The study is nonetheless an outstanding pioneering attempt at establishing a time perspective.

In the late 1920's, Dr. K. P. Emory, also of the Bishop Museum, conducted an archaeological survey of the Society Islands, devoting his attention mainly to the interesting ancient temples found in large numbers along the coastal plains in the interior of these islands. Emory developed a sequence of temple structural forms that coincided in most respects with Handy's earlier work, and his report still stands as one of the most detailed analyses of Polynesian stoneworking techniques and structures.[5]

No stratigraphic excavations have ever been done in the Society Islands in the past, however, so that we possess only a portion of the archaeological picture with our detailed knowledge of native architecture. Such things as artifact types and sequences, information on the native diet from trash-heap analysis, burial practices, and the evolution of the physical traits of the present Tahitians are still to be worked out by excavation. As I write, however, Dr. Douglas Oliver and Mr. J. Green of Harvard University are in Tahiti, preparing to undertake some excavations in Raïatéa and Mooréa. The precise data needed for a complete picture of the prehistory of the Societies may therefore not be too far in the future.

For the present, however, we may draw on the recent archaeological excavations in Hawaii, New Zealand, and the Marquesas as a basis for extrapolation in reconstructing the state of the early culture in Tahiti. Combined with Emory's work on architecture and Handy's material culture studies, a broad picture emerges which is apparently in substantial accord with the data from elsewhere in Polynesia as far as the dynamics of cultural development are concerned.

Fig. 11. Tahitian Inland *marae*, Meetia Island (after Emory, 1930)

The Society Islands were first explored and settled probably in the second or third centuries before Christ, at approximately the same time as the Marquesas were occupied. The discoverers of the Societies issued from the same general Western Polynesian cultural milieu as their Marquesan relatives; therefore, their cultures were probably substantially similar during the initial period of occupation. Oval houses with floors outlined by small stone slabs set on edge are frequently found in Tahiti,[6] both on the coast and inland. These houses, which resemble the earliest Marquesan houses, substantially represent the type erected by the first settlers. They were not, however, replaced in later years by other house types but continued in use until the historic period. Although houses with rectangular floor plans were constructed, they were never able to eclipse the round-ended house completely. The houses were grouped in small clusters of two or three, a pattern that will be seen to recur throughout all of Eastern Polynesia. Early temple structures[7] were simple, low, rectangular stone platforms, or pebble enclosures in which basal uprights stood. Such temples were generally separate from the community meeting grounds, sites of all public ceremonies, which were nothing more than a natural level area.

As in nearly all island occupations throughout Polynesia, the original settlement was probably made by a rather small group, possibly consisting of ten canoes or so. These probably split up upon arrival and settled down in various highly favorable areas to begin their task of wresting an existence from their new and promising homeland. There is some evidence to indicate that the island of Tahiti may have been occupied first and that cultural development there was generally ahead of the other islands in the group. Certainly, however, the difference in time between the settlements of the major volcanic islands would not be excessive, so there is really not too much importance to the question of priority of occupation.

The total tool kit carried to the Societies by the discoverers probably resembled the Marquesan Settlement Period assemblage to a large extent. Many hook types, for instance, which are known only from the early periods of Marquesan prehistory, continued in use in the Societies until later, being diffused from there to Hawaii and New Zealand, while some types even survived into the period of European contact. The adzes of this early period probably included the quadrangular cross-section types, with and without a tanged offset handle for lashing. These continued in use in Tahiti until at least A.D. 900 and probably later. Other types resembled the early Marquesan adzes very probably.

Although no pottery has as yet been found in Tahiti, I should like to go out on a limb and predict that it will ultimately appear in the course of excavations in early living sites. The presence of pottery is not easy to exclude from consideration. The natives, who would logically have the best opportunity to find any archaeological material in the course of their horticultural activities, do not generally look for it and could certainly not be expected to cherish and preserve a miserable potsherd—even if they recognized it as such, which would be highly improbable.

In the second century an exploring expedition from the island of Tahiti sailed north, discovering the great island chain of Hawaii. Latest radiocarbon dates from Hawaii indicate that the first settlements in those islands were established, at least by that date, by a group bearing an essentially Tahitian culture. What prompted the long voyage into the cooler northern waters is hard to say, but whether by intention or accident, the first view of the majestic Hawaiian Islands must have been a thrilling experience for the Tahitian explorers.

The population of the Society Islands began to grow in the original colonies and small satellite hamlets sprouted here and there. Larger populations meant more manpower to build better temples, a fact clearly expressed in Tahitian sacred architecture of this period. Changes were made in the basic form of the early temples.[8] The altars of the temple *ahu* were expanded and elaborated; the platforms sometimes reached three feet in height, with basalt slabs forming the walls within which was piled a mass of earth and debris. The basalt slabs were often covered with thin slabs of coral to give the altar a decorative white veneer. In front of the temple altar a rectangular court appeared, sometimes marked merely by an indistinct stone pavement, but occasionally delimited by a stone wall. Terraces of small size were built for the court in some cases. Within the court, small stones were placed upright at various spots to mark the places of important participants in ceremonies or the positions of ceremonial objects. The joining of the altar with the court probably marks the extinction of the separate vil-

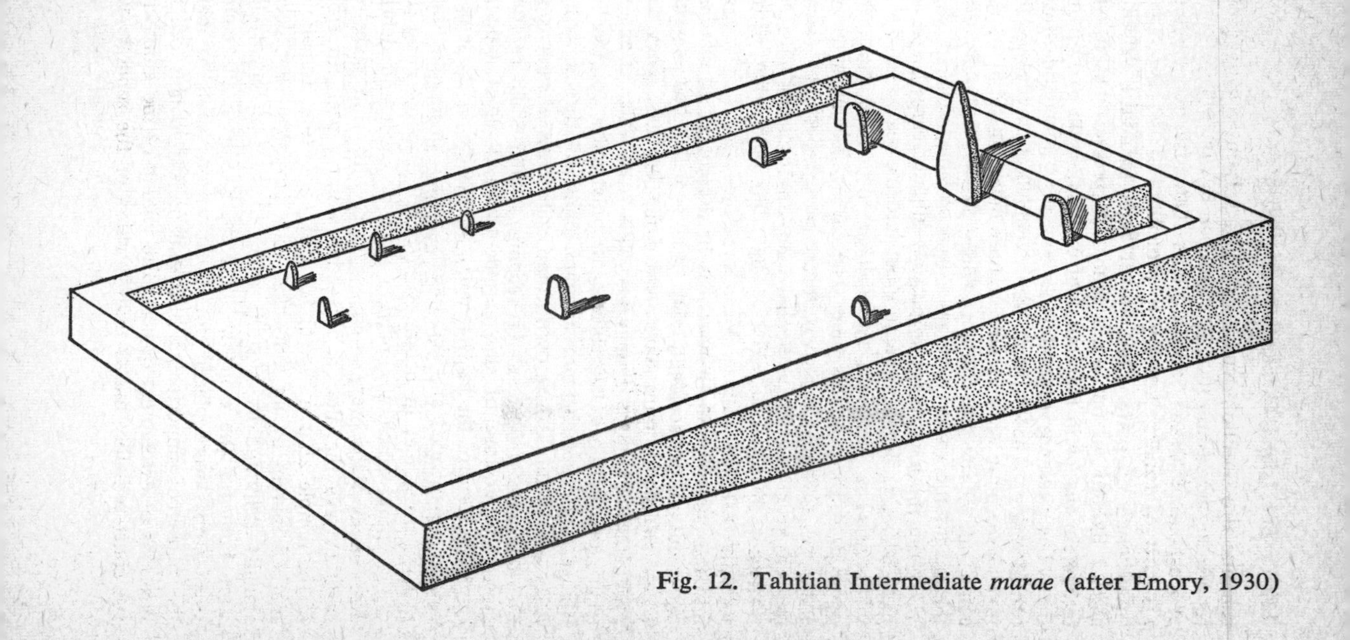

Fig. 12. Tahitian Intermediate *marae* (after Emory, 1930)

lage meeting ground, and the transferral of many profane functions into the sacred precincts of the temple.

The dimensions of these structures ran to a maximum of 120 feet by 59 feet for courts and 30 by 8 feet for altars, which are by no means inconsiderable sizes. Add to this the fact that temples of this type are often found in groups of two or more near hamlets, and we see immediately that the native economy had already reached a rather respectable productivity. If a sizable food surplus did not exist in the first place, permitting a release from subsistence activity for some part of the population, then no structures approaching this magnitude would ever have been possible.

By the ninth century, or possibly slightly earlier, the Society Islanders began to venture out into the sea wastes again in force. The Tuamotu Archipelago may have been discovered by them at this time. The eastern Tuamotu temple structures resemble the early *marae* of the Societies, which has led Emory to postulate that many of the islands in that quarter of the Tuamotu Archipelago may have been settled from the Societies.[9]

The atolls of the Tuamotu group present an enthralling appearance to the present-day visitor with their crystal-clear coral-bottomed lagoons and white beaches. They are by no means easily habitable even today, as water is always short and soil for agriculture is practically nonexistent. Many food crops that are standard elsewhere through Polynesia simply refuse to grow in the coral debris of atoll islets with brackish ground water seeping around their roots.

It was undoubtedly doubly difficult for the first colonies to establish themselves in the Tuamotu Archipelago, but they nonetheless managed to survive, evolving a different economic structure based on the bare necessities of their new environment. New ways were devised to grow taro in pits filled with rotten leaves. Volcanic stones from Tahiti were placed in tree roots to provide silica needed for growth. The Tuamotu houses were of the oval shape, scattered in the usual Eastern Polynesian hamlet settlement pattern. Temples were also dispersed, as in Tahiti, among the hamlets.[10]

Despite the obvious disadvantages of the environment, strong island societies subsequently developed in the Tuamotus, most famous of all being the warlike inhabitants of Anaá. The Anaá warriors raided neighboring atolls in the northern archipelago, carving out a sizable domain and attaining a deserved reputation for savagery in late prehistoric times.

Other Tahitian voyagers may have gone into the Cook Islands; some studies of the temple structures of Tongareva [11] indicate a possible relationship to the Society *marae* of this period.

The Austral Islands, far to the south, may also have been settled from Tahiti, but little is known of them archaeologically. Austral Island temples are considerably different from the Tahitian structures, consisting merely of courts walled on three sides with upright carved slabs placed at intervals.[12] Such an unusual plan may be the result of local elaboration from the basic Tahitian types, however.

On the island of Rapa Iti, a sea-breached volcanic cone with spectacular fairy-tale mountains, the Polynesian inhabitants constructed a large system of fortifications along the crests of the ridges. These ruins were studied by Stokes of the Bishop Museum in the 1920's, but his monograph was never published. Recently the Norwegian Expedition excavated one of the main fortification sites. Radiocarbon dates indicate that the Australs may have been settled as early as A.D. 1300, although the forts were not constructed until much later, approximately at the time of European contact.[13]

Another group of Tahitians explored the sea to the southwest of their island, sailing on until they came in sight of the huge islands of New Zealand, sprawled across the sea like a slumbering monster. Whatever prompted the Tahitians to voyage into this unknown quarter of the Polynesian triangle will remain a mystery. It is relatively certain, however, that this trip was no accident, as there are no winds in Polynesia that blow from the northeast with enough regularity to permit a canoe once blown off course to be carried to New Zealand from the Society Islands.

This discovery set the stage for the development of a very interesting variation of Polynesian culture, for the environment of New Zealand was markedly different from anything the Tahitians had ever seen before.

In the heavy forests were myriads of plants and trees never found on any tropical Polynesian island. Strange wingless birds moved in large flocks through the forest, while spiny lizards, much bigger than the tropical geckos and skinks, scuttled about in the underbrush. On the mountains snow was sometimes seen, and in the southern island great glaciers moved slowly to the sea from mountain valleys.

Elsewhere mineral springs and geysers sent steam clouds into the air. In the waters along the New Zealand coasts, the marine life of tropical Polynesia was replaced by other types of fish and mammals, including the seal.

The effects wrought by this new environment upon the culture of the Tahitian settlers were far-reaching, but beneath these more or less external changes the relationships to Eastern Polynesia are still quite evident in the New Zealand archaeological record, as we shall see below when we discuss the archaeology of those islands in more detail.

About A.D. 1000 or 1100, more changes took place in the *marae* architecture in the Societies as a new type of *marae* evolved, known as the Intermediate type.[14] Like its predecessor, this *marae* was possessed of an enclosed court and an altar, which were considerably larger than the earlier types. The altar no longer consisted of merely a single platform, but often two platforms were superposed, the uppermost being smaller than the base. These temples were often faced with dressed coral blocks, but basalt was still used. On the altar itself the center of the three upright slabs was usually the highest.

According to traditions,[15] a Tahitian chief named Pa'ao is supposed to have introduced the Intermediate type of temple into the Hawaiian Islands, possibly in the thirteenth century. Pa'ao reputedly lived in the district of Uporu in Tahiti and owned lands in the Vavau district. When he landed on Hawaii he finally settled on the northern tip of the island, which he named Uporu after his Tahitian home district. Legends state that Pa'ao influenced Hawaiian native architecture to the extent that the Hawaiian temples, which had been of the open courtless type in this period, were abruptly changed and court enclosures added to keep up with the latest in foreign fashions.

Another legendary account of a Tahitian voyage to Hawaii is to be found in the story of Moikeha, a Tahitian chief who settled on the island of Kauai, possibly building a large Tahitian type of temple there that bears a name cognate to that of a prominent Tahitian *marae*: *Hikina' akala.*[16] Such legends need validation from intensive excavations before they are acceptable, however.

In the Leeward group of the Societies, the architectural advances that originated in Tahiti were not followed slavishly, but an independent development took place in which the temple altars were expanded enormously and courts remained unenclosed. The so-called "international" temple of Taputapuatea,[17] at Opoa, Raïatéa, may have been constructed about the thirteenth century and enlarged again a century later, although the dating is solely genealogical and therefore open to great doubt. Taputapuatea still stands, fortunately, and an excellent description of it and the surrounding ruins is available.[18] The *ahu* is 129 feet long and 24 feet wide. Its sides are formed by standing slabs of rough-cut coral stone that reach 10 feet above the ground surface. Within the outer facing are remains of the façade of an earlier structure, only a few feet smaller than the present structure. The heart of the altar, which may contain even earlier building periods, is filled with stones and coral debris. In the vicinity of this megalithic masterpiece are the remains of three other temples, two of which are approximately 100 feet long while the third is "small"—69 feet in length.

From the fourteenth century on, the development of temple architecture in Tahiti was rapid and spectacular, evolving the structures known as the Coastal *marae*.[19] These *marae* were considerably larger than any of their predecessors, and all details of their construction were more elaborate. The altars were no longer flat platforms but rather flat-topped, stepped pyramids formed of series of superposed platforms of gradually diminishing size. Most altars displayed no more than three or four steps, although a few exceeded this by a large margin. The upright stones that were previously placed on temple altars do not appear on the Coastal *marae*, probably because the stone uprights were replaced with carved wooden uprights. The altar walls were built of worked basalt and coral blocks in the lower portions, with naturally polished stones forming the upper parts. The average size of the altars of Coastal *marae* was 60 feet long, 15 feet wide, and 10 to 12 feet high.

The courtyards of these temples were quite sizable, attaining maximum dimensions of 267 feet wide by 377 feet long. The surfaces of the courts were usually paved with small stones, and basalt uprights marked the positions reserved for important persons or equipment during various rituals. Around the temple courtyard a wall was constructed of shaped basalt blocks, each of which was elongated and rectangular in section, with one neatly rounded end. The blocks were placed with all the rounded ends visible on the exterior of the courtyard wall, the rhythmic repetition of these soft contours in horizontal courses presenting a very pleasing effect. Around the interior of the court and the general precincts of the temple were found other less important components of Tahitian ceremonial sites, such as refuse pits which were dug to hold dangerous cast-off ceremonial objects charged with supernatural force for the uninitiated, or small houses which housed various ceremonial equipment such as drums and images.

The culmination of Tahitian temple architecture was the giant *marae* Mahaiatea, located on the point of the same name in the Papara district.[20] This structure was erected between 1766 and 1768 by the female chief of this district for her son and was visited by Cook during his sojourn in Tahiti. Emory, after examining the site and the historical eyewitness reports concerning its size and configuration, has arrived at a reliable reconstruction of Mahaiatea. The court was 377 by 267 feet; the altar, located at the west end of the court, was 267 feet long, 87 feet wide at the base, and 50 feet high, with ten steps on the side facing the courtyard. The altar was constructed of coral blocks and basalt as in the past, with basalt cornerstones at the angles of each step.

If our use of religious monuments as an index of social elaboration is valid, then, at the time when the Coastal *marae* had evolved, the Society Island culture had become substantially the same as that which was later to be witnessed by the Europeans.[21] The islands were divided into districts, each of which was ruled by a chief who was the senior male of the lineage of that district. The chiefs enjoyed a large measure of power over their subjects, which was backed up by the presence of a group of warriors always ready to enforce the royal will at spear point. Chiefs could appropriate economic goods without ceremony, at a whim, or to serve a real need. They directed agricultural activities to a large extent and supervised the flow of produce from the farmers to the consumers, removing their portion at the same time. There were many insignia which denoted chiefly rank, among them the *Maro 'ura*, a tapa loincloth which was decorated with feathers and bore, according to some authorities, a symbolic representation of the chiefly genealogy. All that a chief touched, including the ground beneath his feet, was *tapu*—charged with chiefly power. In speaking to chiefs, special grammatical forms were used. When a chief or some member of his family passed through one of the so-called life crises (i.e., birth, puberty, marriage, sickness, etc.) the

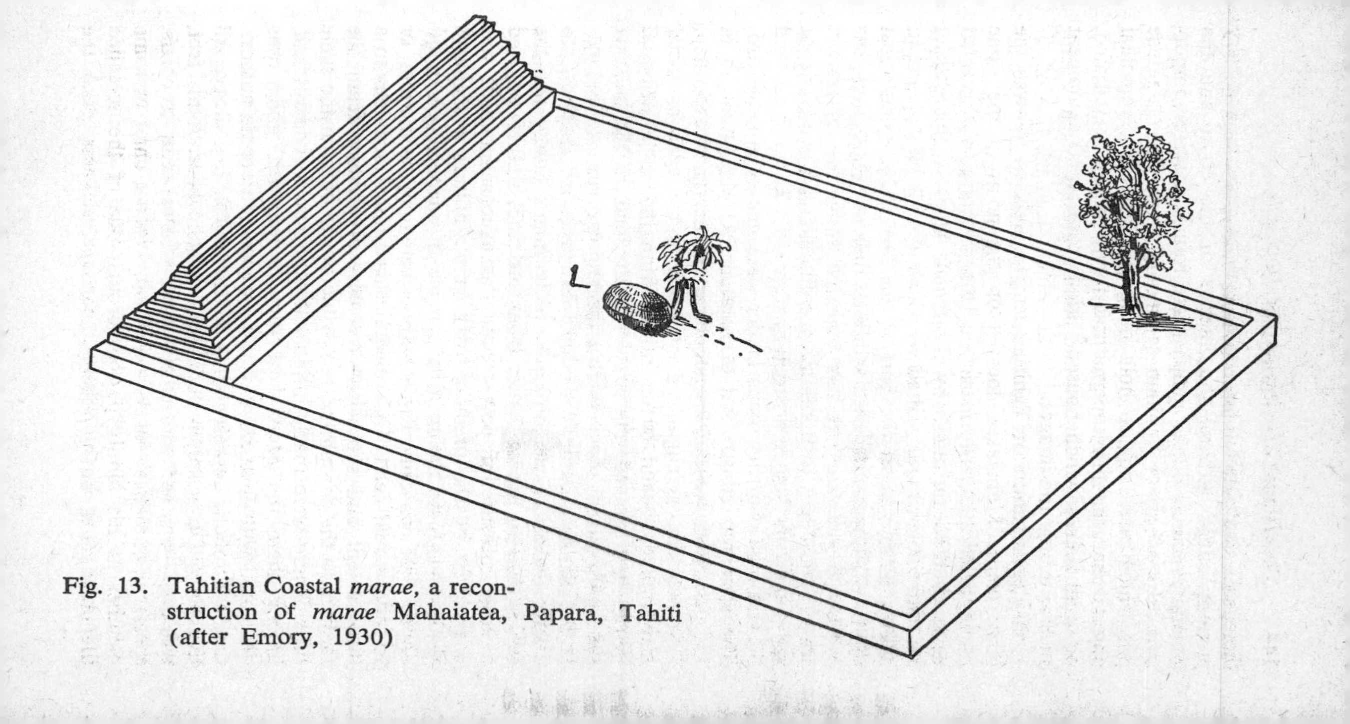

Fig. 13. Tahitian Coastal *marae*, a reconstruction of *marae* Mahaiatea, Papara, Tahiti (after Emory, 1930)

ceremonies of commemoration were elaborate and quite frequently marked by human sacrifices.

The chiefs themselves were bound into groups of a larger order by kinship ties which connected several districts into what might be called a confederation, for purposes of warfare. Below the level of the district or tribal organization were smaller super-family and family groups, each tracing back ancestry to some collateral branch from the line of the royal family, and each associated with certain tracts of land. The rulers of these smaller social groups within the tribe were called the *ra'atira* or subchiefs. They supervised the production within their own properties. These subchiefs were certainly not without real power, however, for they could oppose any moves on the part of the *'ari'i* if such measures appeared unjust. Evidence indicates that the chiefs were by no means oblivious to this potential threat to their well-being and sought to minimize possible causes for dissatisfaction among the landed aristocracy.

At the base of the social ladder were the commoners who composed the bulk of the population and played the main role in production under the direction of the *ra'atira* and the *'ari'i.*

As noted above, the divisions within the tribal structure consisted of successively smaller units down to the level of the family group. Each one of the major divisions from the family of the tribal chief downward was invested with a specific temple of its own, the more minor family temples being erected with a stone from the ancestral temple incorporated into the new structure as a cornerstone.

The productivity of the Society Islands culture was apparently tremendous, being fully capable of supporting a large upper class that did not engage directly in production at all. In addition to the chiefs and subchiefs a large class of religious functionaries existed, some individuals specializing in the religious life completely while others held posts which demanded only part-time participation. These individuals had to be supported, and food offerings to the tribal gods were therefore mandatory. Besides the religious orders there were a number of specialist groups who performed a variety of services, such as canoe building, fishing, etc., in return for pay in kind. Such specialists were seldom completely divorced from subsistence activities, however, as there was not enough demand for their services to permit anything more than a part-time specialization.

With such a well-developed political organization and subsistence economy, it is no wonder that the population of the Society Islands grew to sizable proportions, with the island of Tahiti alone supporting a population of about 204,000, according to Captain Cook. In islands of this type, much of the surface area is uninhabitable owing to the aridity of the high plateaus and the mountainous nature of the island interior. Therefore, a figure of 204,000 for an island of the size of Tahiti indicates a fairly high population density in the actually inhabited areas and consequently a good probability of marked competition for the best ecological areas. This competition frequently took the form of an open warfare which was well organized and bloody. Warriors were armed with javelins, lances of several types, clubs, slings, and shark-tooth swords. On the field they conducted themselves in a loose formation with some division of military duties. Religious practices entered into all phases of warfare from the conception of strategy to the disposition of captives and loot.

Such was the culture of the Society Islands as it existed in the eighteenth century, flowering in the relative isolation of the great Pacific. The people, completely engrossed in the immediacies of everyday life, were blissfully unaware of the disturbances on the continent of Europe that were driving the white men to find new worlds to conquer.

Legend records that, during the last years before the appearance of the Europeans, a strange incident occurred at the temple of Opoa, Raïatéa,[22] in the course of a ceremony for adoration of the gods. A sudden squall, out of a blue sky, removed the branches of a live hard-wooded tree standing in the temple enclosure, leaving only the trunk standing naked. Astonished, the onlookers demanded of each other the significance of this event, until a priest named Vaita spoke, interpreting the event as a message of the gods. Vaita prophesied that the native way of life would soon vanish like the branches on the tree, changed by the arrival of a new people who, although appearing different from the Tahitians, would also paradoxically resemble them in certain respects. These visitors would initiate profound changes in the social order. When asked as to the manner in which this visitation would take place, the priest responded "*Te haere mai nei i ni'a i te ho'e pahi 'ama 'ore*" ("They will come aboard a ship without an outrigger"). Many refused to believe that such a ship would sail until Tamatoa, a chief of Raïatéa, ordered some of his servants to place a large wooden receptacle in the lagoon to see if it would float. The bowl floated, even after Tamatoa had placed some stones inside of it. Convinced that a ship was indeed feasible without an outrigger, the chief declared his acceptance of the prophecy, although others present were not so convinced and threatened Vaita with dire vengeance if the prophecy should not prove true. If the legend is credible, it was not long after that the white sails of the *Dolphin* peeped over the horizon and the charmed freedom of Tahiti was broken forever.

The main points of Society Island prehistory may be summarized thus:

1. The Societies were probably settled at approximately the same time as the Marquesas by a Western Polynesian group possessing a material culture similar to that of the Marquesan Settlement Period.
2. Subsequent isolation and cultural evolution produced divergences in Society Island culture that became evident at an early date.
3. The size and complexity of archaeological religious architecture constitute evidence that the Society Islanders developed a sound economic structure and political organization at an early date and continued to improve their techniques of environmental exploitation until historic times.
4. The Society Islands served as a dispersion point from which Hawaii, some of the Tuamotu Islands, New Zealand, and possibly the Cook Islands were settled.

12

North to Flaming Hawaii

According to an old Tahitian chant,[1] when Ru and Hina discovered earth in the primordial ocean, the great god Maui, the trickster, set sail with his canoes and visited the islands, building temples wherever he stopped. Then the chant continues: *Tae na to'erau, na Nu'u hiva roa e na 'Aihi ahuahu* ("He sailed to the north, to great Nuku Hiva and to flaming Hawaii"). The tropical Polynesian discoverers of the Hawaiian Islands must have been quite awed by the majesty of giant Mauna Loa, the largest live volcano in the world, for references to it and its companions on the island of Hawaii are often found in old Tahitian figures of speech alluding to the Hawaiian group. Equally awesome was the extent of the island chain that rose out of the northern sea, stretching off to the northwest in a 1,500-mile string of increasingly smaller islets. The varied lands of the larger islands were extremely fertile and well watered, presenting an ideal ecological situation for colonization.

Long ago the historical traditions of the native Hawaiians yielded clues to the source from which their islands were settled. David Malo, the well-known Hawaiian historian, wrote in his *Moolelo Hawaii* (*Hawaiian Antiquities*) that the settlers of his home islands came from Tahiti or an adjacent island.[2] Malo had heard references to an island called Tahiti in the archaic Hawaiian chants and legends and had concluded that they referred to the actual island of Tahiti rather than a fictitious place with a similar name. William Ellis, the missionary who was a contemporary of Malo,

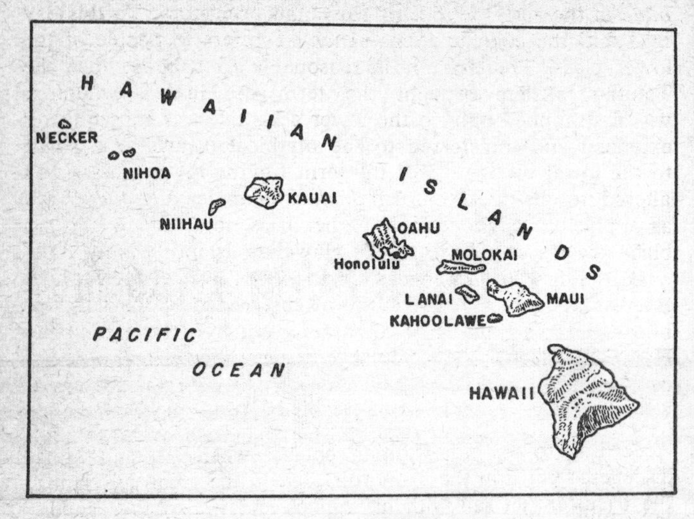

Fig. 14. The Hawaiian chain

reported that the belief was very widespread among the natives that their ancestors had arrived from Tahiti. For many years all speculation about Hawaiian origins were based on evidence derived from legends and traditions.

In opposition to such traditions, a body of lore has been accumulating concerning the *menehune* ("black dwarfs") of Hawaii to whose prowess in architecture many stone monuments in the islands have been legendarily attributed. Certain authorities have even gone so far as to interpret the references to *menethune* in the early Hawaiian legends as being evidence of a population of Melanesians who inhabited the islands prior to the arrival of the Polynesian peoples from Tahiti. Such speculation was well silenced by the recent publication of a very definitive study of the *menehune* legends.[3] It was pointed out that such legends existed in various islands of Melanesia and Micronesia and in other islands of the Polynesian triangle as well as in Hawaii. Apparently all these legends derive from a common substratum of mythology and are reinterpreted in terms of local conditions by various groups. Thus in Hawaii the ancient legends of mischievous and highly talented dwarfs were interpreted to refer to the lower classes, who were probably called *mene-*

hune in the early periods of Hawaiian prehistory. To this day in Tahiti the cognate term *menehune* refers to people of the lower class. Therefore it is reasonable to suppose that the Tahitian settlers brought the term to Hawaii, where it was first applied only to the lower class but was subsequently extended and transferred to the mythical dwarfs as a slight to the lower classes. Later the term for the lower classes was altered to the present form *makaainana,* leaving *menehune* as applicable to the dwarfs alone. It is now certain that no black dwarfs ever lived in the Hawaiian Islands at any time.

In the first four decades of the twentieth century much interest developed in the study of the ancient stone temples, house platforms, and forts that were scattered throughout the Hawaiian Islands. Very extensive surveys were carried out on most of the main islands of the group by Emory, Bennett, McAllister, and other members of the staff of the Bernice Bishop Museum of Honolulu. These surveys involved little excavation, however, but were devoted mainly to recording the fast-vanishing stone structures left by the native Hawaiians and whatever ethnological information could be associated with them. It became apparent during this work that the relationship between Hawaiian and Tahitian cultures which had been claimed by historical traditions might actually exist, as many temple structures found in the Hawaiian group bore a very marked resemblance to Tahitian temples; and it was believed that such resemblance could not be the result of mere chance.

After the end of World War II, a surge of interest in the problems of Polynesian prehistory resulted in the first attempts to apply stratigraphic techniques to the archaeological remains of Hawaii. Heretofore, anthropologists had often maintained that no stratified archaeological deposits could be found in Polynesia. The islands had been inhabited for a relatively short period of time according to them, and therefore no refuse material could have accumulated on archaeological sites. In 1950 Dr. Emory began his program of excavations under the sponsorship of the Bishop Museum, aided by a large number of nonprofessional and student assistants. A rock shelter was selected for the first excavation in this somewhat bold experiment and the excavators were delighted to recover an extremely rich collection of ancient artifacts: fish hooks of bone and shell, adzes, and coral files. As interest in the program grew with continued success, Dr. Emory expanded the scope of his investigations, fielding several teams of archaeological workers formed around nuclei of well-trained anthropological students from the University of Hawaii. With the able assistance of a young Japanese archaeologist, Mr. Yoshiko Sinoto, Emory has accumulated during the past nine years the largest collection of Polynesian archaeological material presently above the ground, and the efforts of the Bishop Museum group show no signs of slacking.

The results of these excavations, coupled with those of the earlier archaeological surveys, permit us now to sketch the outlines of Hawaiian prehistory far more definitively and to indicate, with a much higher degree of certainty, the source of the Hawaiian occupation.

In brief, the results of Emory's work amount to a vindication of the ancient Hawaiian historical traditions of a Tahitian occupation. The dates obtained for the earliest sites by radiocarbon age determinations are approximately A.D. 120 ± 120 years, earlier than even Emory expected for the occupation of the Hawaiian chain and far in excess of the A.D. 900 date generally accepted on traditional evidence.

Two sites on the South Point of Hawaii have contributed much to our knowledge of the early period of Hawaiian occupation.[4] One is a large rock shelter, called *Waiakuhini* in the native tongue, while the other is on a sandy dune deposit. The Sand Dune site at South Point had been occupied by a group of fishermen who leveled off the surface of the dune and laid pavements of coral gravel and small beach stones upon which they constructed their houses.

As a result of prolonged occupation of the site, castoff tools, fish bones, shells, charcoal, and ashes accumulated on the paved floors to a depth of ten inches or more. This debris of habitation yielded a remarkable assortment of artifacts to the Bishop Museum excavators. Over 1,600 finished fish hooks and hook fragments were recovered, in addition to numerous partially completed hooks that had been discarded during manufacture for reasons often known only to the long-dead Polynesian craftsmen who had worked on them. A very sizable proportion of the hooks were of bone of a type used by later Hawaiians for deep-sea fishing; therefore, Emory concluded that the South Point site was inhabited by fishermen who ventured far off the Hawaii coast for their catch.

Besides the numerous hooks, 20,000 files of coral and sea urchin spines were found in the South Point site. These had been used by the fishermen to shape their bone hooks and polish them smooth, once the general plan of the hook had been "roughed out" with a basalt-flake knife. The little dune settlement was occupied for some time and then abandoned, after which the ceaseless winds gradually covered the hut remains with a thick mantle of sand, obscuring them from view completely. It was only shortly before the advent of the Europeans that the sand dune was again a locus of native activity, this time as a burial ground. The deep, soft dune sand over the ancient hut floors was quite easy to dig, and a number of burials were made in the area.

Excavations at the rock shelter Waiahukini demonstrated that the Sand Dune site had been occupied earlier. Tools found at the base of the trash accumulation in Waiahukini appeared at the top of the Sand Dune site deposits, while artifacts from the base of the Sand Dune site did not appear at all in Waiahukini.

Emory was able to show after a few excavations that fish-hook types offered a very valuable index for dating Hawaiian archaeological sites. He found, for instance, that the earliest archaeological sites showed certain varieties of fish hooks that were not present in later sites, and that new types of hooks were invented by the Hawaiians in the course of their prehistory. He was ultimately able to trace the history of each hook type, showing its fluctuation in frequency relative to other types in the total Hawaiian hook inventory. Thus, given the total fish-hook collection from a particular site for typological analysis, he could chronologically place that site relative to other previously excavated sites by virtue of the percentages of the various types of hooks in the collection.

Emory has used the information obtained from these two rich archaeological sites to reconstruct the culture of the Polynesians who settled Hawaii.[5] He believes that the occupation was effected by a sizable, very well-equipped expedition that carried with it all the necessities for life in the form of food plants and domestic animals. Perhaps the actual discovery of the Hawaiian chain was made first by a small exploring party. These explorers may have returned to their home islands with news of the discovery, on the basis of which a major expedition was outfitted to occupy the virgin territory.

Whatever the sequence of events, whether a pioneering group of sailors discovered Hawaii and sailed away to return with an expedition, or whether Hawaii was initially stumbled upon by a large, fully outfitted expedition, the occupation of the islands got off to an excellent start.

The houses of the early Hawaiians were simple affairs, often built on the surface of the earth or occasionally on a crude pavement. They were oval or circular in plan, and the walls were made of wooden poles covered with a thatch of leaves. These houses were dispersed in small hamlet groups consisting of several houses each. Each group probably corresponded to an extended family: a father, his wife and sons, and their wives and children.

The temples of the early Hawaiians were like those of the Tahitian Inland type or the *ahu* of the Marquesan Settlement Period culture; they were small crude platforms or enclosures on which basalt uprights stood. We may presume on the basis of evidence from the other Polynesian islands that temples were constructed in the general vicinity of most of the hamlets.

The discoverers of Hawaii used many tools already familiar to us from the archaeological excavations in the other islands of Polynesia. The Rotating Hook is well represented in early Hawaiian culture, as are the composite tuna hooks. Stone adzes are of the quadrangular tanged variety, quite common in Tahiti.

According to Emory,[6] the total tool assemblage of the early Polynesian settlers of Hawaii (adzes, hooks, etc.) indicates that Tahiti was the source of this migration. In support of the cold facts of archaeology, the data of physical anthropology demonstrate that the Hawaiian native population was physically very similar to the Tahitians, even more so than one would expect on the basis of their being two regional varieties of the same race. The linguist has also made his contribution to the solution of this problem by demonstrating that the Polynesian dialect of Hawaii is more closely related to the Tahitian dialect than to any other Eastern Polynesian tongue.

To summarize the most recent evidence on Hawaiian origins obtained by archaeological excavations, the Hawaiian Islands were occupied by a large, well-planned expedition from Tahiti in the second century after Christ. The initial occupation of the Hawaiian Islands probably followed roughly the same pattern that was evident in the Marquesas; the first settlers logically selected the most favorable ecological areas for their colonies. As the population in these nuclear colonies grew, groups broke away from time to time, establishing themselves elsewhere in order fully to exploit the possibilities of the land, perhaps, or to avoid friction of one type or another within the parent groups. Gradually the population increased through the centuries, spreading over the habitable land of the more favorable islands, overflowing into the less habitable marginal areas of the archipelago. Although more work has been done on the island of Hawaii than on any other in the archipelago, there is evidence from some of the other islands that indicates at least minimal dates for the occupations of the lesser islands.

Attention has recently been focused on the island of Kauai [7] because of some outstanding peculiarities in the subculture of its inhabitants. It appears that Kauai may have been a backwater in which many features of the ancient Hawaiian culture were preserved with extraordinary conservatism. Besides these archaisms, there are also some unusual innovations apparent in the Kauai archaeological record which distinguish it from the other islands of the archipelago.[8] The Kauai Polynesians manufactured a type of poi-pounding pestle of a most interesting stirruplike configuration, differing markedly from the classical Hawaiian knobbed pestle pounder found elsewhere in the archipelago. Kauai was also known for its own distinctive type of double-grooved stone club head. The famous "menehune ditch" on Kauai, an irrigation ditch faced with well-fitted cut-stone slabs, represents one of the most remarkable works of Hawaiian architecture. In their social organization the Kauai Polynesians did not emphasize the distinction between chief and subject that was so common in later Polynesian societies. The Kauai subdialect of Hawaiian preserved the *t* and *r* sounds of Tahitian that had dropped out or had been replaced by sound changes in the development and differentiation of the distinctive Hawaiian dialect. Radiocarbon dates obtained from excavations in the rock shelter of Ha'ele'ele on Kauai indicate that the island was occupied by at least A.D. 1200 if not earlier (A.D. 1239 ± 200).[9]

On the large island of Oahu, the earliest record of occupation so far obtained is from the Kuli'ou'ou Valley shelter, which has been dated at A.D. 1005 ± 180. The Moomomi shelter on Molokai yielded charcoal that was dated at A.D. 1408 ± 300. Although none of the dates listed above may actually represent the earliest occupation of the various islands from which they were derived, they at least serve as a minimal indication of the time lapse between the occupation of the great island of Hawaii and the more diminutive members of the chain. Little has been published concerning the period subsequent to settlement of the islands besides the names of some sites and radiocarbon determinations of their respective ages. Most of the sites of this period excavated to date have been rock shelters; consequently little information is yet available on the distribution of hamlets and ceremonial sites. We cannot, therefore, trace the development of Hawaiian culture through this period or be more specific about population expansion.

A good view of Hawaiian culture of the fourteenth and fifteenth centuries is available, but to obtain it we must travel far out to the northwest along the Hawaiian chain to two barren volcanic islets. The first of these, called Nihoa, is 150 miles northwest of Kauai. Approximately 150 miles farther to the northwest lies Necker Island. Neither of these islands was inhabited when first seen by Europeans, nor have they ever been inhabited since except by the birds that nest in droves on both. In the fourteenth and fifteenth centuries, however, they may have supported a rather sizable population if the archaeological remains found on them by the 1924 Tanager Expedition are representative.[10]

Nihoa is about a mile long and approximately a quarter mile in width, rising some 850 feet out of the sea at its highest point. The north, east, and west sides are steep cliffs dropping into the sea, but the land slopes down to low bluffs on the southern coast of the island and six small hanging valleys open onto a shallow bay where landings may be made. On these slopes the Hawaiian occupants constructed some twelve acres of low agricultural terraces for taro, sweet potatoes, and other crops. Scattered among the terraces are over thirty-five house sites, consisting mostly of rectangular unpaved floors with occupation debris scattered about on their surfaces. In addition to the open house sites there were fifteen rock shelters on the rugged hills of Nihoa that were also inhabited. Fifteen temples were constructed by the dwellers of this barren little islet, all of the familiar Tahitian Inland type as defined by Emory. Small low cairns of stone, rectangular or pentangular in plan, supported coral branches and coral heads, indicating that they were altars of some type (coral branches played an important role in many religious ceremonies throughout all Polynesian societies). Other temple structures were the familiar small terraces or platforms supporting basalt prism uprights.

An astonishing fact concerning the settlement of this tiny and somewhat inhospitable island appeared during the course of archaeological explorations: fresh water supply did not exist in quantity to support life. The only sources of water were a few small springs, the water of which was highly charged with foreign matter and minerals from the excretions of the many birds now nesting on the island. Even if one makes allowances for the absence of such large numbers of birds during native Hawaiian occupation, the volume of water produced by the springs may have been insufficient to support anything more than a small family. According to Emory, however, the population of Nihoa was approximately 200.

From the debris on the exposed house floors and the trash deposits forming the floors of the various rock shelters a large collection of artifacts of various types was obtained, all of familiar types duplicated generally throughout Polynesia. Tanged adzes with quadrangular cross sections were numerous, as were coral files and beautifully fashioned bone hooks in a typically Hawaiian style with gracefully curving points and barbs. Many fragments of cowry shells that had been fashioned into lures for squid fishing were recovered, as were the grooved oval stone weights used for such lures.

A collection of very interesting stone vessels was made from various habitation sites on the island. These had been pecked from large beach boulders by a very painstaking process that achieved quite admirable results. The bowls were generally between 6 and 9 inches tall and between 5 and 7 inches in diameter at the rim, with a lip thickness of about .3 to .5 inch. The weight of the bowls varied considerably, one large specimen attaining a remarkable 56 pounds. The control which the native craftsman exercised over his material is quite evident when one considers the difficulty encountered in hollowing out a boulder by the pecking process to obtain such relatively fragile vessel walls, while not cracking the vessel by an inexpertly directed stroke of the stone pick.

Although the archaeological remains of Nihoa had made it plain that the native population had resided there for some time, very little evidence of human burials was discovered. Only two of the sites investigated by the Tanager Expedition contained human remains, in both instances in very small quantity. There is a possibility that many other burials were interred around the house sites, however, where no test excavations were made, or hidden in the rocks. It is also possible that sea burial was practiced by the ancient inhabitants of Nihoa.

The remains of ancient native occupation on Nihoa parallel closely those found at Necker Island, 150 miles farther northwest. Necker is more barren than Nihoa and considerably smaller in surface area, being 1 mile long and about 400 feet wide, projecting about 278 feet above sea level at a maximum. The south side of the island consists of impassable cliffs, while the northern coast line is accessible, but only when the trade winds are not blowing strongly. The vegetation of Necker is sparse, limited to grasses and scrubby bushes. Only two small water sources are known, both of which provide water unfit for human use at the rate of about five gallons per day or less. The total surface area of Necker is approximately forty-one acres, over which are scattered a rather surprising number of archaeological remains. No less than thirty-three temples were erected on Necker, the erect stone uprights on their altars giving the skyline of the island a serrated appearance to an offshore observer. Eight rock shelters showed signs of habitation, as did some ten possible house-site terraces. Fifteen more terraces probably saw use as garden plots.

The temples of Necker are a little more sophisticated than those of Nihoa while still of the same general type, the so-called Tahitian Inland *marae*. The differences between the buildings found on the two islands may be a result of simple availability of raw materials. Slabs were at hand on Necker for wall construction and uprights, while only boulders and pillow lava prisms were present on Nihoa as building materials. The altars of the Necker temples were long and low, with irregular slab uprights spaced along the rear. The altars faced a level courtyard often raised on a low terrace.

The richest site on the entire island was the 15-foot-by-8-foot rock shelter, Bowl Cave, so called because of the number of stone bowls and bowl fragments found in the trash accumulation on its floor. The artifacts excavated in Bowl Cave —adzes, coral files, basalt knives, squid-luring equipment, etc.—all resemble closely the tools discovered on Nihoa. A noteworthy discovery at Necker, however, was a large number of well-carved stone images of an unusual type. These, unfortunately, were found by members of the party that annexed Necker for Hawaii in 1894. Of the seven recovered, only five found their way to the Bishop Museum. Sailors from a British warship landed in the same year on Necker and evidently found quite a number of images and fragments on one of the temple platforms. Only two of this collection were brought to the British Museum. The total extant collection of Necker images was swelled by some additional fragments recovered by the Tanager Expedition.

The images are all of one general type, ranging from 8 to 18 inches high and manufactured of vesicular basalt. The figures are represented in full length, but hands and feet are not differentiated. Legs are bulky and slightly astraddle, occasionally with lateral ridges across the knees. The arms are short, stumpy, and directed outward from the sides, joining the body in a pair of wide shoulders. The heads of the images are oval, set well into the shoulders without a trace of a neck, giving the little statues the appearance of an eternally frozen shrug of the shoulders. On the flat and oval face a wide, thick-lipped mouth is open and a tongue protrudes. Two ovoid eyes are set on either side of a rectangular nose that issues from a pair of beetle brows. The facial features of the figures are a Hawaiian variation on the basic stylized face motif that is found in the art of Polynesians as well as Melanesians and is believed to have a great antiquity.

On the basis of the archaic temples of Nihoa and Necker, Emory dated the occupation of the islands as being previous to the traditional second period of Tahitian migration, which supposedly occurred around the fourteenth to fifteenth centuries according to genealogies. Recently, radiocarbon age determinations on charcoal collected from Bowl Cave indicated that the islands may have been inhabited about the 1400's, a date in agreement with that obtained by the genealogical method.[11]

The prehistorian is indebted, then, to the ancient Hawaiians who occupied these two barren islands and subsequently departed, leaving behind them a fossilized record of their culture of the fourteenth or fifteenth century for archaeologists to read some 500 years later. This record is actually very neat, uncluttered by the subsequent occupations that occur on most archaeological sites with frequent deleterious effects to earlier deposits.

It was a culture similar to that found on Nihoa and Necker

islands, then, that was spread throughout the whole Hawaiian Island group in the fourteenth century when some rather important events for Hawaiian culture history may have occurred, if tradition is reliable. It was about this time, according to legends, that more frequent contacts with Tahiti were resumed after a lapse of many centuries. In the chapter on Tahitian archaeology we have already had occasion to mention the Tahitian voyagers Pa'ao and Makua Kaumana who sailed to the Hawaiian Islands.[12] Another Tahitian, Moikeha, sailed to Hawaii and remained there. His son returned to the father's homeland and brought back more Tahitians to Hawaii. Traffic flowed not only in a northward direction from Tahiti, however, for there are other legends which speak of Hawaiians visiting Tahiti and other islands. Among these were Hema, a high chief of Maui who died in Tahiti,[13] and Paumakua, a chief of Oahu who sailed to Tahiti and returned with a large white-skinned priest to whom is attributed the introduction of the Hawaiian native custom of circumcision.

On the basis of temples in definite Tahitian style, often supposedly constructed at the command of Tahitian migrants in Hawaii, we might be inclined to place some credence in these legends of Tahitian contact. Final confirmation of such traditions, however, must await stratigraphic excavations in the rich archaeological sites of Tahiti. Only when detailed data on Tahitian artifacts are available will it be possible for us to trace such inter-island contacts in detail by the appearance of Tahitian artifacts in Hawaii or Hawaiian artifacts in Tahiti.

Regardless of the basis for change, whether through resumed Tahitian contact, which is quite plausible, or simply through evolution *sui generis,* the post-fourteenth-century Hawaiian culture began to show some signs of expansion and elaboration in many areas.

Most outstanding of these is the area of religious and ceremonial architecture. In contrast to the Tahitians or Marquesans, the Hawaiians called their temple-ceremonial centers *heiau.* We have seen that up to the fourteenth century *heiau* construction was fairly uniform, but after that a proliferation of *heiau* forms took place, resulting in a rather bewildering multiplicity of variations and totally different types. In general, most of these later temples were built of larger stones than those used in the diminutive earlier models, in addition to being designed on a much more ambitious scale. Thus, Hawaiian temples were following the trends of megalithic architecture that we have seen so far repeated in Tahiti, the Marquesas, and Easter Island. In a classic study of the *heiau* of Kauai, Bennett [14] was able to distinguish five main types of temple structures among the ruins of that island, which can generally be taken as a fair representation of the other islands in the Hawaiian group. Although size variation between temples was great, there were three main kinds of *heiau*: open platforms, walled enclosures, and terraced platforms. The open-platform *heiau* consisted of a platform elevated on three sides, or a terrace. Occasionally a hilltop would be terraced completely around at the same level to form a platform of this type. Walled enclosures were rectangular or square in plan, with internal divisions marked off on paved floors. The walls did not always enclose all four sides and were of varying sizes. The terraced *heiau* was a combination of the open-platform and walled-enclosure types, often consisting of complexes of four terraces, some of which bore walled enclosures or open platforms. Some natural flat areas on hills were also identified as being *heiau,* although they bore no structures of any type.

With the above types as a basic foundation, further elaboration was possible for the native Hawaiian engineers in original arrangements of more minor superstructural parts of the ceremonial complex. Both within and outside the *heiau* precincts, numerous houses were built to shelter the priests who maintained the site or the idols and unused ceremonial gear. Near the center of the uppermost and largest of the terraces of a *heiau* was a square platform which probably served as an altar. Occasionally, stone towers were constructed along the walls of enclosures, possibly for observation of the sea for sea turtles, which played an important part in rituals. Around the sacred precincts, pits called *luakini* were dug to hold discarded refuse from ceremonies, such as broken ceremonial gear and the decaying remains of offerings. The floors of the terraces and platforms of a *heiau* were often marked off into several divisions, which may have been each intended for specific classes of native spectators and participants. The familiar stone prism or slab uprights of the earlier Eastern Polynesian temples are also found in later Hawaiian *heiau*. According to eyewitnesses of the historic period, wooden frame obelisks covered with tapa cloth were erected on the *heiau* grounds; large bundles of staves with tapa streamers attached were planted in the ground. Often wooden slabs carved with faces and other decorative designs replaced the stone uprights on the *heiau* altar. Wooden uprights naturally could not withstand the passage of time, however, and few are now extant. In the vicinity of the temples, and often actually within the precincts, the dead of the upper classes were buried in the earth.

As in other islands of Polynesia, the construction of temples of such magnitude and complexity is indicative of an increase in food surplus and the existence of a strong central authority to manage this food surplus in the support of various community projects. David Malo, the native historian, has left us some comments on the subject of building a *heiau*. Referring to the labor, both physical and ceremonial, which was enjoined by the construction of a *heiau* of the type called *luakini,* Malo [15] says: "It was a great undertaking for a king . . . to be accomplished only with fatigue and with redness of eyes from long and wearisome prayers and ceremonies on his part." Old temples were sometimes chosen as the sites for new structures, but if the old sites available did not suit the priests, an architect was called. He would suggest several designs to the chief, modeling the basic layouts in the earth at his feet, after which the chief selected the design most pleasing to him. The work of construction of the temple was carried out by a corvée directed by chiefs. In addition to the corvée, further demands were made on the populace to supply pigs for the long cycle of ceremonies that were necessary for the consecration of a temple. Large numbers of pigs were slaughtered as offerings at several points during these ceremonies.

The *heiau* of the Hawaiians were found widely dispersed over the islands, but many were located near the shore on prominent points and also on higher ridges inland.[16] Usually hamlets, consisting of a number of house sites, some garden terraces, stone cairns, and possibly some stone-walled pig pens, were found near *heiau.*[17] The native houses of this period displayed as much variation in form as did the temples.[18] Many houses were evidently simply stick-and-thatch structures built directly on the surface of the earth after the surface stones had been removed. These sites can often be recognized as circular stone-cleared areas with small four-stone fire pits in the center. Other house sites were outlined with stones on the ground surface, the boundary stones probably serving to prop up the small branches used for house wall frames. Many houses were built on platforms and terraces averaging about 18 feet in width by 25 to 30 feet in length. The platforms resembled those of the Marquesas in structure and were paved on top. On some terraces and platforms a stone lower foundation wall had been erected for the wood-and-thatch superstructure of the house. This stone foundation ran around three sides of the house. Many sites consisted of a number of interconnected terraces, each of which held one or more houses. Although most of the houses appear to have been rectangular or oval in plan, others apparently were circular. Pile houses of which no surface traces remain may also have been built.

Agricultural garden terraces have already been mentioned in connection with the description of Nihoa and Necker islands. These were low terraces, often with retaining walls of small stones. To supply garden plots with water the Hawaiians constructed large irrigation ditches that linked their streams and garden plots across long distances, thus enabling agriculture on otherwise infertile soil. Perhaps the most famous of these is the "menehune ditch" of Kauai,[19] which displays a facing of neatly fitted stone blocks rivaling the fitted masonry of *ahu* Vinapu at Easter Island. According to the legends this monument was built by the *menehune*, or black dwarfs, to whom the native Hawaiians attributed much of their handiwork. Stone-walled fish ponds were also constructed in rivers and at the seaside to facilitate the capture of fish for food. Food production was further facilitated by the natural endowments of the Hawaiian Islands, which possessed a wide range of ecological niches offering excellent possibilities for adaptation to all the food and useful plants known to the Polynesians. Such fertile lands with their well-constructed terraces, watered by a network of streams and irrigation ditches, combined with the wealth of the sea to give the Hawaiians a bounteous living. The surplus produce allowed them to rear monumental structures for the glorification of their chiefs and gods, as well as to build more gardens and irrigation projects to produce even larger surpluses in a never-ending cycle of increasing production which never did utilize all the available land.

Despite the apparent abundance of habitable land in the Hawaiian Islands, wars were by no means rare. Fortifications of the trench and palisade type found elsewhere throughout Eastern Polynesia appear on the thin Hawaiian ridges and valley rims.[20] The surface around these now-abandoned fortifications is often littered with smooth sling stones, remnants of some long-forgotten battle. Many small rock shelters that have been excavated by Emory and others of the Bishop Museum staff have proven to be refuge caves, inhabited by groups fleeing into inhospitable areas of the islands to escape defeat in war.

The Hawaiians buried their dead in a variety of ways.[21] Bodies were wrapped in tapa or a mat and desiccated, to be later placed in caves or in the earth. Primary earth burials were made in the vicinity of *heiau* for individuals of higher rank, although many burials of both commoner and upper class were made in sand dunes on the beaches, where digging was easier. One such sand dune site, Mokapu on Oahu, was accidentally uncovered during the war, yielding the largest collection of Polynesian skeletons yet recovered. As a result of detailed studies on these skeletons, physical anthropologists will soon be in an excellent position for a detailed description of the ancient Hawaiian physical types. In addition, the skeletons yield much information about common diseases (arthritic lesions are common), native medical practices (broken and set bones are known), and nutrition (dental caries and other indications on the skeleton).

During the course of development of Hawaiian culture, the varieties of tools brought from Tahiti by the first settlers were gradually modified, developing a number of distinctively Hawaiian varieties of fish hooks, poi pestles, net sinkers, etc. Other kinds of tools were dropped completely from the inventory, however, while others were invented in Hawaii.

Much of the material culture of the Hawaiians was made in perishable media, such as wood and vegetable fiber, and naturally very little has survived in the archaeological sites that have been excavated so far. The collections of Hawaiian antiquities of the early historical period that are on view in the Bishop Museum [22] attest to the technical ability of the Hawaiian craftsmen. Mats of intricately woven fine strands, highly polished wooden vessels, beautiful feather plumes and cloaks, geometrically decorated drinking gourds, and elaborate neck amulets in the form of whales' teeth demonstrate clearly what time subtracts from the archaeological record. The Hawaiian preference for artistic expression in such perishable media has left us with little information concerning the history of the development of the unique Hawaiian art style. Our knowledge of this area of native culture received an additional setback when most of the idols and religious paraphernalia were destroyed by the Hawaiians themselves in a fervor to embrace the tenets of Christianity after the arrival of the white man. Some idols and pieces of wooden sculpture did survive the flames of Christianity, but they are quite rare. There is one excellent source of ancient Hawaiian art forms, however, which did survive in an imperishable medium to the present time. These are the multitudinous rock drawings or petroglyphs found in large quantities throughout the islands. These drawings depict men, gods, lizards, canoes, turtles, and many other motifs in an often very attractive style. They were apparently pecked and/or incised into the surface of rocks, as a kind of doodle, by natives passing the time of day, or they may have been placed in some instances to commemorate events or mark certain geographical points of importance. The Bishop Museum staff mapped a collection of petroglyphs of several acres in an area on the smooth surface of a lava flow on the island of Hawaii. The petroglyphs in this particular site had been protected by a mantle of ash from a more recent volcanic eruption. In prehistoric times a native trail passed across the lava flow, and travelers on the route availed themselves of the smooth surface of the stone to sketch designs now and then, with the result that over the years a tremendous collection of petroglyphs accumulated on the surface of the rock. The designs were copied by the Bishop Museum staff, and reproductions of many of the outstanding "works" now grace the covers of Hawaiian Christmas cards.

In our progress so far we have discussed the origin of Hawaiian society and its development up to late prehistoric times. It is clear that this development broadly paralleled that found in the Marquesas, Tahiti, Easter Island, and the islands of Western Polynesia in terms of the interrelationships among the natural environment, the technology, and the productivity of the culture. As the Hawaiians became able to wrest more from their land by improved agricultural techniques and better organization of production, the surplus produce increased, forming the foundation for monumental projects, such as temples and giant irrigation ditches.

Great power would accrue to the chief whose responsibility it was to control this productive potential and administer such a surplus; at the same time, the separation of the chiefly classes from the lower classes would be correspondingly wider with every increase in the economic power of the aristocracy.

Such, indeed, was the case in historic Hawaiian society, as

we know from historical records and the descriptions of native government passed on by Malo and others.[23] The paramount chiefs (*'ali'i*) of the islands were possessed of a tremendous temporal and sacred power. Besides being at the center of the economic structure, they officiated at all major ceremonies and were accorded almost incredible respect. For example, it was only under pain of death that a commoner touched any object belonging to a chief or even allowed his shadow to touch certain of the chiefly possessions. All were required to prostrate themselves before a chiefly person, and honorifics were used when speaking to a chief. All of the special events occurring in the life of a chief, such as circumcision, illness, marriage, and even attempts at procreation of a royal heir, were marked by elaborate ceremonies to insure success. Many types of food were reserved for chiefs, as well as special types of personal ornaments and clothing such as feathered cloaks, whales' teeth amulets, and ceremonial staves. When making a journey, the chief was carried in a kind of chair, for his feet would render sacred (and therefore useless to commoner farmers) the ground which they touched.

The Hawaiian paramount chiefs and their close relatives of nearly equal high rank ruled entire islands or large territorial divisions. The land of each paramount chief was subdivided into smaller districts, each of which was ruled by a subchief (*konohiki*) who traced his ancestry to some collateral branch of the royal line. It was the duty of each of the *konohiki* to oversee his district's production activities and to carry out the periodical collections of food and other products (i.e., mats, tapa cloth, etc.). The *konohiki* would then pass his goods on to the paramount chief, who would reapportion the goods as he saw fit, redistribution following lines of kinship. Although the paramount chiefs possessed great power, theoretically extending to the death decree for relatively minor misdemeanors, the *konohiki* were by no means insignificant. A paramount chief had to be extremely wary of overexercising his prerogatives, as the *konohiki* were quick to sense an affront and could effectively overthrow the high chief without so much as a sideward glance at the vaunted supernatural powers of the chiefly line. Such defiance of authority might seem ill based, but one must consider that the *konohiki* each had very effective control of the males of his district for purely secular purposes. This control could quickly be turned to military ends, however, to bring about the overthrow of the throne.

Warfare, whether of this type or for territorial aggrandizement, was common in Hawaii. Weapons were the standard spears, clubs, and slings found elsewhere in Polynesia. Wooden daggers and small stone-headed clubs were also used. Heavy fiber helmets were worn for protection. The warriors on the field conducted themselves in formation and utilized elementary tactics. As in Tahiti war was surrounded by religious observances from beginning to end.

The majority of the Hawaiian population were commoners (*makaainana*), of course. They were dispersed over the land in hamlets, some of which were growing to fairly large size by the time of white contact in Hawaii. The commoners worked the taro and sweet potato patches, grew yams, bananas, breadfruit, coconuts, and sugar cane, with each crop planted in the area where it would produce the best, from the coastal flats and valley bottoms to the high mountainsides.

Specialists were numerous and varied in Hawaiian culture, foremost among them being the priesthood, which possessed a great deal of power in profane affairs. To mention but a few, architects, sculptors, canoe builders, tattoo artists, fishermen, and even fish-hook makers existed as recognized craftsmen. Of these only a few, such as canoe makers attached to the households of the paramount chiefs, were full-time specialists, while the others practiced their arts by demand.

When the Europeans arrived in Hawaii, the natives were rather quick to adopt the ways of Western civilization, as a consequence of which their aboriginal culture disintegrated rather rapidly. With the passage of the years, immigrants from the Orient, Oceania, and many countries of Europe have moved into the Hawaiian Islands in large numbers. As a result Hawaiian society today is a melting pot of many races and national groups, each of which has contributed to the culture of the whole and has in turn been modified to a certain extent by the other participant nationalities. The culture of the Hawaiians lives on, however, in the native language which is taught in schools and universities, in music and the dance, and in many sporting pursuits such as canoe racing and surf riding.

In review, we have seen that archaeological evidence indicates that the Hawaiian Islands were discovered and settled by a large expedition from Tahiti in the second century after Christ. The original colonizing group grew in size, spreading gradually over the numerous islands of the large archipelago. By the fourteenth century, small groups had settled tiny islands far out on the northwestern end of the Hawaiian chain. As the culture developed and the population increased, a distinctive Hawaiian variety of Polynesian culture evolved, within which many minor local variations were to be found, such as the idiosyncrasies of the Kauai inhabitants.

Contact with Tahiti may have been resumed in the fourteenth century, resulting in an influx of new ideas, which took substance in changes in Hawaiian temple architecture. The changes may also have been a result of internal cultural evolution, however, as further archaeological data are needed to clarify this point.

The later periods of Hawaiian prehistory up to historic times were marked by an increase in population and subsistence production. Large temple complexes were constructed and agricultural projects of startling size were carried through. A highly stratified society grew up, at the head of which stood a sacred chief with a great deal of very practical temporal power, presiding over a graded hierarchy of advisors, subchiefs, priests, craftsmen, and commoners.

13

The Navel of the World

"The Navel of the World" was the grandiose name that the Polynesians of diminutive Easter Island attached to their home of rolling rock-strewn grasslands and dead volcanic cones, lost in the gloomy expanse of the cool southeastern Pacific.

This rather barren and harsh environment, however, gave root to one of the most intriguing and impressive of all the Polynesian cultures. Easter Island society met a tragic end in the nineteenth century, but we are still pondering its most impressive and yet pathetic remnants. The giant stone statues, standing in haughty pursed-lip silence in the midst of ruined temples and houses, the fantastic engravings of birds, bird-men, and gods found on basalt chunks that litter the landscape, and the wooden tablets covered with lines of tiny, finely engraved characters in a forgotten script have always generated a strong attraction for the scholar and the adventurer. Much ink has been spilled on the topic of the Easter Island Polynesians over the years.

The "theories" concerning the derivation of Easter Island culture range all the way from the lost continent of the Pacific,[1] to the Indus Valley in northwestern India,[2] to a race of giants who existed contemporaneously with the dinosaurs. Others have seen the origin of Easter Island society in the aboriginal cultures of Peru;[3] this has been most recently promulgated in the *Kon-Tiki* theory,[4] which will be discussed in a subsequent chapter.

The acceptance of such theories by the public is invariably

due to complete lack of acquaintance with the numerous valuable sources that are available concerning the culture of Easter Island.

The earliest information concerning Easter Island[5] is derived from the journals of Roggeveen, the Dutch sea captain who discovered the island. Captain Cook and his staff, as well as other European navigators of the "Age of Discovery," have left accounts of the culture of Easter Island as they saw it during their brief visits. In the nineteenth century, French missionaries landed to begin the thankless task of conversion. Their first-hand experiences with the aboriginal culture of Easter Island, transmitted to us mainly through the journals and letters of Fr. Roussel, have likewise contributed to the fund of information concerning the native culture of Easter Island. In the late nineteenth century, a German naval officer, Captain-Lieutenant Gieseler, profited from the visit that his vessel paid to the island by collecting artifacts and general information on the culture, in addition to making some excavations. Shortly thereafter, an American warship brought an equally interested naval officer, Paymaster William Thompson, who also made good use of his short sojourn by amassing texts, general ethnological data, and a good collection of implements and *objets d'art* which were subsequently placed in the Smithsonian Institution in Washington, D.C.

In 1914, Mrs. C. Scoresby Routledge led a British Museum expedition to Easter Island for a prolonged session of field work involving an archaeological survey including excavations and general ethnological research. Mrs. Routledge had an opportunity to talk with many aged islanders who in their youth had witnessed the death agonies of the aboriginal society in the epidemics, slave raids, and missionizing of the mid-nineteenth century. Unfortunately, she arrived in time for the death of the last surviving student of the sacred college of the *rongorongo* men, the tribal bards who knew the esoteric script on the "talking boards" that played such an important role in Easter Island ceremony. Only a few all too brief articles and a semi-popular book were produced as a result of this highly successful expedition. Full publication of Mrs. Routledge's data was never realized and her field notes are now lost, probably irretrievably.

In 1934, the Belgian training ship *Mercator* brought the Franco-Belgian Expedition, sponsored by the Musée de l' Homme of Paris and the Belgian Royal Academy. Dr. Alfred Métraux, leader of the party, and Dr. Henri Lavachéry have given the anthropological community and the world a series of articles and monographs detailing the results of their impressive efforts in the areas of art, archaeology, and ethnology.

A Chilean missionary, Fr. Engert, who has spent the greatest part of his life on Easter and has detailed knowledge of the language as well as the remains of the aboriginal way of life, has published a volume of his own researches, which, although it reflects probably only a small fraction of his vast total knowledge of the islanders, is still a very important document.

In 1955, the Norwegian Expedition conducted intensive excavations on several of the more spectacular and important archaeological sites on the island, in an attempt to reconstruct the prehistory of the culture. The scientific team, made up of professional archaeologists from Norway, Chile, and the United States, was apparently quite successful in uncovering stratified cultural deposits and unraveled the developmental sequence of the temple structures and statues which have so long puzzled anthropologists. As yet, however, only one brief scientific report of this work has appeared in print, although publication of the entire monograph is probably no more than a year or two away. This work provides an excellent basis, but much remains to be done before the entire prehistory of the culture is clearly visible.

Little evidence of the earliest occupation was found by the Norwegian Expedition, for the concentration on the more spectacular stone monuments left little time for the equally important exploration of village sites. However, at least one member of the expedition has since returned to Easter Island in order to extract further data from the archaeological record on these problem areas. There is therefore reason to hope that the passage of a few more years will see the publication of the results of these latest archaeological researches, which will serve as a complement to the publications of the Norwegian Expedition.

After the departure of the Norwegians, Easter Island was visited by Dr. Thomas Barthel, a German anthropologist whose main interest was in the famous *rongorongo* script. Barthel had become familiar with cryptographic techniques during World War II and sought to lay a firm foundation for the decipherment of the script that had foiled the efforts of many earlier students. Barthel's work has borne fruit in a monumental volume [6] which clearly indicates the nature of the structural system or "grammar" used in the script and defines the areas in which further research must be undertaken in order finally to arrive at a complete translation of the texts now extant.

Aside from the outstanding names in Easter Island anthropology mentioned above, there are numerous other authors who have made contributions of a lesser magnitude, but to detail these would involve an entire chapter in itself. References to their work may be found in the basic publications listed above.

Thus it is obvious that there is an adequate body of literature available on the Easter Island culture. In fact, there is, surprisingly, more information available on this island than on many of the more accessible islands of Polynesia. Naturally, there are many gaps in our knowledge, and only some of these will ultimately be filled. This situation, however, is far from that pictured by the romanticist or adventurer who must create an aura of mystery and enigma about the "Navel of the World" in order to make his theory more attractive, whatever the basic motivation may be. The mystery surrounding this island is no more impenetrable than that surrounding any other area of the world in which the archaeologists' spades have not been soiled. The ample archaeological resources of Easter Island have been shown to yield to standard archaeological techniques, and the *rongorongo* script is tottering before the first well-aimed attack ever launched at it. Ethnological data are available now and have been for some time. The mystery of this island, then, is largely of an artificial nature, created for specific purposes by nonscientific authors.

For our reconstruction of the prehistory of Easter, we will use in the main the data gathered by the Franco-Belgian expedition, which will be fitted into the outline of stratigraphic sequences uncovered by the Norwegian Expedition,[7] with some modifications to allow for the opinions of other authorities on Polynesian prehistory. From time to time references will be made to the historical oral traditions of the Easter Islanders where they are of interpretive value, although it is necessary to bear in mind that these traditions still largely stand in need of archaeological documentation before they can be accorded any kind of acceptance.

The historical traditions are rather explicit concerning the discovery and settlement of Easter Island and related occurrences.[8] According to the chief Easter Island informant of the Franco-Belgian Expedition, one Juan Tepano by name, the settlers came from a large, warm, verdant island in the west called "Marae Renga." Hotu-Matua, a chief of that island, was forced to flee after a defeat in war, either at the hands of his brother or because of the brother's misconduct with the affianced of a rival chief. A tattooer in the Hotu-Matua's entourage, named Hau-Maka, had a prophetic dream of an island to the east with volcanic craters and pleasant beaches on which six men were seen. Informed of Hau-Maka's dream, Hotu-Matua ordered a canoe to put to sea in search of that island, choosing six men for the exploration party so that the conditions of the dream might be fulfilled. Departing from Marae Renga, the six voyagers were conducted by favorable winds to Easter Island. There the large volcanic craters fitted the description of Hau-Maka's dream, as did the many sandy beaches. After selecting a suitable beach for the chief's residence, the six discoverers sailed to the west coast of Easter Island to await the arrival of Hotu-Matua. Upon doubling the point of Mataveri, however, they perceived the double canoe of Hotu-Matua on the horizon. The chief had followed them. Reaching the beach of Anakena, which had been selected as the most suitable for a chief of the dignity of Hotu-Matua, the crews of the canoes alighted, but at that moment the wives of both Hotu-Matua and his second in command, Tu'u-ko-ihu, gave birth to a prince and princess respectively. After the birth ceremonies the canoes were unburdened of their cargo of taro, yams, bananas, hibiscus, sugar cane, and probably coconuts and breadfruits. Pigs, dogs, and chickens were also put ashore. Thus the settlers began with a full complement of plants and animals necessary to support life, although subsequently many of the plants, as well as the pigs and dogs, became extinct, the former because of environmental difficulties, the latter as a result of accidental or purposeful extermination.

Oroi, the enemy of Hotu-Matua, had not failed to note the flight of the vanquished chief, however. Sensing an opportunity ultimately to annihilate his quarry, he had stowed away at Marae Renga in Hotu-Matua's canoe. After the cargo had been unloaded at Easter and darkness had fallen, Oroi slipped ashore and struck inland. For a long period thereafter Oroi plagued the followers of Hotu-Matua, constantly attempting to trap and kill any unwary wanderers.

Hotu-Matua finally caught and killed his nemesis, however, and peace reigned once again on Easter Island. When Hotu-Matua had grown old and felt the hour of death drawing nigh, he divided the island into equal parts among his sons, each of whom subsequently founded a tribe. Then, climbing the rim of the volcano of Rano-Kao, he called across the miles of sea to his ancient homeland, invoking the gods. Far away in Marae Renga the gods heard and caused a cock to crow as a sign. The sound of this call echoed back to Hotu-Matua, who knew his time had come. He was carried to his house, where he died.

The legend is strange, and stranger still in the form in which Métraux originally recorded it in 1934 from the lips of Tepano. Much of the substance is obviously mythological and pure fantasy, but the chances are rather good that there is a sound framework of truth within the entire legend, to which the more fantastic elements have been attached like brilliant globes on a Christmas tree.

The political circumstances leading to Hotu-Matua's flight from Marae Renga are by no means unusual in Polynesian legends or actual historical records and are perfectly believable. In a similar fashion, the provisioning of the canoes with all necessary food plants and animals for the new colony accords quite well with the archaeological data from other areas of Polynesia where definitely early habitation sites have yielded evidence that such food sources accompanied colonizing or exploring expeditions.

In the chapter dealing with the Marquesas we had occasion to note that in the opinion of Dr. Métraux, the leading Easter Island authority, the land of Marae Renga in the Hotu-Matua legend is one of the islands of the Marquesas. The more recent evidence uncovered by the Norwegian Expedition and Dr. Barthel has not given any cause as yet to alter this view.

The identification of Marae Renga as a Marquesan island was based originally on a number of broad similarities between Easter Island and Marquesan archaeological and ethnological features. Métraux enumerated the following areas of resemblance: the general configuration of the Marquesan temple structures; Marquesan tattooing, which like that of Easter covered the whole body; the Marquesan *tiki* face, resembling closely that of many of the Easter Island petroglyphs; and the importance of genealogical chants and associated symbolic devices which were used by the chanters in both the Marquesas and Easter societies as mnemonic aids.

Now further resemblances are appearing as a result of the stratigraphic archaeology carried out in the Marquesas and Easter Island. These are in the more precise field of similarities between specific artifact types. Most outstanding of these are the virtual identity between the basic stone-adze types of Easter Island and those of the Settlement and Developmental periods of the Marquesas. The oval or circular cross-section adzes found at Ha'atuatua in the Marquesas also appear on Easter, but are extremely scarce elsewhere in Polynesia, occurring only in New Zealand in very small numbers and in the Western Polynesian islands. A very common adze throughout the early periods of Marquesan prehistory is the quadrangular-section untanged type, which also seems to constitute a large percentage of the adzes recovered in the excavations of Easter Island.[9]

Besides adzes we have the evidence of fish-hook types. In the Marquesas it was possible to trace the development of a number of fish-hook types throughout the entirety of the prehistoric period. One of these types (which we called the Rotating Hook), appearing in a high frequency in the Settlement Period, gradually became extinct in the subsequent Developmental Period. Rotating Hooks have a beautifully contoured, almost circular, lateral plan, the shank blending imperceptibly into the base of the hook and continuing in a slightly more restricted curve up to the point, which terminates quite close to the inside of the shank. Of all the varieties of hooks found at Easter Island, large Rotating Hooks are probably the most common.[10] The only difference is that the Easter examples are made of soft basalt, as no pearl shells were available there and wood was too precious on the barren island to use for hooks. Other Easter Island basalt hooks resemble still another Marquesan type, the Incurved Point variety, which has the same chronological distribution as the Rotating Hooks, having become obsolete quite early in Marquesan prehistory.

Further Easter Island similarities to the Marquesan materials are to be found in general artifacts, such as stone squid-lure weights and large, knobbed net weights.[11]

In architecture the resemblances are rather striking. The early oval houses of the Marquesas are almost identical with those of Easter Island in shape and size.[12] Furthermore, the early temple structure on the Ha'atuatua site could represent the basic temple type from which the later Easter Island sanctuaries developed.

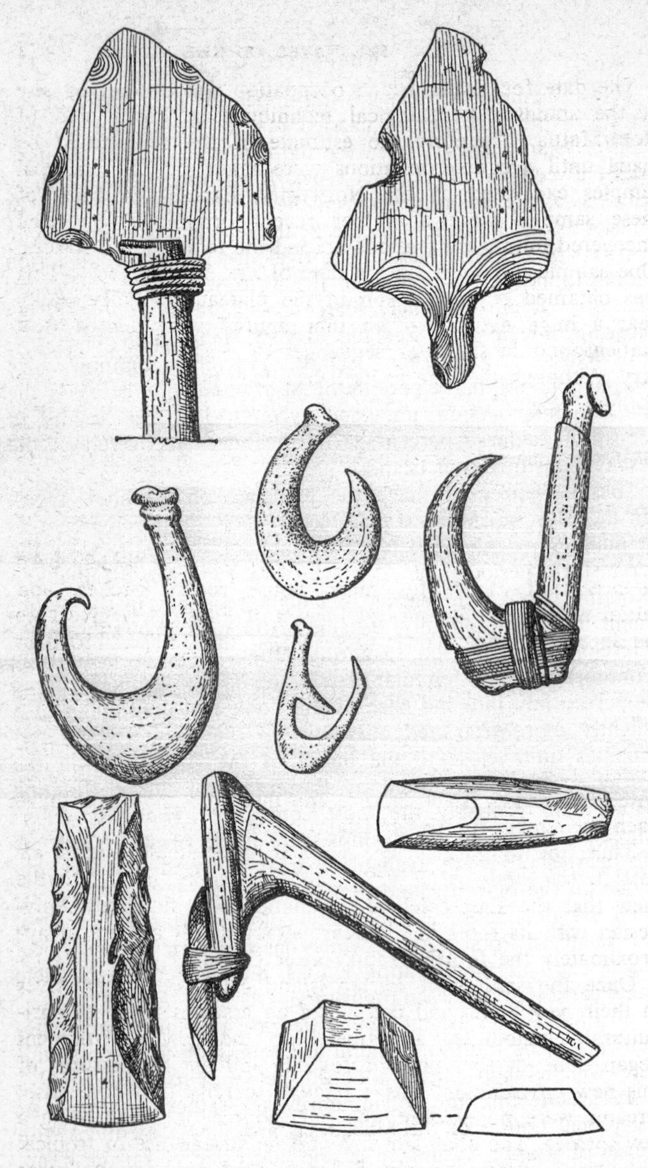

Fig. 15. Easter Island artifacts: Mata'a spear points, hooks of bone and stone, and stone adzes (after Métraux, 1940)

The date for Easter Island occupation was not set by any of the standard genealogical techniques in the legend of Hotu-Matua. Therefore, no estimate of the date could be made until age determinations were made on the charcoal samples excavated by the Norwegian Expedition. Most of these samples were of rather recent origin, having been uncovered during excavations around the temples and statues. One sample, however, gave a date of A.D. 384 ± 120.[13] This was obtained from an oven in the plateau of Poike, quite near a huge natural trench that figured prominently as a battleground in the later sequences of Easter Island prehistory. Although the date in itself has been published, we know nothing about the circumstances under which the sample was collected. It is necessary to know, for instance, what archaeological remains were associated with the sample; more important, the composition of the sample itself must be specified as there is evidence that one particularly common Easter Island plant gives highly erratic dates when subjected to the C-14 technique. This plant, the *totora* reed, was widely used in prehistoric times for mats, house roofs, torches, and burial wrappings. Samples of *tortora* of known age give ages far in excess of actuality; therefore, if the 384 ± 120 date from Poike had been derived from *totora* reeds there would be ample reason for disqualifying it. However, this date does not seem out of line with the Marquesan archaeological evidence which indicates that the Marquesan culture of approximately that epoch possessed a great number of similarities with later Easter Island culture and therefore could well have been the source for Easter Island colonization.

Thus, the authorities who have to date devoted most effort to the study of Easter Island prehistory incline to the view that the Easter Island occupation was definitely Polynesian with its roots in the Marquesas Islands culture of approximately the fourth century after Christ.

Once the settlers of Easter Island established themselves in their new home and completed an assessment of its agricultural possibilities, adjustments to the new environment began. One of the most profoundly influencing features of this new environment was a relative scarcity of wood. Also, streams were nonexistent, the only source of water being a few springs. The abundant fish and molluscan life of tropical Polynesian waters simply did not exist in the cool seas around Easter Island.

A number of food plants brought by the settlers could not

stand the cool rainy winters and hot summers of Easter Island and succumbed, forcing a heavier reliance on the productivity of those food plants that did survive. The soil, however, was fertile and the dry taro, yams, and sweet potatoes brought by the settlers grew quite well, despite the relatively small water supply. Pits were dug and lined with stones to catch rain water and the moisture of the soil, thus providing a suitably damp environment to plant bananas and *ti,* a plant which was used for the manufacture of bark cloth. In the face of the shortage of wood the islanders began to rely on the soft, easily worked basalts and tufts that were present in abundance. Bone, both animal and human, was also pressed into service. The lack of shells suitable for cutting tools was more than compensated by the presence of large deposits of obsidian, from which very fine blades could be manufactured.

During the centuries after initial occupation, these major adjustments and many others of a more minor nature were accomplished by the Easter Islanders. The productivity of their agricultural system began to increase and with it their capacity for supporting various kinds of endeavors not directly related to everyday subsistence. The island and tribal chieftains who were here, as elsewhere in Polynesia, the focal points of the economic structure, began to utilize the surplus of production for the endowment of various community projects, among them the construction of larger and more elaborate religious buildings and the sculpture of stone statues to be displayed in association with such buildings.[14]

The complete sequence of development for Easter Island temples is yet to be published. However, there is evidence that by approximately A.D. 1000 [15] they had already attained quite respectable dimensions and a high degree of elaboration. There were several types of temples, each of which may have had its own specialized usage in the ceremonial life of aboriginal Easter Island, but the predominant type is the so-called image *ahu* [16] upon which huge stone heads were erected. These *ahu* consisted of a central elevated rectangular stage or body, which formed the main portion of the temple and upon which the statues were ultimately erected. On either side of the central stage, lower winglike structures extended laterally. All image *ahu* were constructed with a common orientation; the *ahu* faced inland and the back wall of the stage and wings faced the sea. The greatest care was lavished on the construction of the seaward *ahu* walls, stone blocks and slabs intended for this façade being chosen for their finish and fit. The inland face of the *ahu*, on the other hand, was not perpendicular or stepped like the Tahitian temples but consisted of an inclined plane descending from the stage and wings, gradually merging with the ground surface of the temple forecourt. The presence of the inclined plane constitutes the only major difference between Easter Island *ahu* and those of other islands of Eastern Polynesia. The precise course of its development is not clear at present, but one thing is reasonably sure: the addition of the inclined-plane façade to the Easter Island *ahu* is inextricably related to the size of the statues that were placed on the *ahu*. Surely, without an inclined plane it would have been impossible to position a giant twenty-ton head on a relatively narrow *ahu* stage. In Eastern Polynesia in general the only features appearing on the *ahu* were much smaller wooden, basalt, or coral-stone uprights which could be handled with comparative ease.

The image *ahu* were constructed on a flat foundation pavement. The wings and stage consisted of retaining walls and finished paved surfaces around a rubble core. Most of the retaining walls of the large *ahu* contained at least some dressed stone blocks and slabs, mixed with unshaped stones.[17] There are a few extremely fine examples of image *ahu* whose retaining walls were constructed entirely of very precisely carved stone slabs fitted to each other with incredible exactness.[18] Of these, perhaps the *ahu* Vinapu is the most famous, and it was only natural that the attention of the members of the Norwegian party should have been focused on this outstanding achievement of Polynesian architecture. Excavations in the various components of the Vinapu complex uncovered evidence of three successive periods of construction within that *ahu*.[19] In the first of these periods, the finely fitted seaward wall of the *ahu* was erected, while subsequent stages utilized less well fitted or natural stone masonry. The date of the earliest stage of construction at Vinapu was fixed by radiocarbon dating at approximately A.D. 850, and claims have been made that the fitted-stone masonry techniques preceded the use of natural stone everywhere on the island. Such conclusions, however, are probably somewhat premature, as many of the other image *ahu* of equally imposing size, but less interesting construction, were not excavated by the Norwegian Expedition. Therefore, the apparent sequence of structures established mainly at *ahu*

Vinapu may be only a part of the sequence, and the virtuosity displayed in fitted masonry may actually be the result of a longer development. Such masonry should by no means be considered to be absolutely unique in Polynesia. Fitted masonry also appears in ancient Hawaiian irrigation-ditch walls and temples, in temples on the tiny volcanic island of Mehetia, south of Tahiti, and in two late house structures in the valley of Atuona on Hiva Oa in the Marquesas.[20]

Leaving the dispute concerning the possible priority of the fitted masonry structures to be settled by further archaeological excavation, we can state with assurance that by A.D. 850, at least, the basic form of the image *ahu* had evolved from its Eastern Polynesian antecedent and was well along a separate course of development. Cut stone was used in many of the *ahu* in varying quantities with varying degrees of competence. Later developments of the image *ahu* are still not known in detail. It is certain, however, that many of the larger *ahu* were still being elaborated at the time of the Europeans' arrival, as many *ahu* walls display cut-stone curbs from house foundations exactly like those seen and described by Cook as being in use in the eighteenth century. The Easter Islanders evidently were not always sufficiently motivated to cut new stone for their *ahu* but simply destroyed available house foundations to obtain blocks that were already cut.

There are several other types of *ahu*, about the history of which much less is presently known. The least common of these is the rectangular *ahu ava'anga*.[21] This type of temple exists in a large range of sizes. It is essentially a rectangular platform with a burial vault in the middle. Almost as rare in occurrence is the *ahu poepoe*[22] or boat-shaped *ahu*. The ends of the stages on the *ahu poepoe* are raised like canoe ends. Mrs. Routledge found historic European artifacts in structures of this type which she excavated, indicating that the type may have been a late development. Another possibly late type is the semi-pyramidal *ahu paepae*,[23] which consists of a large stone cairn with wings and an inland ramp. Métraux found that these were often constructed of stones torn from the large image *ahus*, which in themselves might have been of late construction.

The houses of the Easter Islanders[24] were undoubtedly built on the ground surface during the early period of occupation of the island. As the use of cut stone became more common, however, narrow stone curbs were shaped to serve as house foundations. Sockets were cut into the curbs at intervals for the thin poles that served as wall braces and rafters to the long, oval houses. Small stone pavements were placed before the house doors. As elsewhere in Eastern Polynesia, the houses were not grouped in organized villages but scattered in small groups or hamlets. The location of the hamlets was likely determined by the position of the garden plots of the house owners, and also by considerations of defense, for there were no natural barriers to protect the outlying settlements as in the Marquesas Islands.

The evolution of the striking Easter Island monumental statuary has been somewhat illuminated by excavation of the Norwegian Expedition at Vinapu. There, a less common type of statue was excavated in association with the fitted-masonry period of construction. The statue was apparently an elongated pillarlike figure from which the head had been removed.[25] It had evidently been erected in the forecourt of the temple rather than on the *ahu* stage. Other unusual statues were found, among them a kneeling figure, the first known on Easter Island.[26] The significance of aberrant types such as these has yet to be published. The well-known beetle-browed, lantern-jawed busts of Easter Island with their red-stone headpieces are apparently the final form of the monumental sculpture sequence on the island. These date from the seventeenth century, perhaps, or later.

An intriguing area of Easter Island archaeology is presented by the petroglyphs found in great profusion on boulders, *ahu*, statues, cave walls, and even stone implements. A monumental study of these highly artistic designs was published by Lavachéry of the Franco-Belgian Expedition.[27] Most numerous among the petroglyphs is that of the so-called *makemake* mask, a stylized representation of a wide-eyed face with an elongated nose. Variations of this are found throughout Polynesia (in the Marquesas, Tahiti, and Hawaii) and even occur in the islands of Melanesia (in New Caledonia and Fiji). It has been theorized that such a mask was one of the motifs in the artistic vocabulary of the original Malayo-Polynesians who first occupied Melanesia and Polynesia.[28]

Also found in the petroglyphic art of Easter Island are numerous representations of bird-headed human figures—references to the famous annual bird-man ceremonial which took place at Orongo. Other common motifs are representations of tuna and other marine life, outrigger canoes, and

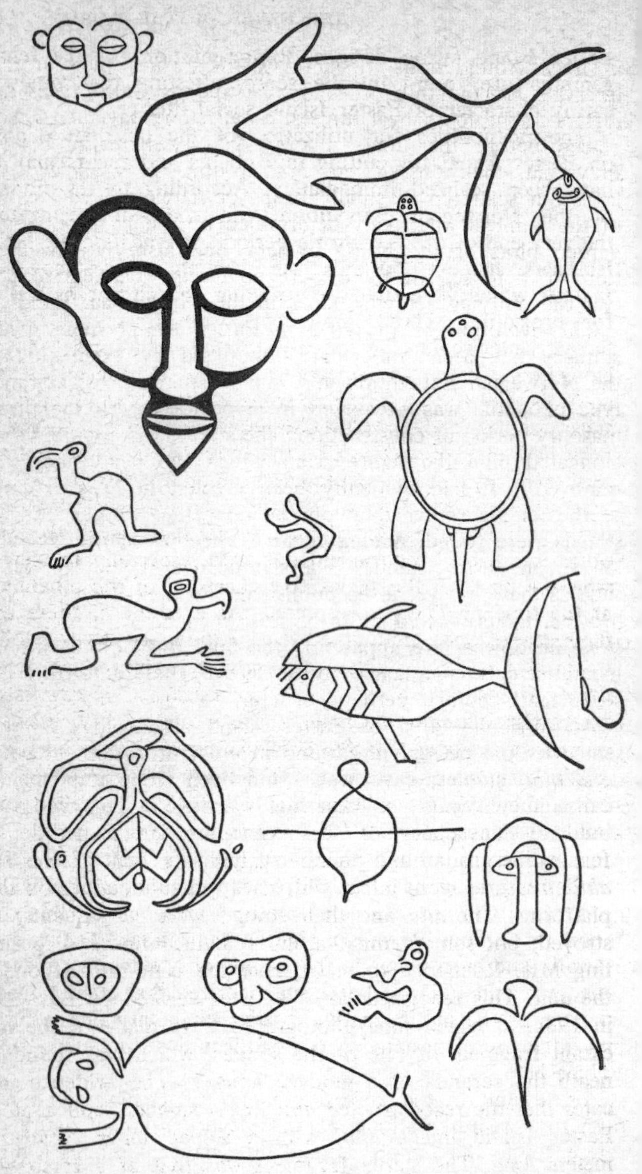

Fig. 16. Easter Island petroglyphs (after Lavachéry, 1939)

Easter Island tattoo designs. Representations of the female genitalia are found by the score, attesting the somewhat earthy character of Easter Island social life.

The possibilities for utilization of the obsidian deposits on Easter Island for cutting implements and spears may not have been realized immediately. According to the findings of the Norwegian Expedition, this did not occur until the very end of the prehistoric period. At that time the Easter Islanders made thousands of obsidian tools, known as *mata,*[29] which were used for scraping and cutting as well as for projectiles. These implements were irregular, roughly flaked, semicircular, or roughly pointed implements with an elongated stem on the side opposite the "cutting edge," if it could be called that. There is some debate as to whether the stems themselves might not also have seen use as drill points. Besides the very common *mata,* other variously shaped cutting and scraping tools were made from obsidian. (See Fig. 15.)

During the evolution of the distinctive Easter Island culture it would have been rather unusual if at one time or another intertribal conflicts did not arise, especially in view of what we know of the sanguinary character of the inhabitants at the time of European contact. As a result of these conflicts there were undoubtedly repetitions of that familiar Polynesian scene of the beaten chieftain and his warriors fleeing the wrath of the enemy in search of a new island where they alone could rule. It was probably as a result of one of these flights that the island of Pitcairn was inhabited.

When the mutineers from the *Bounty* first landed on Pitcairn, they found evidence that others had preceded them but had since departed. Stone adzes were found on the surface of the ground and remains of huts were still visible. Two *ahu* structures were intact with hard red tufa statues on their platforms. The *ahu* and their statues were subsequently destroyed; but some remnants still remained in 1914, permitting Mrs. Routledge to reconstruct the condition of one of the *ahu.* This reconstruction was later verified by Lavachéry in 1934, at which time photographs were made of the only extant fragment of one of the statues, which was found beneath the veranda of a modern house.[30] The evidence indicates that the reconstructed *ahu* was a smaller replica of the Easter Island image *ahu,* with a sloped inner façade 12 meters long. The statue fragment was that of a torso with large hands clasped on its abdomen, also similar to the statues of the late image *ahu* of Easter Island. The head had unfortunately been broken from the short, thick neck; therefore the identification of the statue as definitely of the Easter Island variety is impossible. The chances are good, however, that it did possess the well-known beetle-browed scowl of the typical stone giants of the "Navel of the World."

The original settlers of Pitcairn may have been refugees from Easter Island, then,[31] if the above data are correct. What caused them to abandon the relative safety of Pitcairn and strike out to sea again is anyone's guess. By the time of the arrival of the *Bounty* mutineers, however, the soil of Pitcairn had not been printed by a human foot for many a year, and the fate of its former inhabitants was one of the great mysteries sealed up in the sea.

Summarizing the development of Easter Island's culture, it is clear that the general sequence of events followed was a duplicate of the sequences of other islands. As productivity increased, the upper classes of the society utilized their control over the surplus food production to support temple building and monumental stone sculpture. The lack of wood on Easter Island directed most of this artistic effort into more enduring stone, the result being the efflorescence of megalithic art on Easter Island.[32] The point has been well made that in other Polynesian islands a chief could use the surplus production of his subjects to construct more agricultural projects, but in Easter Island the poorer quality of the soil and limited water supply made this impractical. The efforts of the chiefs and family heads were therefore directed toward architectural projects as a means of building their all-important prestige.

The large *ahu* were well under way by A.D. 850 and were subsequently enlarged frequently. During some part of the period of *ahu* building, fitted stone masonry was used in the construction of a few large *ahu*. Subsequent structures, although utilizing cut stone, did not incorporate fitted masonry. In the earliest *ahu* the statues may not have been placed on the stage but in the forecourt. It was only in late prehistoric times that the statues were elevated to the *ahu* stage.

In the seventeenth and eighteenth centuries, the population of Easter Island was growing cumbersome, possibly numbering as many as 4,000 divided among the ten tribes.[33] The definite scarcity of arable land aggravated the effects of the increase in population, with the result that warfare became quite common. Each of the island tribes was ruled by a chieftain who theoretically was subject to the *ariki-mau* or ceremonial chief of the senior tribe. The *ariki-mau,* however, possessed little temporal power, being often taken prisoner and used as a pawn in the intertribal strife.

A large number of able-bodied men of this period were practically full-time warriors, while the legends contain numerous references to vicious intertribal warfare. It was at this time that the natural ditch isolating the headland of Poike from the other parts of the island was deepened and widened.[34] The ditch figures in an extremely interesting legend of a battle between two factions called the Long Ears and the Short Ears.[35] By a ruse, the Long Ears were trapped and driven into a conflagration in the Poike ditch, which had been filled with brush for the occasion by the Short Ears. This legend has been cause for endless debate, for many have taken it as evidence of the existence of two different populations on the island. If the reference to ear length is of any validity, however, this battle must have taken place after Captain Cook's visit, because he records seeing numerous individuals with pierced, stretched earlobes. It should be noted that the vocabulary that Cook collected during his visit was exclusively Polynesian, so that if any other ethnic group existed on Easter Island in the eighteenth century it must have been of Polynesian origin also.

In the intertribal wars a favorite form of insult and revenge was to topple the ancestral statues from the platforms of the loser's *ahu,* thus humiliating their ancestors. This desecration was well under way even in Cook's day, as he noted that *ahu* were frequently in poor repair. Thus, not only natural forces and curious white men, but the islanders themselves aided in the destruction of their own heritage.

Tribes that were defeated were often depleted considerably by the slaughter of their aged and children. They were then put to work for the victors.[36] Many caves in the volcanic core of Easter Island were used as shelters by refugees hiding from these incessant fights.

Despite the constant warfare and destruction, it must be remembered that a great amount of very constructive work was carried on also at this time. *Ahu* were still built and the huge statues of the "typical" Easter Island variety date from this period.

The Europeans appeared on this bloody scene in the eighteenth century, but they were generally ill received by the population. In the mid-nineteenth century, slave raiders from

Peru carried off 1,000 of the population to work on the guano islands off the South American coast. Only a hundred returned, bringing to those left behind the inestimably valuable gift of European diseases, chief among which was smallpox. This reduced the population in a horrible epidemic, which was followed by a famine. At this point, the culture of Easter Island began to die, as the population ravaged by disease and still disturbed by bloody warfare simply lost all interest in perpetuating their way of life any more than was necessary to survive.[37]

To gain an overview of the prehistory of Easter Island, let us now retrace in steps to emphasize the main points of the sequence as they are presently known:

1. Easter Island probably was occupied by a group of Marquesans in the fourth century after Christ.

2. By A.D. 850 the economic basis of the budding society was well established. Large temple structures were built with statues standing in the forecourt. Fitted masonry may have been used.

3. Temple architecture continued to develop and increase in complexity, while new temple types evolved. Masonry techniques began to degenerate, however, fitted masonry being replaced by dressed blocks and unworked stone.

4. In the final period of Easter Island prehistory, population growth reached a critical point with a consequent increase in warfare. In this period the great statues now seen on the image *ahu* were carved. Obsidian-pointed weapons were used. Although much monumental construction took place, many temples and statues were also damaged or destroyed during these tribal wars.

5. The native culture was severely impacted by slave raids of the nineteenth century, followed by epidemics, famine, and missionaries and the culture disintegrated.

A recent and important development for Polynesianists and linguists in general is the work of Dr. Thomas Barthel on the Easter Island *rongorongo* script.[38] This script, part of the esoterica taught to the priests in the sacred college of the Easter Island religious orders, had been a puzzle to anthropologists for many years and constituted the basis for a number of rather wild theories of Easter Island cultural origins. Barthel's approach to the problem was systematic. He acquired all known examples of this script and developed a sign catalogue. He then tracked down several manuscripts that contained dictations given by a nineteenth-century

Easter Islander, which were purported to be a rendition of the contents of a particular tablet. These dictations had been taken by Bishop Jaussen of Tahiti, who had become interested in the problems of the script and contacted a supposedly well-informed Easter Islander in a colony of them brought as laborers to Tahiti. Barthel laboriously compared the contents of the unpublished dictations with the signs on the tablet, arriving at the conclusion that Jaussen's informant was not well grounded in his esoterica but at least had some knowledge of the script. From certain consistencies in the dictations, it was possible to establish some sign equivalencies and further to associate the purely objective analysis of the signs themselves with the dictations and other texts, thus making an excellent start at deriving the system or "grammar" behind the script.

According to Barthel, the Easter Island script is not a pictographic system, but has a definite format with good possibilities of expressing varieties of concepts. The script itself consists of a limited vocabulary of some 120 basic elements which are combined to make 1,500 to 2,000 composite forms. Ideograms, associated with a definite semantic content, form the bulk of the script. Some ideograms, however, have more than one meaning, and often the multiple meanings are related. Natural elements are often simple to recognize. Colors are shown by objects which display them as a characteristic; supernatural entities are depicted by one of their attributes or main aspects. The signs can also be used phonetically in a series, each giving some phonetic value required to form a word in a kind of rebus writing.

There are very definite difficulties awaiting those who attempt to push toward a complete translation of the script. Many difficulties lie in the script itself; there are no signs to indicate grammatical particles, which are all important in Polynesian languages. Furthermore, there is a tendency to abbreviate or condense the text in spots, and a predilection for the use of circumlocutions and figures of speech which may be quite abstruse, as in any language. There is also no way of distinguishing personal or place names from ordinary words by use of an index sign that would function like an Egyptian hieroglyphic determinative.

Other difficulties are historical in origin; there is only a very small amount of the script extant, which increases the probability of error for any statistical approach, and there are many gaps in our knowledge of Easter Island culture that might aid in interpreting oblique references in the script.

The texts deal mainly with traditions of a historical nature and rituals, but there is also a remnant of a kind of catalogue of tablets and their contents. Barthel believes that the texts involve a form of Polynesian close to the historic dialect of Easter Island. The script itself is a part of ancient Polynesian culture that was lost elsewhere but retained on Easter Island.

Thus, this brief summary of Easter Island prehistory comes to an end. It should be obvious now to the reader that the "mysteries" of Easter Island are fictional creations, with no basis in fact. Problems definitely exist, it is true, but many can be solved ultimately by the application of a scientific approach, rather than the direct intuition of the visionary whose "solution" only creates more mysteries. The use of such a scientific approach will yield information which to me, at least, is far more wonderful and fascinating than a carload of romantic theories. There are problems, however, that may never be solved. Let them come, for we do not claim to possess all the answers. Our only goal is to move, by small steps, a little closer to the ultimate truth.

14

The Moa and the Maori

The Polynesian discoverers of the islands of New Zealand were undoubtedly quite pleased at the prospect of the vast new land which they had come upon with its forest of tall trees, its hot mineral springs and lakes, rolling grasslands, and far to the south, mighty glaciers in the high mountain valleys. To the navigators from tropical Polynesia the landscape was no less unusual than its animal inhabitants, however, among which were stately, long-necked, wingless birds, walking on strong, slender legs that raised their small wicked-beaked heads above the stature of a man. These strange earthbound feathered creatures, moving through the plains and forest of primeval New Zealand in large flocks, must have been equally startled at the appearance of man on the scene, for throughout millennia they had been the largest of all creatures in these islands, which had never before echoed to the sound of human voices.

The Polynesians lost little time in attaching a name to the former rulers of this new land. The name, *moa,* perhaps displays a bit of ancient Polynesian humor, as elsewhere in Polynesia it designated the diminutive but proud jungle cock.

The tropical Polynesians were probably also quick to determine whether the moa was of food value. Indeed, a moa or two were probably turning slowly over a fire under the hopeful eyes of a group of very hungry seafarers within a short time after the first double canoes had been beached. The anticipation of the onlookers was undoubtedly rewarded by an abundance of quite tasty meat, and thus began a very close association between man (as the hunter) and moa (as a food source) which was to last for centuries, ultimately resulting, however, in the complete extinction of the bird a century or so before the arrival of the Europeans. This relationship resulted in considerable changes and alterations in the regional variation of Polynesian culture that evolved in New Zealand. Furthermore, it was the finding of moa bones after the European occupation of New Zealand that first alerted scholars to the possibility of time depth in Polynesian prehistory, and so by acting as a stimulus to very significant scientific research, the moa, even in death, continued to exert an influence on the inhabitants of the land which it once ruled.

As a result of extensive study of moa remains recovered in New Zealand, scientists today can be fairly precise about this bird and its genetic affiliations.[1] With the Australian and African ostriches, the emu and the cassowaries of New Guinea, the moa are known as struthious birds (struthiones), that is, they lack the keeled breastbone found among their winged relatives. Although the early Polynesians were inclined to group all moa together, detailed skeletal studies indicate that a number of genera and species of that bird had evolved in primeval New Zealand. A number of moa have been found in peat bogs in a relatively good state of preservation. After these specimens were carefully dissected, the contents of their gastrointestinal systems were analyzed. It was found that the moa evidently preferred a forest environment, living on shoots, twigs, and leaves. Abandoned nests and unhatched eggs have been recovered in isolated shelters formerly inhabited by these animals. The nests, of twigs, were two or three feet in diameter and six inches deep. Each contained a few eggs. Of the total number of eggs produced, however, only a few hatched, because other fauna, quite fond of the contents, destroyed a large number.

In the 1840's, when many of the other native cultures of Polynesia were still very much alive, New Zealand had already been occupied by Europeans, and scientists were devoting attention to the natural history of the islands. At that time the moa was physically extinct and perhaps had been so for over a century, existing only in a few proverbs and legends of the living Maori. In the course of exploration, study, and construction, moa bones were found in several places [2] and almost immediately were recognized as belonging to a large bird of some type. The precise conditions of the early moa finds are not at all clear, and it is therefore impossible to say whether any evidence of human contemporaneity had been uncovered with them. It was not too long, however, before man's presence became abundantly evident, as moa remains associated with oven pits were found by Mantell in 1847 at Awamoa, South Island. Besides a number of drilled moa eggs, a few stone artifacts were found at this site, but they were crude flake knives; no polished stone adzes were recovered. This led Mantell to postulate that the moa had been killed off by the earliest wave of Polynesian aborigines arriving in New Zealand. These early Polynesians were envisioned as substantially different from the Maori inhabitants of the historic period, who used polished stone adzes. Interest quickly heightened as a result of these finds, which were followed in close succession by further discoveries of moa remains and human artifacts.

In 1870 a bombshell was dropped in the midst of this atmosphere of interest by one Julius von Haast, who had located a very large archaeological site on the Rakaia River in Canterbury. The site consisted of an extensive midden deposit of moa bones and numerous ovens. In excavating the Rakaia midden, von Haast believed he had found evidence that New Zealand had been inhabited in very remote geological time by a race of "autocthones" who had migrated in on dry land before the island had been separated from the Asian mainland by a rising sea. Von Haast believed the moa to be an ancient animal. Therefore, he reasoned that human artifacts with moa remains must also be ancient. It has been remarked [3] that he never considered the possibility that his assumption of great antiquity for the moa might have been wrong. In the Rakaia midden numerous stone flake knives appeared around the ovens where the moa had been cooked. In other areas of the site, where the inhabitants had built their houses, fewer moa bones appeared and the tools were mainly polished stone adzes. The difference between the crude stone flakes in the trash heaps and the adzes in the other areas of the site led Haast to postulate further that the people who had eaten the moa on the premises were possessed of a paleolithic chipped-stone-tool type of culture. In contrast, he attributed the polished stone adzes to a much later reoccupation of the same area by the Maori. Von Haast's views touched off a storm of rather bitter controversy that stimulated archaeological excavation of many sites, resulting in an accumulation of archaeological artifacts from a number of early sites. It also sparked a feverish search for references to the moa in Maori oral tradition. In the course of this work it became quite obvious that the aborigines who had slaughtered the moa at Rakaia, and in many other sites that had been investigated, were identical with the aborigines who had made the polished stone adzes on the site. Therefore it was impossible to cling to the belief that these aborigines were a paleolithic race of great age. Von Haast was ultimately driven to admit that the "autocthonous" inhabitants of New Zealand whom he labeled as Moa-Hunters were on a cultural and technological level with the Maori; but he never would admit that the two groups were genetically related, and steadfastly maintained that a large but unspecified span of time separated Moa-Hunter from Maori.

As a result of the attempts by von Haast to attribute great age to the Moa-Hunters, a typical scientific reaction took place. The opposing forces refused to admit that the Moa-Hunter remains were older than 550 years, and maintained further that the Moa-Hunters were actually identical with the Maori, a position that was actually untenable even with the unscientific approach to archaeology which was utilized during the last decade of the nineteenth century.

In the early 1900's a new theory concerning the source of the Moa-Hunters was promulgated by two scholars of Maori tradition, Elsdon Best and C. Percy Smith. According to these authorities, the Moa-Hunters were actually a Melanesian people, which in those days implied a more pronounced difference than at present. This theory, of course, provoked another healthy controversy which may, however, have resulted in a second polarization of opinions along another axis such as that noted in the disputes over von Haast's claims. H. D. Skinner of the Otago Museum led the opposition to the claims of Melanesian origin. Under his direction and sponsorship much research was done and archaeological excavations were carried out in many early sites such as Waitaki, Papatowai, and Shag River, by David Teviotdale and other workers. The number of known Moa-Hunter sites multiplied rapidly, with a consequent increase in knowledge of the Moa-Hunter culture. Duff has pointed out, however, that despite the pressure to identify the Moa-Hunter with Melanesians or with the Maori, no attempts were made by Skinner and his group to specify the degree of similarity between the Moa-Hunter and Maori cultural inventory. Gradually, the Melanesian theory lost credence and the belief in Maori–Moa-Hunter identity gained ascendancy, only to tumble in its turn before new information derived from excavations in the thirties and forties, which began to demonstrate irrefutably that: (1) there was a very definite difference between the historic Maori culture and that displayed in the Moa-Hunter sites, and (2) that this difference was at least partially a result of time depth.

Outstanding in the field of Moa-Hunter archaeology is Dr. Roger Duff of the Canterbury Museum, whose volume on the culture of the Moa-Hunter is a must for all students of Polynesian prehistory. Duff's painstaking analysis of certain aspects of the archaeological remains formed the basis for a realistic assessment of the role of New Zealand in the prehistory of Polynesia. Recently Duff has been joined by Mr. J. Golson, of the University of Auckland, who has applied the refined techniques of the best British archaeologists to the problems of Polynesian archaeology both in New Zealand and in Western Polynesia, as we have already had occasion to note.

The large collections accumulated in the nineteenth and early twentieth centuries have taken on more meaning now as a result of these recent excavations, which have acted as a kind of framework to integrate and order the artifacts amassed by the untrained collectors of the past.

The name of Moa-Hunter, designating the early inhabitants of New Zealand who derived much of their sustenance from moa flesh, has survived through the years of controversy and the pendulum swings of scientific opinion since it was first applied by von Haast.

Radiocarbon dating has been introduced, yielding some very interesting results for the age of New Zealand's earliest human occupation. There has even been an attempt to establish a scale for tree-ring dating, a technique based on counting and matching growth rings in wood, pioneered in archaeological explorations in the American Southwest. Stratigraphic excavations of the numerous sizable middens has replaced the helter-skelter "adze hunting" of the early collectors, and a great deal of attention has been devoted to an analysis of tools and ornaments in terms of their form and extra-New Zealand relationships. The burials excavated in many of the early sites have been studied carefully by standard anthropometric techniques.

On the basis of over a century of work supported by the

latest of scientific techniques, what then is the status of New Zealand archaeology as it stands at present? What, for instance, can be said of the discoverers of New Zealand and their origin?

New Zealand was discovered and settled by an expedition from tropical Eastern Polynesia, probably from the Society Islands group. It was these Polynesians who became the Moa-Hunters of New Zealand archaeology when they began to adjust to the peculiar food resources of their new environment.

The date of Moa-Hunter arrival in New Zealand is probably about A.D. 1000. Our earliest radiocarbon date from a Moa-Hunter site is A.D. 1125 ± 50,[4] obtained from a sample collected at the famous Wairau site, which has probably contributed more to our knowledge of the Moa-Hunter culture than any other site excavated to date. There is a very definite possibility that this site was not inhabited at the outset of Polynesian occupation of the island, as the artifacts discovered there show a familiarity with the stones of the region and their properties that bespeaks at least some previous residence in the area. One does not become conversant with techniques of miniature stone carving overnight; the art of working New Zealand greenstone is not quickly acquired, either. It is for these reasons that I believe New Zealand may prove to have been inhabited at approximately A.D. 1000.

(It is interesting to note that Maori legends of the discovery of New Zealand indicate a similar date on the basis of genealogical lists depending, of course, on the arbitrary value that one selects as the equivalent of one generation.)

Moa-Hunter sites [5] are generally located on the coast near the mouths of rivers. Particular preference seems to be shown for sites located on points jutting out into river mouths, enclosing small lagoons on their landward sides. The main reason for coastal settlement was evidently the fact that at the time of Polynesian occupation, the moa were concentrated on the coastal plains and the downstream areas of the major rivers. Sites located on river-mouth spits and bars would, of course, be ideal for moa "drives," as the moa could very easily be trapped with sea, river, and lagoon enclosing them on three sides while their pursuers advanced along the bar, the only escape route. In addition to the availability of the moa, the seaside and river-mouth sites offered other advantages—abundant fish of many varieties, shellfish, and numerous water birds. All told, it seems that the Moa-Hunter camps were most intelligently placed.

Excavations in the Moa-Hunter sites most recently investigated have failed to uncover any definite house structures.[6] Post-molds have been noted in profusion, but they do not fall into any consistent pattern, and it is therefore impossible to say what the Moa-Hunter domiciles looked like. One might feel rather justified in assuming that the houses were of the general archaic Eastern Polynesian type previously noted in Tahiti, Easter Island, the Marquesas, and Hawaii, characterized by an oval "boat-shaped" or rounded-end floor plan with small wall braces set into the earth and curving up to meet at the crest of the roof. The Moa-Hunter settlements probably consisted of a number of these houses with a nearby oven area and undoubtedly an adjacent temple of a type similar to the very simple Tahitian Inland Temple as defined by Emory. Such temples are known from the later Maori culture, but have yet to be found on a Moa-Hunter site. The ovens of the camps were merely large pits in which the moa were cooked on hot stones, covered by a mantle of earth. In addition to the oven pits, other rectangular storage pits, probably for root crops,[7] were scattered around the sites. The majority of the sites are located on elevated bars and ridges, and drainage among the houses was a problem in the sandy soil. Therefore, shallow canals for drainage purposes were sometimes dug.

As we have noted, the Moa-Hunter groups relied to a great extent on the moa for their food. The bird was large and appeared in great numbers. Its flesh was probably susceptible to a variety of preservative techniques that would permit the surplus kills of one day to be stored against future need. The standard root and tree crops of tropical Polynesia may have been carried by the discoverers in their canoes; but if they were, they failed to survive the New Zealand climate. The only root crop of which we have evidence in the archaeological record is the sweet potato, and that must be regarded as tentative.[8] It is also probable that the abundance of game and wild plant foods in the newly found islands was such that the tropical cultogens were felt to be superfluous and, consequently, may have been abandoned. There is no evidence that the pig or the jungle cock, incongruous passengers on most if not all of the Polynesian colonizing trips, ever arrived in New Zealand. It is possible that these animals were eaten during the course of the voyage, however, or that they were allowed to die off in New Zealand in the first rush of enthusiasm for the more productive moa. Despite the absence of the pig and the fowl, the dog was definitely present among the passengers of the discovering canoes and survived through to the coming of the white man. Dogs were of obvious utility in moa hunting, and this may account for their survival.

The most characteristic and significant tools in the varied assemblage that the Moa-Hunters used were stone adzes, personal ornaments, fish hooks.[9] The adzes are of the familiar Polynesian types: quadrangular in cross section (with and without the stepped or shouldered tang); triangular in cross section (with or without tangs); and even a few oval section gouges have been recovered. The adzes of the Moa-Hunter have attracted much attention, as they are frequently found in archaeological sites and especially fine specimens are often included with burials as grave furniture. Many outstanding examples are made of the semiprecious nephrite or greenstone. The workmanship displayed by the specimens illustrated in Duff's volume[10] is of quite high standard. Duff believes that the adze assemblage displayed by the Moa-Hunter Polynesians is a good representation of the basic Eastern Polynesian adze types from which the characteristic local variations of each island group and archipelago developed at a later date.

Moa-Hunter personal ornaments[11] have been mostly recovered from male status burials. They are quite distinctive expressions of certain very ancient basic and widespread Polynesian symbols, the whale tooth and the "reel" or "spool." Throughout Eastern and Western Polynesia and Melanesia, the teeth of whales are signs of rank and prestige par excellence. Even today, in Fiji, it is forbidden to export the large sperm whale teeth that are still used among the Fijians as awards for outstanding services. In early times in New Zealand whales were in short supply evidently, and softer stones were worked into the shape of whales' teeth to compensate for the shortage of the real article. Necklaces and bracelets of several such teeth, long, slender, and gently curving, have been found in Moa-Hunter burials. Shorter, heavier stone whales'-teeth amulets were also worn.

The so-called "reel" or "spool" ornaments are cylindrical or barrel-shaped beads with ridges encircling the body of the bead at various points. Occasionally the ridges are lightly notched. These were worn alone or in combination with a whale's tooth to form a necklace. They were made of various types of stone, segments of moa and dog-leg bone shafts, and fossilized *Dentalia* shells. Bilobed pectoral amulets were also worn, and one excellent example of a polished serpentine plaque with two large fish in relief has been recovered.[12]

Besides these interesting and very attractive personal ornaments, there were a large number of less striking but equally significant implements in the technological armory of the Moa-Hunter. Fish hooks are not found so frequently in excavation in early New Zealand sites as they are in the Marquesas and Hawaii, for example. Nevertheless, they are definitely present in very familiar forms. The composite bonito or tuna hook of Western and Eastern Polynesia is well represented. However, the shank of this type of hook was made of soft stone by the Moa-Hunters in the absence of the pearl shell and whale ivory usually utilized for that purpose in tropical Polynesia. The points of the composite hook were formed of durable moa bone. One-piece bait hooks were made from sections cut from the heavy limb bones of the moa in styles reminiscent of the hooks of the Marquesas, Easter Island, and Hawaii.

Besides these more specific tools, the Moa-Hunters possessed a large number of generalized implements for cutting and scraping. The flint obsidian and slate found in New Zealand offered ample sources for edged tools to be manufactured for woodworking, butchering, hook manufacture, and the working of soft stone. Other kinds of stone—basalt, sandstone, and other coarse varieties—were used for abrading tools in finishing stone and wooden objects.

At the Wairau site [13] a large number of early Moa-Hunter burials were uncovered. They were, of course, all Polynesians of a physical type fully in keeping with our expectations for Polynesians of that era.[14] The burial customs of these people are somewhat unusual, however, and merit mention here. The male of the species received the lion's share of attention in death. He was carefully laid out in full regalia in any one of several positions, usually extended on his stomach or back. Adzes and other belongings were placed with him, if he was of consequence. Indeed, the presence of such artifacts indicates some definite differences in prestige within the social groups that inhabited New Zealand at the time. This situation contrasts sharply with that of the Marquesas, where few goods of any type were placed with the dead except in the period immediately preceding the arrival of the white man. Once the males of the Wairau Moa-Hunter group were tucked away beneath the sand, however, they did not repose undisturbed. An ancestor cult was evidently part and parcel of Moa-Hunter spiritual life. A grave was left long enough for the corpse to reach an advanced state of decay, after which someone was saddled with the delectable task of delving in to retrieve the maggotty skull of Uncle Te Whanga or whoever it might be. The graves of Wairau showed definite signs of having been disturbed for the removal of skulls. Often the neck ornaments and adzes which had been placed near the head of the corpse had been disturbed and neatly redeposited after the head had been extracted. In other cases the skull had been removed, but the lower jaw had become separated and was left in the grave. The use of skulls in ancestral worship was very common in the Marquesas and in other islands of Polynesia. The skull was of greatest importance generally, because it was believed that the head was the seat of all of a person's supernatural power or *mana*. Therefore, to preserve the skull of a deceased family head would be to preserve intact, or nearly so, whatever *mana* he had accumulated during the course of his life, as a benefit to his progeny.

In contrast to the male burial practices, the females and children of the Wairau dwellers got cavalier treatment after passing into the great beyond, for they were tamped unceremoniously into hastily prepared pits in the midden with little or no equipment for the trip. One infers that women meant as little in the long view to the Moa-Hunters of 1,000 years ago as they mean today to most of the living Eastern Polynesians.

The Moa-Hunter culture—an A.D. 1000 Tahitian culture transplanted into New Zealand's unusual environment—has been described above. This culture was distributed over the extent of New Zealand, although it was mainly concentrated in the South Island. There is evidence that the North Island was not inhabited very heavily by the Moa-Hunters, although some sites have recently been located there.[15] The remote Chatham Islands to the southeast of the South Island of New Zealand were occupied at approximately the same time as the South Island; but the culture in the Chathams remained strangely atavistic, and when the islands were invaded by the Maori in 1830, the Chatham inhabitants were still leading an existence quite similar to that of the Wairau dwellers many centuries earlier.

The Moa-Hunters were very dependent on the moa, for as the years slipped by and a diminution in the moa population became evident on the coast, the Moa-Hunters penetrated the interior, searching for refugee flocks of the large birds.

Recently sites have been located in the mountainous regions of New Zealand where hunting parties evidently camped during long expeditions after moa. One site of this type is Hawksburn,[16] where a six- to seven-inch deposit of midden material and stone knives had accumulated as a result of constant visits of hunting parties since A.D. 1300 to 1400.

During this period of moa withdrawal to the interior, changes in the culture of the native population were also taking place. According to tradition, after the initial occupation of New Zealand, a few centuries elapsed; a few voyagers from Tahiti began to appear sporadically. This irregular contact culminated in a major migration from Tahiti, called the "Great Fleet," which supposedly occurred in A.D. 1350. From this migration, modern Maori trace their ancestry, reckoning their family trees from the occupants of the various canoes which supposedly composed the Fleet. In the past, much faith has been placed in this legend of Tahitian contact, for the very obvious reason that it has such reality to the Maori themselves. According to reconstructions of New Zealand prehistory, it was the Fleet migration that resulted in implanting in Tahiti the cultural entity which finally evolved into the historic Maori. Those who subscribed to such views believed that the Moa-Hunter culture did not have the capability of evolving into the Maori; consequently, it was necessary to invoke outside assistance to obtain the necessary Maori end product given the basic Moa-Hunter ingredients.[17] Recently, however, views have changed considerably and at least one authority[18] has stated the conviction that the Maori culture is a result of direct evolution from the Moa-Hunter without benefit of exotic stimuli. The catalyst for this evolution is simply the unusual environment of New Zealand, with its range of adaptive possibilities and resources far surpassing that of the tropical Polynesian islands. The present writer inclines to the latter view for several reasons. First, it would be relatively impossible for a small migration, as the Great Fleet was actually depicted, to have effected a change in the basic orientation of the pre-existing native culture. Secondly, the differences between the poles of Moa-Hunter and Maori are really very minor when one views them against the large number of similarities. Therefore, it seems plausible to interpret Maori culture as a direct outgrowth from the Moa-Hunter basis.

It is unfortunate, however, that at precisely this point in New Zealand prehistory our documentation from the archaeological record fails us. Very few sites have been excavated of what might be termed an intermediate or transitional period between the Moa-Hunter and Maori cultures, and no representative classic Maori sites have ever been excavated! The lure of the moa bones and the absorbing problems of the origin of New Zealand's early aborigines have so affected the concentration of effort in prehistoric studies in that country that the more recent periods have simply been neglected. The New Zealand archaeologists are quite aware of this lacuna in their data, however, and it will certainly not be too long before the situation is ameliorated by a series of excavations on representative Maori sites, which will fill in the upper sections of the prehistoric sequence. As a matter of fact, excavations on Maori fortification sites are already being conducted with results that will be discussed at more length below.

A general view of the developments during the intermediate and late periods can be pieced together from several sources including excavations at sites that were occupied over a long period of time from the twelfth to the seventeenth centuries (Pounawea, Papatowai, Hinahina).[19] Surface collections and ethnological data such as legends support this construct. In an analysis of the middens at Pounawea, Papatowai, and Hinahina, a steady decline in the frequency of moa bone was found in the upper layers of the occupation debris, accompanied by a commensurate increase in the amount of fish and shellfish remains. These excavations indicate that by perhaps A.D. 1500 the moa were becoming very scarce, as a result of which the attention of the aboriginal population was being forcibly diverted to other sources of protein for their diet, namely the abundant riverine and marine life. With this increase in dependence on the sea for food, the settlements that had been established inland for the purpose of hunting the vanishing moa were vacated as the population gravitated toward the coast again in order to be close to the main source of food supply.

At this period the dependence on agriculture may have also increased, although there is as yet no evidence in the archaeological record. It must be noted, however, that such evidence is generally quite hard to obtain in the absence of specific agricultural and food-preparation tools in imperishable stone, bone, or shell. Such are unfortunately not found in New Zealand.

By the 1500's it can be said that the South Island Moa-Hunter culture had been transformed into something qualitatively different as a result of the changes in its environmental situation, coupled with the internal evolutionary alterations in its own technology. In isolated pockets of the South Island, however, some marginal groups may have remained quite conservative, maintaining a basically Moa-Hunter culture into the seventeenth century. In the cultural backwater of the Chatham Islands, such conservatism was extreme until the Maori conquest in the early nineteenth century brought radical "modernization."

For the purposes of description we will call all that transpired after A.D. 1500 "Maori," although it is plain that the period may be subdivided as a result of further work.

The population of this later stage of New Zealand prehistory had grown markedly from the earlier small bands of Moa-Hunters. Tribes were evidently of a very respectable size, and the size of settlements increased as a consequence. In such a situation of increased population density, it is natural that the best areas for human habitation would become highly valued. As many of the optimal habitation areas in New Zealand were in virgin forest land,[20] clearing and preparing such areas for habitation represented a sizable investment of effort, thus tending to produce a reluctance on the part of the inhabitants to move once they were well settled in a good location. There were, of course, groups who were not so territorially well endowed as others, and they naturally sought to better their conditions by conquering the better cleared lands and driving out the previous owners. These defeated expatriates had to find some place to settle, and they in turn had to prey on other tribal groups to re-establish themselves. The result was that there were constant conflicts, as stronger and weaker groups jockeyed for the prime habitation sites. Each time a tribe was conquered and driven off its land, a chain reaction was set off in which a weak group would ultimately be forced into the virgin forest areas to clear a new tract of land by dint of hard labor which the more powerful tribes scrupulously avoided.

The conditions of intertribal warfare in New Zealand are adequately reflected by the number of fortified village sites which dot the landscape.[21] Called *pa* in the Maori dialect as elsewhere in Polynesia, these sites were found in locations providing the best natural defenses. Some *pa* were permanently inhabited, while others were used only during time of war for refuge. In such cases the *pa* were situated near the open village sites called *kainga*. The fortification systems of the *pa* were basically the same as those noted elsewhere in Polynesia, but they were larger and carried to a greater degree of elaboration by the Polynesians of New Zealand. Intricate systems of palisades, scarps, terraces, and ditches protected the approaches to *pa* situated on high hills or ridges. The interior of such *pa* were further subdivided into a number of divisions that would allow the defenders to carry on their fight even though the enemy had breached the outer defense ring of palisades and trenches. The surface area of fortified sites was often astonishingly great, one site containing 100 acres. Fortifications were also built in the lowlands, ringed by ditches, earthworks, and palisades. Natural features, such as rivers, were utilized for further protection, forts often being constructed on narrow meanders where they were surrounded on three sides by swift, deep streams. In such cases the landward approach was cut off by a deep ditch which could be crossed only on a narrow exposed ramp. Within the fortifications, houses were constructed and large storage pits were built for food to be conserved against the possibility of sieges. The houses were of a semi-subterranean type, with floors dug into the earth a foot or more, rectangular in plan.

It is probable that the villages situated near the forts consisted of a number of such semi-subterranean houses in no particular organized arrangement, with a larger meeting house among the domiciles. Nearby, an open area would be reserved for dances and public ceremonies. Small temples of the very simple Tahitian Inland type, still in use at this late date, were probably situated near the villages or within the village *pa* for better protection.

The tools and art of the Maori [22] can be differentiated from those of the Moa-Hunter by a number of salient features. The beautiful and often large adzes of the earlier period are replaced by tools of a generally similar type but of differing proportions and finish. The Maori developed a number of techniques for sawing and polishing nephrite that resulted in highly finished adzes of this beautiful stone. The whale-tooth and reel ornaments worn by Moa-Hunter males were almost completely replaced by very characteristic Maori forms, the most outstanding of which are the types called *hei tiki* (tiki amulet) and *hei matau* (hook amulet). Many of these objects were made of finely worked greenstone. The Maori did not use the composite bonito hook, as did their predecessors, but developed a variety of other hook types to replace it and at the same time improve their utilization of the marine life of New Zealand. Weapons of war are common in the Maori period, the most interesting of these being the *pata* short-bladed club which, as we have previously noted, is a direct descendant of the south coastal China weapon of the upper Neolithic. A very distinctive art style developed in New Zealand utilizing the spiral and scroll as dominant motifs. Woodcarving was very advanced, and everyday articles were often elaborately carved. House posts and walls, canoe prows, food funnels, bird snares, and other such objects were highly decorated. The distinctive New Zealand version of the universal Polynesian tiki developed into a wide-eyed beaked creature with an elongated tongue rolling out onto its chest in a sinuous curve.

It was this society that the British encountered in the eighteenth century when they discovered and subsequently colonized the islands of New Zealand. It was no easy task to colonize the Maori, however, for they were quite accustomed to warfare on a reasonably grand scale. The Maori warriors, their faces incised with the ghastly *moko* tattoo designs, proved to have courage and a strange kind of sportsmanship that made the British military might look somewhat sickly. The Maori characteristically were quick to note the obvious advantages of firearms and immediately acquired some of their own. They also were not slow to realize the effect of cannon on their *pa*, and set about to redesign their defensive system to provide maximal protection against the weapons of the Europeans. They retained the very pragmatic but gallant approach to warfare which their native culture had imparted to them, with the result that the British could never decisively defeat them and were often at a moral, as well as a military, disadvantage.

Maori tribesmen once surrounded a group of Britishers and kept them pinned down for days until their ammunition ran out. While the "thin red line of heroes" was making ready to "put up a good show at the end," the Maori, who had realized the situation, sent an envoy to the British position. He suggested that the British accept some Maori ammunition so that the highly entertaining fight might continue on a more equal basis! In another incident, the situation was reversed and the Maori were encircled in the great *pa* of Ruapekapeka,[23] which was one of the newly rebuilt Maori fortifications, specifically designed to withstand European cannon fire. Trenches with salients and re-entrants ran between the serried stockades, while subterranean shelters protected the Maori from British explosive projectiles. The British troops bombarded Ruapekapeka for ten days with three thirty-two-pound guns, one eighteen-pounder, two twelve-pounders, seven smaller brass cannon, and some rocket launchers. Periodic infantry assaults on the *pa* were beaten off with regularity, however, as it became obvious that the Maori were not impressed by the firepower that was directed on them. After ten days the Maori decided to vacate the *pa* and did so, emerging virtually unscathed, leaving the British the fort for which they had already paid so dearly in men and ammunition.

The Maori have integrated with the culture of the European colonials, but have managed to retain their language, art, and ethnic identity. They ceased to fight the British long ago, and have performed nobly in two world wars side by side with British troops, terrorizing the enemy with the same grimaces and war cries as were used in the days of old when Maori warriors did not know the ways of the white man's warfare.

The Maori people have produced many capable professional men. As an anthropologist, I think first of the great anthropologist-physician Sir Peter Buck, whose Maori name, Te Rangi Hiroa, is familiar to anthropological students everywhere. Buck spent a lifetime in the aid and study of his people—not only the Maori but all Polynesians. His fine volume on Polynesia, *Vikings of the Sunrise,* is the best work available for a grasp of the culture and traditions of the Polynesians as a whole.

At this point let us pause to recapitulate the prehistory of the New Zealand Maori insofar as it is known.

1. The islands of New Zealand were settled at approximately A.D. 1000 by a migration that probably originated in Tahiti. The Polynesian settlers made their camps along the coast, becoming very dependent on the large indigenous struthious birds, moa, for their subsistence. Tremendous amounts of moa bones litter the surface of old archaeological sites of this period. Settlements were small, consisting of a number of simple houses (probably oval in plan), some earth ovens, and a few storage pits for root crops. Moa-

Hunter adzes were mainly quadrangular or triangular in section, with or without the lashing grips. The ornaments worn by these people were whales' teeth, real or artificial, and stone or bone "reel" ornaments. No weapons or signs of warfare are known at this period.

2. As the moa became scarcer and moved inland to seek refuge, the Polynesians followed them, establishing some inland settlements.

3. By A.D. 1500, the moa were to all intents and purposes extinct, and the inland villages were abandoned as the population moved out to the coast, shifting the emphasis of their subsistence pattern to marine animals. The Maori culture of the historic period has its roots in this era of the return to coastal villages and a fishing economy caused by the loss of the moa as a food source.

4. The Maori culture was characterized by strong tribal organization and well-built fortifications near villages. Warfare was common. Tools and personal ornaments differed from those of the Moa-Hunter culture. A very distinctive art style developed with a florescence of woodcarving and working of semiprecious stone.

15

New World Contacts

Up to this point we have been first concerned with establishing in terms of space, time, and culture the origin of the parent group or stock from which the Polynesian race diverged. We have traced the movements of this stock from Asia through the western Pacific to the fringes of the Polynesian triangle and then followed, in more detail, the migrations of the divergent Polynesian race within the island world in which they are presently found. Such migrations covered a tremendous span of ocean, from the coast of Asia to remote Easter Island; even the point-to-point distances involved in various stages of the journey are of very respectable magnitude. For example, considering the geography of Polynesia alone, it was necessary to travel some 2,200 miles from the nearest Polynesian outpost to reach Hawaii; Easter Island is 1,500 miles away from its nearest neighbor; while Pitcairn, Chatham, the Australs, and the Marquesas are also isolated from their nearest neighbors by hundreds of miles of open sea.

Despite the distances involved in such voyages, not to mention the technical and human factors affecting the success of the undertakings, the Polynesians obviously were capable of the task of exploration and discovery which they themselves apparently set, as attested by their colonization of all the habitable islands of Polynesia. Indeed, Polynesian archaeological remains have even appeared on islands that are quite definitely on the borderline of human habitability. Such are the low, sun-drenched coral islands along the equator north and west of Tahiti, where temples, adzes, and other artifacts bear witness to brief Polynesian occupancy.[1]

The evidence of archaeology suggests, then, that the Polynesians did a large amount of voyaging, a portion of which was probably nondirected, simply looking for new lands. If such voyaging was done within the island triangle, carrying the Polynesians to the last island outposts between the cultures of Asia and the New World, is it not also possible that some contacts may have been made with the New World? The answer, of course, is decidedly in the affirmative. It is unfortunate, however, that information on such contacts is meager and not always acceptable without some reservations. This information is derived from two main sources: traditions and archaeology.

In discussing the traditional evidence for Polynesian voyages to the New World, we must constantly bear in mind the strictures applying to such evidence, which have been discussed in a previous chapter. These qualifications do not completely negate the value of oral traditional histories, however, but merely indicate the caution necessary in the use of such data.

In the Marquesas[2] there is a legend of the great double canoe *Kahua* which was constructed by the Naiki tribe in the important valley of Puama'u on the island of Hiva Oa. This canoe was the biggest ever to be launched in all the Marquesas. Its hull was so deep that the bailing crews could not reach over the gunwales to empty their bailing scoops, but had to climb the sides. On the platform that connected the twin hulls of this vessel were a shelter and a number of silos of woven palm leaves and poles, built to hold the fermented breadfruit paste which was the staple of Marquesan diet. According to the legend, the ship sailed from Puama'u toward the northwest to visit the island of Nuku Hiva, possibly because several tribal groups in that island were closely related to the Puama'u tribe, bearing the same tribal name. Representatives of these Nuku Hivan tribes may have been included in the crew. Departing from Nuku Hiva, the great *Kahua* sailed to the east until it arrived at the shores of a large country designated in the legend as *Te Fiti*. (To the east of the Marquesas the only land to be found is the coast of northern Peru and Ecuador. Therefore, if the legend is reliable, it would seem that the Marquesans did touch the New World.) The legend goes on to say that after remaining a time in the land of *Te Fiti,* the Naiki of

Puama'u refitted their ship and returned to Hiva Oa, leaving some of their number behind, however, to live and die among the inhabitants of what may have been the South American coast. It is certainly unfortunate that we know no more about the voyage of the *Kahua,* for more details as to the date, the route, the land of *Te Fiti,* its people, and so on, would aid greatly in verifying the legend.

From the island of Rarotonga comes another legend of Polynesian discovery of the New World. This is reported by Dr. Thomas Davis,[3] half Rarotongan himself, who has a sound knowledge of his own native culture as well as of the art of seamanship. According to Davis, there is a Rarotongan legend of a large-scale expedition led by Maui Marumamao from the island of Raïatéa in the Society group to the east, past Easter Island to a "land of ridges"—probably the Andean range lying along the coast of Peru. After remaining some time in Peru, Maui died; but his son Kiu took command of the group, and it embarked again into the Pacific to return to Polynesia. Although the legend, as Davis has presented it, leaves much to be desired, it would still be well worth the effort of tracking down, recording it in the vernacular, and comparing it to other legends from Rarotonga, as well as those from elsewhere in Polynesia, in the hopes of determining whether it is a latter-day post-European creation or an actual aboriginal tradition.

When dealing with the archaeological evidence of Polynesian contacts with the New World, we are on somewhat firmer ground than when working in the rather nebulous domain of traditions. Nevertheless, the archaeological data possess their own disadvantages, as we shall see below, and there is ample reason for caution here.

A number of Polynesian artifacts have been found on the coast of South America—some in surface collecting, others supposedly in archaeological contexts. Of these, perhaps the most interesting are the Easter Island *mata* (obsidian spear heads),[4] unmistakable in form and material, which were recovered from a prehistoric Indian tomb on the Chilean coast. These artifacts would appear to be prime bits of evidence on which to build a sound case for a Polynesian visit to South America. However, as Métraux has pointed out, these spear points are found by the thousands on Easter Island and many have been brought back to Chile during more than half a century by sailors and other visitors to Easter Island. That such artifacts might appear then near or in Indian archaeological sites in Chile might be merely an accident, or it might be a purposeful fraud in which the artifacts were planted in a site to be discovered by a trusting collector. Elsewhere, stone adzes of indubitable Polynesian type have been picked up on the surface in Chile [5] and also in northern Argentina, according to Dr. Rex Gonzalez, noted Argentinean archaeologist and physician. A Maori fighting club of the flat-bladed *patu-patu* variety was recovered from another Indian site on the South American coast.[6] Imbelloni, a well-known Argentinean anthropologist, has drawn attention to additional evidence indicating a Polynesian contact in South America.[7] He pointed out that among the aborigines of Chile, stone adzes similar to Polynesian types are used in certain ceremonies, being referred to in the native dialect as *toki*, a word quite similar to that denoting "adze" in Polynesia (Marquesas—*toki*; Tahiti—*to'i;* Hawaii—*ko'i,* etc.).

All of the scattered archaeological finds of supposed Polynesian artifacts noted above suffer from a very serious drawback, however. In every case, the finds were not made by trained personnel and the archaeological context of the artifact is completely uncertain; therefore, one must always be aware of the possibility that such finds may be the result of archaeological materials brought back to South America by Europeans in relatively recent times.

The realm of botany yields additional information pointing to Polynesian contacts with the New World. The famous sweet potato, often cited as evidence for Peruvians' reaching Polynesia, may be in actuality an Old World plant of African or Asian origin, as we have noted in a previous chapter. Should such be the case, then the pre-European appearance of the sweet potato in Peru would be obvious evidence of a Polynesian contact.

The Polynesians may only have been one of several Asian groups who touched the shores of South America, however, and their role in trans-Pacific contacts may have been subordinate to that of other peoples from the Asian mainland. Some recent information from the jungles of Yucatán has a possible relation to the problem we are discussing.[8] There, in the ruined cities of Chichén Itzá, Palenque, Piedras Negras, and Tula, a complex of art and architectural elements has been isolated which shows a possible connection with the cultures of Southeast Asia. This complex consists of a number of Mayan art forms, such as the lotus plant, the foliated cross, the cross-legged or reclining figure, and the phallus, as well as various types of attached wall pillars, roof vaults, colonnades, etc., which are used in a fashion reminiscent of features of Indian and Southeast Asian Buddhist architecture. The complex appears in Yucatán about A.D. 700, a time when similar manifestations were already present in the Southeast Asian area. Dr. Gordon Ekholm, who has drawn attention to this complex, which he calls "Complex A," suggests that it may have been introduced into Mexico from Asia by direct voyages. The contact between the Mexicans and the Southeast Asians was probably not of an extended nature. Possibly, it was a type of missionizing attempt by the Buddhist visitors from across the Pacific. (The ships that were in use at this time on the coast of Asia were quite large and could carry passengers and supplies far in excess of those transported by several of the largest Polynesian double canoes put together. They were, therefore, quite capable of making the trip across the Pacific.)

The people who carried Complex A to the coast of Mexico would probably have passed through part of the Polynesian triangle in their voyages. If this was the case, then an excellent possibility would have existed for the Polynesians to gain knowledge of the great continent to the east of their islands, if they themselves did not already know of its existence, and learn the courses to steer to reach that land if they so desired. This, of course, is all conjecture, and Complex A still stands as a theoretical construct, in need of additional archaeological documentation from sites on the coast of Mexico. The possibility of such Asian contacts is tantalizing, however, and might well reward further work.

In general, it might be said that the problems of Polynesian contact with the New World will only be solved by careful attention to the excavations in stratified sites on the coast of South America where such contacts would have been the most frequent, had they occurred. The obstacles in the way of such work are great, however. First, the nature of the archaeological remains on the coast of Peru are such that the usual Polynesian artifacts would be completely lost. Peruvian sites are usually large and often littered with huge quantities of clay potsherds, for the Peruvian Indians were among the greatest potters the world has known. Many of the sites have ruined buildings of great size which further complicate the surface. In such a welter of archaeological remains it would be extremely difficult to spot the thin midden layer, speckled with broken shell and stone flakes, that would signify a Polynesian camp site.

Attention to food-plant remains preserved in many of the dry midden sites on the Peruvian coast may solve once and for all the problem of the sweet potato in South America.

Other sources that might yield clues to possible Polynesian contacts in the early Spanish Colonial period are the documentary records kept by the Spanish priests and officials after the conquest of Peru. Obscure diaries, chronicles, or letters might contain information of inestimable value on this topic.

To recapitulate, the information that we possess from Oceania concerning the Polynesian voyages indicates that they were capable of extended trips. It is therefore conceivable that they might have pushed eastward and touched the coast of South America at one time or another.

Polynesian legends, botanical evidence, and archaeological finds on the Peruvian coast demonstrate that such contacts may have occurred. However, this evidence is not of an extremely reliable nature, and further work is needed before any definite statements can be made. Suffice it to say for the present that contacts were quite possible and that they may have occurred; the "where" and "when" must be answered by future workers.

16

The "Kon-Tiki" Myth

The natives of the atoll of Raroia in the Tuamotu Archipelago of French Oceania were quite surprised one day to see a strange sail appear on the horizon. Gradually the sail approached, bringing into view a most unusual-looking sea craft, far different from the copra schooners and trim cutters that usually plied their trade among those islands. The vessel supporting the sail was riding low in the water, the waves almost level with her deck. A flimsy house of leaves, like a matchbox on a plank, stood on the deck behind a mast that supported a large sail bearing a strange emblem. As the Raroians watched with interest, the odd craft kept its heading, coming ever nearer to the vicious reef that encircled the island without displaying any attempts to escape the crashing surf that heaved against the jagged coral rampart. The crewmen of the sailing raft were obviously unable to control their vessel with any degree of precision, and the raft, moving closer to the reef, was finally caught by a swell and heaved upon the coral, tumbling occupants, canned food, radio equipment, and other gear in every direction. At last it settled in the shallows behind the reef crest in a heap of wreckage. The five occupants of the raft, tall, tanned, bearded, and fortunately unhurt, picked themselves up gingerly and began to collect their belongings from among the spiny sea urchins and sea slugs on the floor of the tidal shallows.

For Thor Heyerdahl, the leader of this group of hardened mariners, this day was memorable in more than one respect. He and his companions had just completed a voyage of 101 days from the coast of South America aboard the now half-wrecked balsa-log raft *Kon-Tiki,* and their arrival on Raroia wrote *finis* to a voyage of hardship and danger. More important, however, was the fact that Heyerdahl, in successfully drifting on the raft between South America and Polynesia, had secured additional proof for a theory for which he had long tried unsuccessfully to win scientific acceptance among the anthropologists of the world.

Heyerdahl's theory, familiar to many laymen through the popular account of the *Kon-Tiki* voyage,[1] concerned the origin of the Polynesian race. Differing with the anthropologists, Heyerdahl believed that the Polynesians did not come from Asia, but were rather American Indians who had sailed from the coast of the New World, which was admittedly much closer to the Polynesian triangle than the coast of Asia. Such a theory was by no means new. It had first been developed in 1803 by a Spanish missionary in the Philippines, Father Joacquin M. de Zuñiga in his book *Historia de las Islas Philipinas,* who proposed an American origin for the natives of those islands. The theory attracted the Polynesia scholar-missionary, William Ellis, who could not completely accept it as applicable to the Polynesians. In more recent times the possibility of Polynesian-Peruvian relationships has been resurrected on several occasions, but it has never received any serious consideration.

According to Heyerdahl's hypothesis, two separate groups of Indians were involved in this population of the islands of Polynesia. First, a group of Peruvian Indians *drifted* out on their rafts from the coast of Peru into the islands of Eastern Polynesia, touching Easter Island and subsequently moving westward through the Marquesas and the Societies right to the western border of Polynesia. Secondly, a group of Indians from the Pacific Northwest of the United States and Canada forsook their cedar trees and totem poles and paddled to Hawaii in their dugouts, after which they gradually filtered into the southern islands of the Polynesian triangle, mingling with the Peruvians who were already dwelling in that area. This obviously presupposes an advanced muscular development for the paddling arms of Northwest Coast Indians, but such strength is certainly no more remarkable than the lengthy patience displayed by the undersized Peruvians on their drifting itinerary through the islands.

The foundations of this theory are somewhat heterogeneous and even include some scientific observations and facts, the most significant of which are the prevailing southeasterly winds and currents in Polynesia, the remote possibility of Peruvian origin of the sweet potato (which is unconditionally accepted by Heyerdahl), and the similarity of Polynesian and Peruvian blood-type distributions.

Heyerdahl pointed out that the winds and currents are mostly against any voyages from Asia to Polynesia, but that the same winds and currents would aid voyages from South America to Polynesia. Therefore it would have been simpler to have populated the Polynesian triangle from the Peruvian coast. But this is not proof that such a migration did occur, for prevailing southeasters do not in any way present an obstacle to sailing canoes or other sailed vessels. Tacking and laying close to the wind were both possible in a Polynesian canoe. The fact that the trade winds quite frequently reverse themselves for long periods is further overlooked by Heyerdahl, and the possibility of using the eastward-flowing equatorial countercurrent is not discussed. Both of these are obviously major factors in attempting to prove the impossibility of eastward voyages in Polynesia.

High on the list of Polynesian-Peruvian parallels is the now-famous sweet potato which bears, both in Peru and in Polynesia, the name *kumara* or some derivation thereof. We have already had an opportunity to discuss the controversy concerning the sweet potato in the chapter on Polynesian environment and have indicated that the plant and the name are probably of Old World origin and may have been introduced into Peru by Polynesian voyagers before the Spanish Conquest or by Spaniards themselves in the colonial period.

Another major prop for the Heyerdahlian theory is the similarity between the blood types of the Peruvians and the Eastern Polynesians. We have noted in a previous chapter that very disparate races may have similar blood-type frequencies and that blood typing alone is meaningless for a comparison of two groups of people, if their morphological characteristics are dissimilar to begin with. There is little resemblance between the short, coppery, barrel-chested Peruvian with round head, straight hair, and slightly hooked nose and the tall, brown, stocky Polynesian with a wide range of head shape, wavy black hair, and a rather flat, wide nose.

Heyerdahl has unwittingly provided in his own work some of the most telling evidence against the use of blood types for determination of racial connections. In the course of the work of his Norwegian Expedition on Easter Island and elsewhere in Eastern Polynesia[2] blood samples were collected for typing from supposedly selected natives on all the islands visited. On the island of Nuku Hiva, where I was residing at the time, the selection of donors was not very rigorous, consisting merely in rounding up of the available Marquesans in the vicinity of the Taiohae Valley dispensary—some twenty-four in number. The results of the serological studies done on these samples indicate that the tested Marquesan group resembles those of the other islands of Eastern Polynesia quite closely.

This seemingly innocuous fact becomes suddenly inexplicable in light of the fact that none but possibly two of Heyerdahl's Marquesan blood donors were of pure Polynesian ancestry.

In over a year of residence on Nuku Hiva, I learned the native language and got to know a large number of the 980 inhabitants. I had an opportunity to examine old church documents that go back to the beginning of French occupation of the island, recording marriages of natives and Europeans, deaths and births. My wife also collected a number of reproductive histories from native women, obtaining further information about genealogies in this fashion. On the basis of my knowledge of these people, there are only 4 individuals out of the 980 who can claim pure Polynesian ancestry with some degree of assurance. Of these 4, only 2 were available for Heyerdahl's tests, the others being in remote parts of the island. There are some 13 other individuals who have made claims to an untainted Polynesian genetic heritage, but their immediate Asian or European ancestry is too well known to their neighbors to remain a secret for long.

One specific "pure Polynesian" who contributed to the blood-type study that day in Taiohae was the wife of my head workman, Tahiahei Puhetini. Dear Tahia went along for the ride, so to speak, and gave a cc. or two of vital fluid to science. It would be difficult to describe her actual ancestry in a brief fashion. She is the granddaughter of a Castilian Spaniard, Alvarado by name, who jumped ship in the Marquesas to live out his life there, and left behind a sizable number of progeny and a wicked reputation. Her father, half Marquesan, married a woman who was also a half-breed herself, with the result that Tahia and her sisters were endowed with a light skin and completely European features. If her blood type resembles that of any pure Polynesian, it does so by sheer chance, because she is genetically and physically half European. The others who contributed their blood were also of mixed racial ancestry. The amount of racial crossing which has gone on in Taiohae and on the island of Nuku Hiva in general can be shown by a brief sketch of Taiohae history since European contact.

The population of Nuku Hiva, particularly of Taiohae Valley on that island, has been exposed to European genetic admixture since the late eighteenth century, when sailors from early whaling vessels went ashore there. Later, in 1813, an American Navy squadron arrived and stayed at Taiohae for fifteen months, during which time an additional increment of Caucasoid genes was introduced into the population. Further deserters from whaling ships formed a large element in the population in 1840 when the French occupied the island and placed a military garrison, backed by a naval force, at Taiohae. The French troops remained for many years, during which time a considerable amount of miscegenation naturally took place between French and Marquesans. In the late nineteenth and early twentieth centuries, Chinese laborers were brought in, many of whom married native women. Martiniquan Negroes were also used as laborers on one plantation for a period, as a result of which a few half-Negro children were born.

During all this time, of course, foreign ships were always present, bringing sailors who were always looking for female companionship. It is obvious that anyone who wishes to find a true Marquesan in such a polyglot group is going to have to do more than merely ask for all Marquesans to step forward, or ask the local French doctor who does not speak a word of the native language and may have only been there a short time himself. Even to ask the missionaries to name the true Marquesans is most foolish, for they, of all people, know least about who *really* sired the Polynesian babies they baptize.

Thus, it is plain that blood-type distribution studies are not always reliable as proof of racial connections and that a racially mixed group may often resemble the type distributions of another possibly pure group. In this case it is of course doubtful whether any of the groups sampled in the entire blood-typing program are even close to 100 per cent pure Polynesian in their structure, and the resemblance between the various groups may actually be a result of the fact that they all have a fairly equal amount of foreign blood, especially Caucasoid and Mongoloid admixture. The above incident shows clearly how far afield it is possible to wander using blood types alone in attempts to prove racial connections. It is further an object lesson in the use of stringent controls for any scientific study. Whatever the subject involved may be, if it is worth study, then data-collection techniques merit the closest of controls. Without such controls experiments are merely wasted effort, no matter how pleasing the results may be to partisans of particular views.

In addition to these main points discussed above, Heyerdahl has adduced a large number of cultural "resemblances" between the cultures of Peru and Polynesia, which he claims as further evidence that the Polynesians are actually American Indians. A few of these resemblances actually do exist, but they are nonsignificant and generally involve traits found all over the world. Other causes of this similarity may also be due to the fact that both the Polynesians and the American Indians are of general Asiatic origin, although the earliest Indians in the New World may have departed from Asia to cross the Bering Straits as many as 25,000 years ago. Heyerdahl is quite enthusiastic over the fact that the Polynesians, the Peruvians, and other American Indians all formerly marked the summer and winter solstices[3] (as an aid to regulating their agricultural calendars). This is supposed to be an extremely important fact in showing a definite relationship between Polynesian culture and that of the New World. The resemblance crumbles immediately, however, when it is recalled that observance of the summer and winter solstices was found universally in the ancient and primitive cultures of Asia, Africa, the Mediterranean, and Europe. The fact that solstices were marked in Polynesian and Peruvian societies is no more an indication of the later connection of those two cultures than it is an indication of their relationships with any of the other cultures of the world.

Most of the other numerous "resemblances" between Peru and Polynesia, however, are far less credible than even the above example. Facts are taken and artistically presented to serve the purpose of showing Polynesian-Peruvian relationships, when in truth the opposite is the case. A few examples of this will show the technique quite clearly. Speaking of the Polynesian water craft, in an attempt to prove that Polynesians used rafts instead of canoes (rafts being a unique Peruvian trait, of course!), Heyerdahl says: "The Tahitian name for a raft-ship was *pahi*. . . ."[4] Actually, however, the Tahitians had no "raft-ships" as a matter of record, and the word *pahi* really means "double canoe" and has also been applied in modern times to the European type of ships.

Again, in the field of language we are told[5] that the

Marquesans have a predilection for beginning their valley names with the prefix *hana,* such as Hanamenu, Hanahei, and so on. *Hana,* by a "well-known Polynesian sound change," is supposedly related to the Quechuan word *sana,* which means "paradise." This therefore purports to demonstrate once again a relationship between Peru and Polynesia. The word *hana* is actually the southeastern dialect equivalent of a word which appears elsewhere in the Marquesan archipelago as *haka, hanga,* and *ha'a.* It means "bay," referring specifically to the body of water rather than the land surrounding the water. It has no relation to any word for "paradise" and there is no "Polynesian sound change" that would produce *sana* from *hanga, ha'a,* or *hana.* A change from *h* to *s* exists in the Samoan dialect, however, but is strictly a regional dialect variation, not characteristic of all Polynesian languages.

Evidence against the Peruvian origin of the Polynesians is naturally quite voluminous; but evidently Heyerdahl has not read many contrary arguments, for they are seldom mentioned. Thus, in trying to convince his readers that Polynesian is not an Asiatic language, Heyerdahl states: ". . . the Polynesian language was only remotely related to the Malay tongues."[6] Nowhere in the extensive bibliography which he included in his *American Indians* volume is there any reference to the numerous works on the Polynesian languages and their genetic affiliations with Malay. Dempwolff, Dyen, Schmidt, and other Polynesian linguists are completely ignored as though they did not exist.

One could devote several volumes the size of Heyerdahl's single "scientific" tome to a cataloguing of his gratuitous uses of scientific data. There is, however, little value in being more exhaustive than is necessary to give a brief indication of the "methodological approach" characteristic of the *Kon-Tiki* theory. The above examples suffice to show what sort of evidence was utilized in formulating the theory.

Let us pause briefly to examine the *Kon-Tiki* raft itself, however. Did not Heyerdahl really prove by his voyage that Peruvian Indians could have reached Polynesia on such rafts? The answer is, flatly, negative.[7] The *Kon-Tiki* raft is a type of craft developed by the Peruvians *after* the Spanish brought the use of the sail to them. Although the Peruvians did use rafts to voyage off their coast long before the white men ever came, such rafts did not use sails, but were propelled by paddles. Sailing rafts of the *Kon-Tiki* type were never used by prehistoric Indians. Furthermore, the Peruvian

Indians, whether using sails or paddles, or just drifting, never had the benefits of canned foods, modern solar stills to make drinking water from the sea, radios, maps, and navigation instruments, and a knowledge of where they were going. All these were used by the *Kon-Tiki* crew, and it must be said that without them the voyage would have quickly ended in tragedy. When the *Kon-Tiki* ran afoul of Raroia's reef there were 1,500 cans of food[8] still aboard her. Therefore, one presumes that for the crew life was not possible, sustained on what the sea yielded alone. Why should it then have been possible for the less well-equipped, sail-less Indians?

In sum, the *Kon-Tiki* voyage was not a fair test of the sailing ability of the ancient Peruvians by any means and proved only this: that by using a modern, post-European-contact type of sailing raft with navigation aids and modern survival equipment, men can survive a 101-day voyage between Peru and Polynesia.

It is needless to say that when the Heyerdahl theory hit the press, the reaction of the scientific community was uniformly negative. The same thesis had been raised a few times before, as I have previously noted, and Heyerdahl's version was the same old story, decked out in newer trappings and backed by a high tide of sensational publicity. The manner in which fact had been fitted to the Procrustean bed of the Peruvian migration theory failed to win Heyerdahl any followers among scientists, who are accustomed to demanding a high degree of objectivity from themselves as well as their colleagues. A few scientists devoted some effort[9] to pointing out in scientific journals various of the numerous inconsistencies and shortcomings of the theory and the evidence upon which it was based. The publication of the *Kon-Tiki* theory did stimulate further scientific work in the area of Polynesian anthropology, which of course resulted rather in an increase in the evidence marshaled against the theory than contributed to its support. The public, completely unaware of the detailed literature of Polynesian and American Indian anthropology, was quite willing to accept the hypothesis as it was presented in the numerous popular publications concerning the raft voyage. The glamour of such an undertaking, the undeniable hardships imposed upon the crew, and their great courage in opposing the mighty Pacific on such a flimsy craft obviously added to the attraction of the theory, if it was not indeed the main cause for its popularity.

After the initial burst of popular enthusiasm immediately following the voyage, public interest tapered off gradually while scientists continued their labors, occasionally pausing to punch a few more holes in the theory which had never been more than Swiss cheese, anyway.

Heyerdahl, however, was not resting, and in 1956 he led the Norwegian Expedition to Polynesia. (We have already had occasion to discuss their work on Easter Island.) The expedition's purpose was to delve into the prehistory of Eastern Polynesia, concentrating on Easter Island in particular. That information lending support to the *Kon-Tiki* theory should be found by such an expedition was, naturally, not too much to expect. The most recent Heyerdahl opus, entitled *Aku-Aku,* is a result of this work, serving as our main source of knowledge of the work of the expedition members on Easter Island and elsewhere. *Aku-Aku* is of the same tradition as the previous works, differing only in that it is more extreme in its position. The general style of the work was set long ago by such hoary favorites of the travel-thriller devotees as *Green Hell* and *All the Rivers Ran East.* The aura of mystery surrounding Easter Island is built up to a fantastic extent with practically no references being made to any of the first-class anthropological studies which have been carried out on Easter by Métraux, Lavachéry, Routledge, and others. Although Heyerdahl avoids mentioning such sources, he obviously is acquainted with them, as anyone who has read Métraux's works will note upon perusal of *Aku-Aku.*

Having thus established for the uninformed reader that Easter Island and its culture are *terra incognita* to the anthropological world, Heyerdahl proceeds to tell what *he* was able to find out by his own special methods during the expedition's five-month sojourn. The Easter Islanders, of course, regurgitated the sum total of their esoterica for this impressive visitor, and he was shown all manner of secrets heretofore hidden from the eyes of white men. These included ancestral caves, reached only by perilous routes deep beneath the island surface, crowded with odd sculpture of *aku-aku* or demons; the secrets of how the great statues were moved and raised; the secret of the Easter Island script; and a number of other outstanding firsts. As a matter of fact, one would gather the impression that the Easter Island natives had done an Ed Sullivan type of spectacle for Heyerdahl, staging the "History of Easter Island" with the original cast and a score by Tiomkin.

Amidst all these accomplishments are some rather disturbing features. The stone sculptures discovered [10] deep in the ancestral caves are the crudest of frauds of a type made every day by Easter Islanders for sale to tourists and sailors. The poor proportions, the abominable sculptural technique, and the obviously contrived forms of these "masterpieces" mark them as bogus even in a photograph. Compared to the fine, delicate woodcarving from the pagan past of the "Navel of the World," these stone figures are monstrosities. It is heartening, however, to see that the natives of Easter Island recognized so quickly the possibilities for pulling such a stunt, and one is impressed by the creativity of their imagination in this as well as some of the other "secrets" which they revealed.

As to the secret of the Easter Island script, Dr. T. Barthel's work on Easter Island after the departure of the Norwegian Expedition has indicated the true nature of the system of signs used on the *rongorongo* boards. The results of this work, as pointed out in a previous chapter, indicate that the script was brought to Easter Island by the earliest settlers and is of Polynesian origin.

Aside from the interludes of excitement and suspense, the book contains the usual sort of statements. For instance, Heyerdahl credits himself with doing the first archaeology ever done in the Marquesas.[11] He was some thirty-seven years too late. Ralph Linton took that honor in 1919, and I personally was doing the first stratigraphic excavation on Nuku Hiva a month before Heyerdahl's ship dropped anchor in Taiohae Bay. The honor of "first" should be and is truly meaningless, anyway; there are far more desirable adjectives, but not so easily won.

Heyerdahl goes on to claim to be the first white man to see the well-known two-headed statue in the valley of Taipivai, Nuku Hiva.[12] Actually, this statue was first seen by Karl von den Steinen, the famous German ethnographer, in 1898, and duly noted in his volume on Marquesan art. Von den Steinen was unfortunately prevented from photographing it by the superstitious fear of his native guide.

Again Heyerdahl claims discovery of the large fort of Morongo Uta on Rapa Iti.[13] This site was mapped and well studied by J. G. Stokes of the Bernice Bishop Museum in the 1920's, but the report was never published. No attempt was ever made by the museum officials to hide the fact that Stokes worked there.

The general picture of Easter Island prehistory imparted in *Aku-Aku* is that the islands were first settled by Peruvian Indians and later invaded by Polynesians (who were in actuality Northwest Coast Indians) at the very end of the prehistoric period. Borrowing from an old Easter Island legend of warfare between two factions who were called, respectively, the Long Ears and the Short Ears, Heyerdahl identifies the Long Ears as the Peruvians and the Short Ears as Polynesians. He shows a few pictures of supposedly pure Long Ears still living on Easter Island—who, I might add, are remarkably Caucasoid in appearance. He attributes this to the fact that the Peruvian conquerors were not really Indians after all, but white men with red hair. (Is there a Nordic hypothesis hidden here?) The fact that no prehistoric Caucasoid population is evident in Peru anywhere is of course immaterial to the theory. The sudden appearance of white men in the Heyerdahl theory is most confusing, as Heyerdahl has tried so desperately to show that Polynesian blood is similar to American Indian blood in type distributions. What racial relationships do these whites have to the Indians, then? Do they possess the same blood types as the Indians? If so, then blood type and physical phenotype certainly do not go together, which contradicts his theory.

The date of settlement of Easter Island is set at A.D. 380 by a radiocarbon date of completely unspecified context, already discussed above. The culture of the Peruvian settlers is, according to Heyerdahl, that of the epoch known to South American archaeologists as the Tiahuanaco period. The Tiahuanaco culture, however, arose in the highlands of Bolivia (near Lake Titicaca) at approximately A.D. 750; thus the Peruvians arriving at Easter Island brought the Tiahuanaco culture some 400 years before it even existed, a great feat even for the fabulous Peruvians! What is even more astonishing, however, is the fact that these Peruvians brought with them the technique of building fitted masonry walls which did not appear in Peru until even later, in approximately A.D. 1500.

Although possessing this remarkably developed (and absolutely anachronistic) stone-working technique, the Tiahuanaco discoverers of Easter Island were strangely lacking in all things typically Tiahuanaco. The Tiahuanaco period is characterized by an abundance of beautiful pottery bearing elaborately painted decorations of felines, anthropomorphic deities, and buzzards. No pottery was found on Easter Island, however. On the Tiahuanaco site itself in Bolivia are the ruins of large buildings and several large statues. There is no resemblance whatsoever between the Easter Island statues, portraying nearly naked human beings, and those of Tiahuanaco, representing anthropomorphic cat-fanged beings heavily clothed in elaborate raiment. The statues of Easter and Tia-

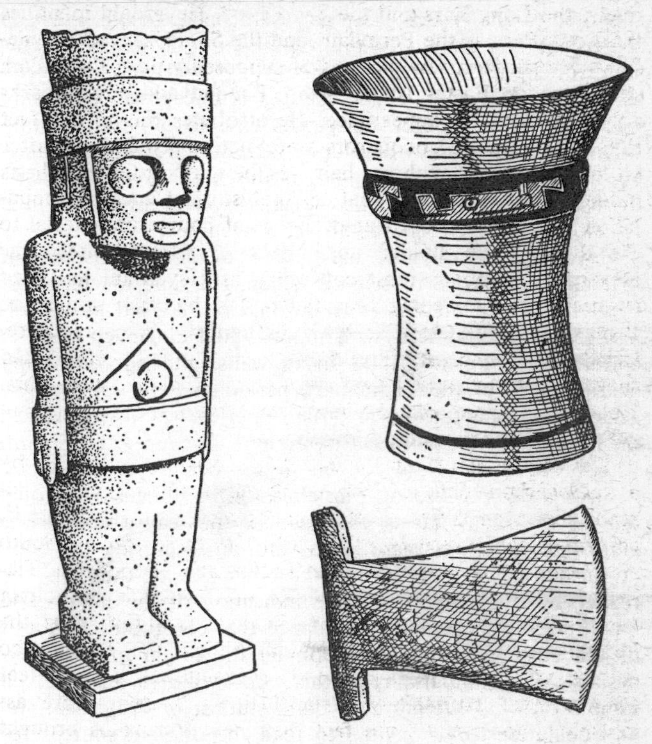

Fig. 17. Tiahuanaco figure, pot and axe (Courtesy of American Museum of Natural History, New York)

huanaco are both of stone, however, but surely this is not very significant.

As to the buildings of Tiahuanaco, they do not resemble in the least the Easter Island *ahu,* which are puny by comparison with the immense rectangular Akapana by Lake Titicaca and its huge, neatly carved monoliths held together with poured copper cleats.

Further characteristics of the Tiahuanaco culture are its beautifully woven fabrics produced from a variety of plants with many techniques. No such things have ever been found on Easter Island.

The migration which carried this paradoxically non-Tiahuanaco group of Tiahuanaco Indians to Easter Island was supposedly led by the great god Viracocha, to whose name Heyerdahl has obligingly prefixed the title Kon-Tiki. Actually, worship of Viracocha, a creator high-god, may date back as far as A.D. 750 in Peru, but this is uncertain. Viracocha was apparently an Inca deity who rose to importance only when the Inca empire developed after A.D. 1500,[14] and may even be a tribal deity limited to the Inca alone. Certainly there is no evidence that he was a real man, any more than Apollo or Zeus is believed to have been real.

Heyerdahl's Peruvians must have availed themselves of that classical device of science fiction, the time machine, for they showed up off Easter Island in A.D. 380, led by a post-A.D. 750 Incan god-hero, with an A.D. 750 Tiahuanaco material culture featuring A.D. 1500 Incan walls, and not one thing characteristic of the Tiahuanaco period in Peru and Bolivia. This is equivalent to saying that America was discovered in the last days of the Roman Empire by King Henry the Eighth, who brought the Ford Falcon to the benighted aborigines.

Such a nimble use of Einstein's fourth dimension is only one of the many facets of *Aku-Aku* that cause concern to anthropologists, but there is no value in discussing the book at further length here. As to the other side of the coin, the reader by this point has some indication of the nature and amplitude of the scientific evidence that constitutes the basis of the current scientific opinion on the origin of the Polynesians. The bibliography of this work will give only a small sample of what literature awaits a student of Polynesia, and anyone interested is invited to read the original sources for himself.

In conclusion, the *Kon-Tiki* theory is seen as a *revenant* from the past, clothed in a more attractive shroud. Its basis is mainly the success of a modern raft voyage that could not even hope to prove anything concerning ancient Peruvian navigation. The meager scientific evidence for the theory is weak, even in the few instances where it is completely acceptable. Otherwise, the similarities which are purported to show Polynesian-Peruvian relationships are completely equivocal. The *Kon-Tiki* theory is about as plausible as the tales of Atlantis, Mu, and "Children of the Sun." Like most such theories it makes exciting light reading, but as an example of scientific method it fares quite poorly.

17

In Retrospect

In the course of this book a wide variety of sources have been evaluated for the evidence that they contribute on the problems of the origin and prehistory of the Polynesians. The information derived from these sources has been discussed and interpreted to provide a broad view of the topic. Two tasks remain: a summarization of the high points of Polynesian prehistory and a discussion of some of the problems in that field that are still awaiting illumination and solution.

The data of linguistics, physical anthropology, ethnology, archaeology, botany, and zoology have all unanimously pointed toward the South China and Indochina coastal regions as the place of origin of the ethnic stock from which the Polynesians as we know them today ultimately diverged. In this area, during the third millennium B.C., a population developed from components of earlier Caucasoid, Negroid, and Mongoloid races. The language or languages that this group spoke were related to the Malayo-Polynesian language family. They had a Neolithic subsistence pattern of root-crop agriculture and stock raising, but also depended on the sea to a large extent for food. They were consequently excellent seafarers. The Malayo-Polynesians were on a definitely lower level of cultural development than the complex late Neolithic proto-Bronze Age societies which were arising contemporaneously in the Huang Ho delta in northern China. In 1800 B.C., when the Chinese empire crystallized in the Huang Ho Shang Bronze Age culture and began to expand in all directions at the expense of neighboring social groups, a chain reaction was touched off; populations disturbed by this expansion were forced to move into other areas already occupied, or accept as the alternative absorption into the Chinese state. The comparatively weaker and poorly organized aboriginal groups of the South China coast were affected by these events as northern refugees began to penetrate into their area. As a result they too began to move from their village sites, taking to the sea to find a home on the offshore islands or move down the coast a few miles. Gradually, in this fashion, the Malayo-Polynesians passed from the mainland of Asia, probing deeper into the Pacific that always lay before them like a multidirectional road to anywhere. The archaeological records of the islands of the western Pacific indicate that the main route followed by the Malayo-Polynesians was through the Philippine Islands and then south into Melanesia and Papua.

Distinctive Polynesian types of artifacts, such as tanged and stepped adzes, tapa-cloth beaters, and fighting clubs, permit us at least to trace this route in general terms although precision is impossible in the current state of archaeological knowledge.

By A.D. 1000 at a minimum, the Melanesian islands of Fiji and New Caledonia, on the fringe of the Polynesian triangle, were occupied by Malayo-Polynesians. Possibly by 750 B.C., the inhabitants of Fiji had explored the sea to the east and discovered the islands known today as the Tongan and Samoan groups. These islands were subsequently occupied, and it is at this point that the ancestors of the modern Polynesians branched from their parent stock, which was of course already considerably ramified as a result of the continual movements through the islands of the western Pacific.

The settlers of Western Polynesia did not remain long in their new-found homes, however, as restless splinter groups soon began to search in the sunrise for lands farther to the east, discovering some of the islands of Eastern Polynesia. The Marquesas were settled by the second century B.C. and Tahiti was undoubtedly settled by approximately the same date, if not somewhat earlier. From these two major "seedings" within the eastern half of the Polynesian triangle, the occupation of the other islands in that area was accomplished. The population of the Marquesas grew rapidly, and soon the canoes were heading off again into the unknown, carrying

Marquesan explorers to settle Easter Island, Mangareva, and the eastern islands of the Tuamotu Archipelago.

Colonization parties crossed the 2,200-mile stretch of open sea between Tahiti and Hawaii by A.D. 100. Others reached New Zealand, far to the southwest, at the end of the first millennium after Christ, while still others discovered the Austral Islands and settled the western Tuamotu Archipelago. This process of island jumping along the major archipelagoes of Eastern Polynesia was probably still going on when the Europeans sailed into the Pacific from the west coast of South America in the sixteenth century.

In this fashion, the Polynesians managed to occupy all the habitable islands of the Polynesian triangle and visit those that could not support human life. Perhaps the most remarkable thing about the entire migration is the relative speed with which it took place, despite the fact that the Polynesians were obviously not particularly interested in making a quick crossing. Between approximately 1800 and 200 B.C. the greatest part of the Pacific had been spanned by the swift-sailing double canoes, while the contemporary cultures of the Mediterranean and Near East were still regarding as major undertakings their relatively short voyages along the coasts of the Mediterranean and the Indian Ocean.

The island societies which were established during the course of this great series of migrations display some interesting similarities in terms of cultural development. The islands were generally occupied by sizable, well-equipped expeditions, so the archaeological record reveals. In some instances, such expeditions were apparently undertaken by tribes who had been beaten in war and forced to flee or face annihilation at the hands of their enemies. Once the colonies were established, population growth appears to have been generally quite rapid (thus enhancing the possibilities of human microevolution and the consequent development of regional physical variations between various populations). A striking feature of the archaeological record is the close adaptation to local environmental differences that each society displayed. Through the basic Polynesian technology the cultures were closely linked to the environment, small environmental differences in resource distribution often producing very marked differences in population distribution and sociopolitical organization. Warfare apparently was always an important factor in Polynesian culture, but it came to play an even more important role on the various islands of Polynesia as populations expanded, approaching the limits of the technology to support the burden in the given environment.

Where conditions permitted the creation of a surplus of subsistence production, it was utilized by the upper classes for self-aggrandizement. In Eastern Polynesia, at least, such glorification found expression, in part, in the construction of elaborate monumental religious structures and sculpture in wood and stone, commissioned by chiefs and dedicated to familial or tribal deities. The tendency toward extreme elaboration of the entire religious complex in Polynesia is also very noteworthy.

Having reviewed, perhaps all too briefly, the course of Polynesian prehistory, let us now pass to the subject of future work. Some of the problem areas may have already been touched upon in a cursory fashion at one point or another throughout the book. Others, however, have not been introduced up to this point.

It is obvious that the main obstacles blocking the route to a more complete and reliable reconstruction of Polynesian prehistory are the lacunae in the archaeological record within Polynesia, in the islands of the western Pacific, and on the coast of Asia. Perhaps it is far too much to hope for that we shall ultimately be able to be as specific about Polynesian prehistory as the archaeologists who specialize in the American Southwest can presently be about their chosen area, but there is much room for a compromise between the extremes of reconstructions as detailed as the Southwestern stratigraphic sequences and the present state of many large islands of the western Pacific where no excavations have ever been carried out. What is needed, then, is an extensive archaeological program beginning in the Polynesian triangle itself and working back across the Pacific toward Asia. This archaeological program should feature stratigraphic excavations which should by no means be confined to habitation sites alone. Although the lure of a rich midden heap is often too much to resist, the archaeologist must also devote much attention to any architectural remains that are present, such as temple complexes, dance plazas, or just large house platforms. All cultural remains should be subjected to a rigorous analysis to determine precisely which kinds of artifacts are of the most utility in the construction of archaeological sequences. It is not enough for an archaeologist to choose to devote the majority of his attention to stone adzes, for instance, or statues alone, when we need information on all phases of Polynesian archaeological cultures. The history of each artifact type should be traced as precisely as possible; house structures should be carefully excavated and studied and architectural sequences developed. Settlement patterns deserve close attention. Analyses of midden trash should be carried on with the study of the architectural remains, as a detailed knowledge of native diet often illuminates important factors of cultural evolution.

Within the Polynesian triangle one of our most pressing needs is for detailed knowledge of the archaeology of the Society Islands. This particular need will be soon remedied by a Bishop Museum Expedition under the leadership of K. P. Emory, which arrived in Tahiti in April of 1960 to begin an extended program of excavations. Perhaps equal in importance to the need for knowledge of the Society Islands prehistory is the necessity for continuing and extending the stratigraphic program begun by Golson in the Samoan and Tongan groups of Western Polynesia. Such excavations should be paralleled by further work in Fiji, especially in the Lau Island group of that archipelago through which the Western Polynesian islands were inhabited.

The Tahitian, Western Polynesian, and Fijian data are, as noted, most needed. On lower levels of importance there are many more islands about which relatively little is known archaeologically. It would obviously be most desirable if we could excavate on every island of Polynesia, but that is patently out of the question; therefore some restriction and direction of effort are indicated so that duplication of effort and dissipation of scarce funds for research are prevented. Along these lines it would probably be most economical to turn our attention next toward the Cook Islands, especially Rarotonga, after we have further knowledge of the Societies, Western Polynesia, and Fiji. Other islands where excavation might also handsomely repay the effort are Mangareva, Raïvavaé, and Mangaia.

From Polynesia and adjacent Melanesia we should then ideally move farther westward to Papua, Indonesia, and the Philippines, ultimately arriving on the coast of Asia with the entire sequence of Malayo-Polynesian migrations worked out in some detail.

The territory to be covered in this area is tremendous, however, and the archaeological resources of much of that territory are still completely unknown. In all of New Guinea, for example, the archaeological excavations to date might be counted off on the fingers of one hand. It will therefore be many years before a suitable knowledge of the archaeology of the Papuan Islands can be acquired as a basis for further detailed work on specific problems. The number of archaeological subcultures to be found in the large archipelagoes of the western Pacific are likely to prove confusing and resist any sort of synthesis for some time after initial excavations are begun. Although the Philippines and Indonesia are relatively well known by comparison to Papua, there are still many regions of both archipelagoes that have yet to be explored to permit even a preliminary assessment of archaeological potentialities.

Let us return for the moment to Polynesia, however, and enumerate some of the benefits that would derive from a program of excavations such as has been suggested here. Armed with large collections of well-documented archaeological material from the major islands of Eastern and Western Polynesia, we can begin to trace the ebb and flow of cultural evolution within Polynesia. We know that all the Polynesian societies are ultimately traceable to a single group or at least a small number of groups who settled in Western Polynesia. We presume with reason that their culture was uniform. From this basic cultural complex arose all the regional varieties of Polynesian tools, ornaments, houses, canoes, etc., that were in use when the Europeans discovered Polynesia. Once we are able precisely to state in detail what the basic Polynesian cultural complex was like and possess in addition the intervening steps of cultural development between that and the historic period cultures of Polynesia, we will be able to trace the relative rates of change of various aspects of material culture and the frequency of original technological inventions. As the environmental matrix of each of these cultures is well known, we will further be able to specify the kinds of interaction that took place between material culture and environment. From this analysis of cultural evolution and differentiation we may be able to formulate general laws of cultural evolution and its causation that will be applicable to all cultures regardless of location.

Detailed studies of the artifact inventories of the various archaeological cultures of Polynesia will also enable us to detect cases of contact between separate island cultures, if such occurred. We are currently at a loss for an explanation when an unusual artifact appears in a Polynesian archaeological site on Island "X," let us say. Often, we can say "such and such is also found in Tahiti," but if the item is rare in its Tahitian appearances we still do not know whether it originated in Tahiti or whether its appearance both there and in Island X is a result of trade with another island, "Y," which is still unknown.

A particularly interesting problem, possibly involving cultural contact on a large scale, is that of the stone structures of Eastern Polynesia. First, of course, one must trace the Western Polynesian antecedents of these stone temples and house platforms and attempt to explain in some fashion why they reached such a level of formal elaboration in Eastern Polynesia. It is also necessary to explain why such structures appear at roughly the same time throughout Eastern Polynesia. Was there a great amount of inter-island contact or is it necessary to invoke some hypothetical and highly improbable basic urge to pile stones? Another alternative might be that the parallel development of stone structures is an example of regional variations of the same culture reacting in a similar fashion to a similar set of socioenvironmental stimuli.

In the field of ethnology much remains to be done, despite the fact that almost all of the Polynesian cultures now existing have undergone fairly heavy acculturation. The tasks now at hand are mainly of a research variety, although there is little doubt that field work among modern Polynesians will still turn up interesting new material. The ethnologist can contribute his knowledge of the functioning of historic and ethnographic native cultures to the study of cultural change and stability that was suggested above. Much also remains to be done in a re-evaluation of presently existing data in terms of recent theoretical formulations concerning, for example, the role of subsistence and surplus in cultural evolution and the development of features of political organization.

An especially interesting field open to ethnologists is that of the systematic study of Polynesian legends. The wealth of texts available is simply crying for depth studies based on sound methodological principles of historic document evaluation and criticism. Comparative studies of the totality of available traditions would permit the reconstruction of a Paleo-Polynesian mythology, thereby enabling us to note which traditions are local developments and which are merely very ancient themes re-elaborated in local terms. It might be possible, for instance, to even isolate a set of myths peculiar to specific areas of Polynesia alone.

A related area which is practically virgin territory is that of stylistic and formal analyses of Polynesian oral literature. What, for instance, are the principles of construction of a creation chant? What kind of meter and foot are used? Do creation chants throughout all of Polynesia follow a set pattern or a series of patterns? How are these patterns distributed? Coupled with this problem, and reaching into the realm of the linguist, are studies of word frequency, phrase structure, etc. Although all of the possibilities for research in the field of traditions involve library work of a humdrum nature, they definitely would yield a large dividend, as armed with such analytical data it would be possible to establish stringent criteria for the acceptability of Polynesian legends on their own terms rather than on the basis of some poorly formulated set of criteria which may be colored by personal bias. It would then probably be possible to exclude from consideration a number of currently accepted traditions, thus narrowing the field of choice for those who seek support for theories of a more far-reaching nature.

In the field of linguistics much remains to be done on historical problems. There is a need for refinement of glottochronological techniques for application to Polynesian languages. First, a number of field studies should be done on modern Polynesian languages to establish the phonetic systems in objective, modern terms, thus replacing the utilitarian but nonscientific standard orthographies. Comparisons of sound systems up to the present consist of little more than a comparison of letters of the old standard orthographies. This obviously leaves much to be desired. There is a further reason for studies of modern languages, namely the compilation of standard-usage vocabularies. In glottochronological work it is necessary to know modern usage for calculation of intercorrelations of core vocabularies of the languages involved. For many Polynesian languages standard usage is not available, and the researcher is forced to consult a dictionary where there may be as many as five or ten synonyms for the same word. Which word does one select? Depending on the arbitrary choice, the intercorrelations may be larger or smaller than is actually the case. Standard-usage vocabularies would obviate such a disturbing choice and introduce more reliability into the calculations upon which age determinations of dialect divergence are based. Glottochronology would further profit by improved controls for dating of relatively recent dialect divergences. Originally intended for dating linguistic ramifications of a much more ancient order than that of some of the Polynesian dialects, glottochronological techniques may lack accuracy in situations without great time depth. Perhaps revisions of core vocabulary lists are in order, or perhaps a rigorous testing of currently used formulas by advanced statistical methods.

An intriguing problem is posed by the Easter Island script. With a basis now firmly established upon which further work may build, decipherment of the entire corpus is only retarded by lack of funds. There are a number of avenues of approach: statistical analyses of the script frequencies; analyses of other Polynesian traditional evidence, as described above, to form a basis for the prediction of possible word combinations and frequencies; and comparison with other Asian script systems.

In physical anthropology the problems are no less broad and absorbing. The racial history of the Polynesians should be known in much greater detail. The Polynesians entered the Polynesian triangle with a large but definitely finite number of possibilities in their genetic pool. The first migrants to leave this group removed some possibilities from the gene pool. With each successive occupation of each additional island, random or non-random samples were withdrawn from the original population or the subpopulations which had themselves previously diverged from the settlers of Polynesia. By microevolution occurring within the genetic parameters of each of these splinter groups, the modern Polynesian physical variations arose. We need amplification of our data at every step along the route of Polynesian racial development in the form of representative skeletal collections made from precisely defined archaeological contexts in the major island groups of Polynesia. We can trace then the relative rates of change of the multitudinous physical characteristics. An interesting part of such a study would be blood serology work on ancient human skeletal material. As blood types can be determined by various biochemical tests on archaeological Polynesian bone samples, we could trace the process of differentiation through which the Eastern Polynesians developed their modern frequencies.

With this discussion of some of the major problems of Polynesian prehistory that are still awaiting solution, we terminate our exploration of the Polynesian past. Such an ending is altogether fitting, however, for although science has advanced our knowledge of this subject by a tremendous increment since the days of William Ellis and Abraham Fornander, there is still much to be done, and it is therefore best to close facing the tasks of the future, rather than contemplating the accomplishments of the past. That which remains is fully as demanding as that which has already been done, and it is certain that in the course of future research additional, presently unforeseen, problems of an even more stimulating nature than those now recognized will arise to tax the abilities of the anthropologist. The answers to some questions, of course, may be irretrievably lost in the mists of the past, but many other problems will ultimately yield to the attack of science. Let us hope that there are many individuals who will prove equal to the challenge of the future, and will pursue the long-erased tracks of the Polynesians on the beaches of Asia and the islands of the Pacific to further exciting and important discoveries.

Bibliography and Notes

Chapter 2

1. J. E. Hoffmeister, "Geology of Eua, Tonga," *Bernice P. Bishop Museum Bulletin 96,* Honolulu, 1932; P. Marshall, "Geology at Rarotonga and Atiu," *B. P. Bishop Museum Bulletin 72,* Honolulu, 1930; J. H. Stark and A. L. Howland, "Geology of Borabora, Society Island," *B. P. Bishop Museum Bulletin 169,* Honolulu, 1941; H. Williams, "Geology of Tahiti, Mooréa and Maiao," *B. P. Bishop Museum Bulletin 105,* Honolulu, 1933; L. J. Chubb, "The Geology of the Marquesas," *B. P. Bishop Museum Bulletin 68,* Honolulu, 1930; J. M. Obelianne, "Contribution à l'étude géologique des îles de l'Océanie Française," *Sciences de la Terre,* Vol. 3, Nancy, 1955.
2. N. Newell, "Questions of the Coral Reefs," *Natural History,* Vol. LXVIII, No. 3, March, 1959, pp. 120-28.
3. R. Carson, *The Sea Around Us,* New York, Oxford University Press, 1951; New York, New American Library (Mentor Books), 1954, p. 76.
4. E. D. Merrill, *Plant Life of the Pacific,* Washington, D.C., 1945, Ch. 12; S. Ekman, *Zoogeography of the Sea,* London, Sidgwick & Jackson, 1953, pp. 18, 72; and L. G. Hertlein and W. K. Emerson, "Mollusks from Clipperton Island," *Transactions of the San Diego Society for Natural History,* Vol. 11, 1953.
5. E. D. Merrill, "The Botany of Cook's Voyages," *Chronica Botanica,* Vol. 14, Nos. 5/6, 1954, p. 191.
6. *Ibid.,* pp. 171, 321.
7. K. Skottsberg in *The Natural History of Juan Fernandez and Easter Island,* Vol. 1, Series 20-56, 1920, p. 18.
8. E. D. Merrill, "Merrilleana," *Chronica Botanica,* Vol. 10, Nos. 3/4, 1946, p. 338.
9. R. Spier, "Some Notes on the Origin of Taro," *Southwestern Journal of Anthropology,* Vol. 7, 1951.
10. Li Chi, *et al.,* "Ch'eng-Tzu-Yai: The Black Pottery Culture Site at Lung-Shan-Chen in Li-Ch'eng-Hsien, Shantung Prov-

ince," *Yale University Publications in Anthropology,* No. 52, 1956, p. 152; W. Fairservis, *The Origins of Oriental Civilization,* New York, New American Library (Mentor Books), 1959, pp. 89, 99-100.

11. S. C. Ball, "Jungle Fowls from the Pacific Islands," *B. P. Bishop Museum Bulletin 108,* Honolulu, 1933.
12. T. D. Carter, J. E. Hill, and G. H. H. Tate, *Mammals of the Pacific World,* New York, The Macmillan Company, 1946, pp. 114-15.

Chapter 3

1. E. A. Hooton, *Up from the Ape,* New York, The Macmillan Company, 1946, pp. 616-18.
2. R. T. Simmons and J. J. Graydon, "A Blood Group Genetical Survey in Eastern and Central Polynesia," *American Journal of Physical Anthropology,* Vol. 15, No. 3, 1957.
3. T. Heyerdahl, *American Indians in the South Pacific,* London, George Allen and Unwin, Ltd., 1950.
4. Hooton, *op. cit.,* p. 557, Table 9.
5. C. Coon, S. Garn, and J. Birdsell, *Races,* Springfield, Ill., C C Thomas, 1950, p. 48.
6. J. Birdsell, *Papers on the Physical Anthropology of the American Indian,* New York, The Viking Fund, Inc., 1951, pp. 1-20,
7. Hooton, *op. cit.,* pp. 617-18.
8. *Ibid.,* p. 621.
9. H. Mansuy and M. Colani, "Néolithique inférieur (Bacsonien) et Néolithique Supérier dans le Haut Tonkin," *Memoirs du Service Géologique de l'Indochine,* Vol. XII, Fasc. 3, Hanoi, 1925; E. Patte, "Le Kjökkenmödding Néolithique de Bau Tro A Tau Toa près de Dong-Hoi (Annam)," *Bulletin du Service Géologique de l'Indochine,* Vol. XIV, Hanoi, 1925.
10. H. L. Shapiro, "The Physical Anthropology of the Maori-Moriori," *Journal of the Polynesian Society,* Vol. 49, No. 1, 1940, p. 10.
11. Coon, Garn, and Birdsell, *loc. cit.;* Birdsell, *op. cit.,* pp. 15-16.
12. D. Black, "A Study of Kansu and Honan Aeneolithic Skulls," *Palaeontologica Sinica,* Series D, Vol. VI, Fasc. 1, Peiping, 1928, p. 81.
13. H. L. Shapiro, "Physical Differentiation in Polynesia," *Papers of the Peabody Museum,* Harvard University, Vol. 20, 1940, p. 3.
14. *Ibid.*
15. H. L. Shapiro, "The Physical Relationships of the Easter Islanders," *B. P. Bishop Museum Bulletin 160,* Honolulu, 1940, p. 29.

16. H. L. Shapiro, "The Anthropometry of Puka Puka," *Anthropological Papers of the American Museum of Natural History,* Vol. XXXVIII, Part III, 1942.
17. L. Sullivan, "Marquesan Somatology," *B. P. Bishop Museum Memoirs,* Vol. 9, No. 2, Honolulu, 1923.
18. A. Montagu, *Introduction to Physical Anthropology,* Springfield, Ill., C C Thomas, 1951, p. 282.

Chapter 4

1. History of Polynesian language studies after: G. Grace, "The Position of the Polynesian Languages within the Austronesian (Malayo-Polynesian) Language Family," *International Journal of American Linguistics,* Memoir 16, Bloomington, Ind., 1959, Ch. I; O. Dempwolff, "Vergleichende Lautlehre des austronesischen Wortschatzes," *Zeitschrift für Eingeborenen Sprachen,* Beihefte 15, 17, 19, 1934-38.
2. I. Dyen, *Proto-Malayo-Polynesian Laryngeals,* Baltimore, Johns Hopkins University Press, 1953.
3. P. K. Benedict, "Thai Kadai and Indonesian: A New Alignment in Southeast Asia," *American Anthropologist,* Vol. 44, 1942.
4. S. H. Elbert, "Internal Relationship of the Polynesian Languages and Dialects," *Southwestern Journal of Anthropology,* Vol. 9, 1953.
5. M. Swadesh, "Lexico Statistic Dating of Prehistoric Ethnic Contacts," *American Philosophical Society Proceedings,* Vol. 96, 1952.
6. Grace, *op. cit.*
7. Elbert, *op. cit.*
8. Grace, *op. cit.*
9. T. Barthel, "Grundlagen zur Entzifferung der Osterinselschrift," *Abhandlung aus dem Gebiete der Auslandskunde,* Vol. 64, Reihe B., Hamburg, 1958.
10. E. S. C. Handy, "Marquesan Legends," *B. P. Bishop Museum Bulletin 69,* Honolulu, 1930, p. 30; T. Henry, "Tahiti aux Temps Anciens," *Publications de la Société des Oceanistes,* No. 1, Paris, 1951, pp. 196-97.

Chapter 5

1. W. Ellis, *Polynesian Researches,* 4 vols., London, 1836.
2. A. Fornander, *An Account of the Polynesian Race,* 2 vols., London, 1880.
3. C. P. Smith, *Hawaiki, the Original Home of the Maori,* 2nd ed., New Plymouth, New Zealand, 1904.
4. E. Tregear, *The Maori Race,* Wanganui, New Zealand, 1926.

5. E. S. C. Handy, "Polynesian Religion," *B. P. Bishop Museum Bulletin 34,* Honolulu, 1927; "History and Culture in the Society Islands," *B. P. Bishop Museum Bulletin 79,* Honolulu, 1930.
6. R. Duff, *The Moa Hunter Period of Maori Culture,* Wellington, New Zealand, 1950, Ch. 9.
7. K. von den Steinen, "Marquesanische Mythen," *Zeitschrift für Ethnologie,* Vol. 65, pp. 1-44, 326-73.
8. K. von den Steinen, *Die Marquesaner und ihre Kunst,* 3 volumes, Vol. 3, Berlin, 1928, p. 64.
9. A. Krämer, *Die Samoa Inseln,* 2 volumes, Vol. 3, Stuttgart, 1902, p. 465.
10. D. Porter, *Journal of a Cruise Made to the Pacific Ocean by Capt. D. Porter in the Years 1812, 13, 14,* Philadelphia, 1832.
11. Père M. Gracia, *Lettres sur les îles Marquises,* Paris, 1843, p. 17.
12. F. W. Christian, "Notes on the Marquesas," *Journal of the Polynesian Society,* Vol. 4, 1895, p. 194.
13. F. Gräbner, "Die Melanesische Bogenkultur und ihre Verwandten," *Anthropos,* Vol. IV, 1909.
14. R. Linton, "The Material Culture of the Marquesas Islands," *B. P. Bishop Museum Memoirs,* Vol. 8, No. 5, Honolulu, 1923.
15. E. G. Burrows, "Western Polynesia," *Ethnological Studies,* Gothenburg Ethnographical Museum, Sweden, 1938.

Chapter 6

1. W. Fairservis, *The Origins of Oriental Civilization,* New York, New American Library (Mentor Books), 1959, pp. 89-102; L. Ward, "The Relative Chronology of China through the Han Period," *Relative Chronologies in Old World Archaeology,* ed. by R. W. Ehrich, University of Chicago Press, 1954, pp. 131-38; and Kwang-Chih Chang, "China, Far East: Area 17," No. 1, 1959, *Council for Old World Archaeology Survey,* Cambridge, Mass., 1959, pp. 1-11.
2. Li Chi, *et al.,* "Ch'eng-Tzu-Yai: The Black Pottery Culture Site at Lung-Shan-Chen in Li-Cheng Hsien, Shantung Province," *Yale University Publications in Anthropology,* No. 52, 1956.
3. Kwang-Chih Chang, "A Brief Survey of the Archæology of Formosa," *Southwestern Journal of Anthropology,* Vol. 12, No. 4, 1956.
4. D. J. Finn, "Archæological Finds on Lamma Island near Hongkong," Pts. 1-13, *The Hong Naturalist,* 1932-36.

by Capt. D. Porter in the Years 1812, 13, 14, Philadelphia, 1832.

5. B. Danielsson, *Work and Life on Raroia,* London, George Allen and Unwin, Ltd., 1956, pp. 49-50.
6. Handy, *op. cit.,* p. 157.
7. Malo, *op. cit.,* Fig. 4.
8. Porter, *op. cit.,* p. 259.
9. Handy, *op. cit.,* p. 157.
10. A. Krämer, *Die Samoa Inseln,* 2 volumes, Vol. I, Stuttgart, 1902, pp. 259-60 t. 97.
11. Danielsson, *op. cit.;* and Porter, *op. cit.,* pp. 72-74.
12. E. S. C. Handy, "Marquesan Legends," *B. P. Bishop Museum Bulletin 69,* Honolulu, 1930, p. 130.
13. H. D. Skinner, "The Morioris of the Chatham Islands," *B. P. Bishop Museum Memoirs,* Vol. 9, No. 1, 1923.
14. H. Laval, *Mangareva: L'Histoire Ancienne d'un Peuple Polynésien,* Braine-le-Comte, Belgium, Maison des Pères de Sacrés Coeurs, 1938, p. 246.
15. Handy, *op. cit.,* 1923, p. 137.
16. Dennis Wing-son-lou, "Rain Worship Among the Ancient Chinese and the Nahua-Maya Indians," *Bulletin, Institute of Ethnology, Academica Sinica,* No. 4, Autumn 1957, pp. 93-94.
17. Krämer, *loc. cit.*
18. R. M. Wheeler, *Rome Beyond the Imperial Frontiers,* Harmondsworth, England, Penguin Books, Ltd., 1955, Ch. 14.
19. K. P. Emory, personal communication.
20. A. Sharp, *Ancient Voyagers in the Pacific,* Harmondsworth, England, Penguin Books, Ltd., 1957.
21. *Ibid.,* p. 30.
22. K. Luomala, Review of *Ancient Voyagers in the South Pacific,* by A. Sharp, *American Anthropologist,* Vol. 60, No. 4, 1958, p. 776.
23. Sharp, *op. cit.*
24. T. Henry, "Tahiti aux Temps Anciens," *Publications de la Société des Océanistes,* No. 1, Paris, 1951, pp. 413, 483, 547, 581; Malo, *op. cit.,* p. 6; Laval, *op. cit.,* pp. 53, 348-49; and Handy, *op. cit.,* 1923, pp. 10-12; *op. cit.,* 1930, pp. 127, 130.
25. J. Cook, *The Voyage of the Endeavour, 1768-1771,* Vol. 1 of *Journals of His Voyages of Discovery,* ed. by J. C. Beaglehole, London, Cambridge University Press, 1955, p. 147, n. 3.
26. R. E. Bell, "New Zealand," *Asian Perspectives,* Vol. II, No. 1, 1958, p. 91.
27. A. Métraux, "The Ethnology of Easter Island," *B. P. Bishop Museum Bulletin 160,* Honolulu, 1940; and T. Bar-

thel, "Grundlagen zur Entzifferung der Osterinselschrift," *Abhandlung aus dem Gebiete der Auslandskunde,* Vol. 64, R. B., Hamburg, 1958.

Chapter 8

1. A. Thompson, "Earth Mounds in Samoa," *Journal of the Polynesian Society,* Vol. 36, 1927; and D. Freeman, "The Vailele Earth Mounds, O le Fale o le Fe'e and the Fale Mauga," *Journal of the Polynesian Society,* Vol. 53, 1944. For the data on recent work in Samoa and Tonga, I am indebted to Mr. J. Golson, of the University of Auckland, for the use of his "Report to Tri-Institutional Pacific Program on Archaeological Field Work in Tonga and Samoa."
2. W. C. McKern, "Archæology of Tonga," *B. P. Bishop Museum Bulletin 60,* Honolulu, 1929.
3. E. W. Gifford, "Archaeological Excavations in Fiji," *University of California Anthropological Records,* 13:3, 1951, Fig. 1A; E. W. Gifford and Dick Shutler, Jr., "Archaeological Excavations in New Caledonia," *University of California Anthropological Records,* 18:1, 1956, p. 65, Pl. 8-h; and F. Sarasin, *Ethnologie der Neu Caledonier und Loyalty Insulaner,* Munich, C. W. Kreidels Verlag, 1929, p. 104, t. 50, Fig. 11.
4. P. Buck, "Samoan Material Culture," *B. P. Bishop Museum Bulletin 75,* Honolulu, 1930, Pl. IV-C.
5. Gifford, *op. cit.,* p. 208; and Gifford and Shutler, *op. cit., Bulletin 75,* Honolulu, 1930, Pl. IV-C.
6. A. Krämer, *Die Samoa Inseln,* 2 volumes., Vol. 1, Stuttgart, 1902, p. 337, Bilder 136-37.
7. R. Duff, *The Moa Hunter Period of Maori Culture,* Wellington, New Zealand, 1950, pp. 162-71; and Buck, *op. cit.,* pp. 330-47.
8. McKern, *op. cit.,* pp. 5-7, 63-66.
9. *Ibid.,* pp. 74-75.
10. *Ibid.,* pp. 80-82.
11. *Ibid.,* pp. 63-66.
12. M. Sahlins, *Social Stratification in Polynesia,* Seattle, American Ethnological Society, 1958, pp. 22-37.
13. McKern, *op. cit.,* pp. 74-75.
14. *Ibid.,* pp. 80-82.
15. *Ibid.,* p. 121.
16. Gifford, *op. cit.,* pp. 235-37; and Gifford and Shutler, *op. cit.,* pp. 93-95.
17. Sahlins, *op. cit.,* pp. 201, 216, 241, 245.
18. J. Cook, *The Voyage of the Endeavour, 1768-1771,* Vol. 1 of *Journals of His Voyages of Discovery,* ed. by J. C. Beagle-

hole, London, Cambridge University Press, 1955; and W. Mariner, *An Account of the Tongan Islands in the South Pacific Ocean,* 2 vols., Edinburgh, 1827.

19. Krämer, *op. cit.;* E. W. Gifford, "Tongan Society," *B. P. Bishop Museum Bulletin 61,* Honolulu, 1929; and M. Mead, "The Social Organization of Manua," *B. P. Bishop Museum Bulletin 60,* Honolulu, 1929.
20. Sahlins, *op. cit.,* pp. 181-217.
21. Mead, *op. cit.;* and Sahlins, *op. cit.,* pp. 29-37.

Chapter 9

1. Prof. Dr. T. Barthel, personal communication.
2. B. Danielsson, *Work and Life on Raroia,* London, George Allen and Unwin, Ltd., 1956.
3. K. P. Emory, "The Archaeology of the Pacific Equatorial Islands," *B. P. Bishop Museum Bulletin 123,* Honolulu, 1934.
4. K. von den Steinen, *Die Marquesaner und ihre Kunst,* 3 volumes, Berlin, Vol. 3, 1928, p. 52; and Danielsson, *op. cit.,* p. 53.

Chapter 10

1. K. von den Steinen, *Die Marquesaner und ihre Kunst,* Berlin, Vols. 1 and 2, 1925; Vol. 3, 1928; E. S. C. Handy, "The Native Culture of the Marquesas," *B. P. Bishop Museum Bulletin 17*, Honolulu, 1923; "Marquesan Legends," *B. P. Bishop Museum Bulletin 69,* Honolulu, 1930; "Tattooing in the Marquesas," *B. P. Bishop Museum Bulletin 1,* Honolulu, 1922; "Music in the Marquesas," *B. P. Bishop Museum Bulletin 17,* Honolulu, 1925; "String Figures from the Marquesas and Society Islands," *B. P. Bishop Museum Bulletin 18,* Honolulu, 1925; *L'Art des Iles Marquesas,* Editions de l'Art et d'Histoire, Paris, 1938; and R. Linton, "The Material Culture of the Marquesas Islands," *B. P. Bishop Museum Memoirs,* Vol. 8, No. 5, Honolulu, 1923. For additional references refer to complete bibliography in Von den Steinen, *op. cit.,* Vol. 1, 1925.
2. See, for example 2 volumes, London, 1813; U. Lisiansky, *Voyages Around the World in the Years 1803, 4, 5, and 6,* and in the Ship "Neva," London, 1814; D. Porter, *Journal of a Cruise Made to the Pacific Ocean by Capt. D. Porter in the Years 1812, 13, 14,* Philadelphia, 1832; M. Radiguet, *Les Derniers Sauvages* (1842-1854), Paris, Editions Ducharte et Van Buggenhoundt, 1929; and Père M. Gracia, *Lettres sur les îles Marquises,* Paris, 1843.
3. R. Linton, "The Archæology of the Marquesas Islands," *B. P. Bishop Museum Bulletin 23,* Honolulu, 1925. For a complete report of stratigraphic excavations in the Marquesas

see R. C. Suggs, *The Archaeology of Nuku Hiva,* Ph.D. dissertation, Dept. of Anthropology, Columbia University, 1959; in press, American Museum of Natural History.

4. For a description of this technique see J. Ford, "A Surface Survey of the Viru Valley," *Anthropology Papers of the American Museum of Natural History,* Vol. 43, Part I, 1950.
5. H. L. Shapiro and R. C. Suggs, "New Dates for Polynesian Prehistory," *Man,* January 1959.
6. G. G. Reichard, *Melanesian Design,* 2 volumes, New York, Columbia University Press, 1933, Ch. III.
7. A. Métraux, *L'Ile de Paques,* Paris, Librairie Gallimard, 1941, pp. 181-82.
8. B. Danielsson, *Work and Life on Raroia,* London, George Allen and Unwin, Ltd., 1956, p. 41.
9. H. Laval, Mangareva: *L'Histoire ancienne d'un peuple Polynésien,* Braine-le-Comte, Belgium, Maison des Pères de Sacrés Coeurs, 1938, pp. 1-2.
10. K. P. Emory, "The Archæology of Mangareva and Neighboring Atolls," *B. P. Bishop Museum Bulletin 163,* Honolulu, 1939, p. 49.
11. Porter, *op. cit.,* pp. 101-02; Handy, *op. cit.,* 1923, pp. 203-05; and Père S. Delmas, *La Réligion òu Le Paganisme des Marquisiens,* Paris, 1927, pp. 85, 120-22.
12. Linton, *op. cit.,* 1925, pp. 77-78, 162, Pls. VI A, B and VII A; and Von den Steinen, *op. cit.,* 1925, Vol. II, pp. 78-86.
13. Handy, *op. cit.,* 1923, p. 223; and Delmas, *op. cit.,* 1927, p. 7.
14. Von den Steinen, *op. cit.,* 1928, Vol. II, p. 33.

Chapter 11

1. T. Henry, "Tahiti aux Temps Anciens," *Publications de la Société des Océanistes,* No. 1, Paris, 1951, pp. 21-26.
2. *Ibid.;* E. S. C. Handy, "History and Culture in the Society Islands," *B. P. Bishop Museum Bulletin 79,* Honolulu, 1930; W. Ellis, *Polynesian Researches,* 4 volumes, London, 1853; and J. Cook, *The Voyage of the Endeavour, 1768-1771,* Vol. 1 of *Journals of His Voyages of Discovery,* ed. by J. C. Beaglehole, London, Cambridge University Press, 1955.
3. Henry, *op. cit.,* pp. 449-62.
4. Handy, *op. cit.;* E. S. C. Handy, "Some Conclusions and Suggestions Regarding the Polynesian Problem," *American Anthropologist,* Vol. 22, No. 3, 1920; and E. S. C. Handy, "Polynesian Religion," *B. P. Bishop Museum Memoirs,* Vol. 34, Honolulu, 1927.
5. K. P. Emory, "Stone Remains in the Society Islands," *B. P. Bishop Museum Bulletin 116,* Honolulu, 1933.

6. *Ibid.*, p. 44.
7. *Ibid.*, pp. 23, 38, 50-53.
8. *Ibid.*, pp. 38, 50.
9. *Ibid.*, p. 50; and K. P. Emory, "Tuamotu Stone Structures," *B. P. Bishop Museum Bulletin 118,* Honolulu, 1934.
10. B. Danielsson, *Work and Life on Raroia,* London, George Allen and Unwin, Ltd., 1956, Ch. II.
11. P. Buck, "The Ethnology of Tongareva," *B. P. Bishop Museum Bulletin 92,* Honolulu, 1930, pp. 178-79, Figs. 20, 22.
12. R. T. Aitken, "The Ethnology of Tubuai," *B. P. Bishop Museum Bulletin 70,* Honolulu, 1930, p. 107.
13. K. P. Emory and Y. Sinoto, "Radiocarbon Dates Significant for Pacific Anthropology," *Pacific Science Association Bulletin,* Vol. 11, No. 3, Supplement, 1959, pp. 11-12.
14. Emory, *op. cit.,* 1933, pp. 31-32, 53.
15. *Ibid.*, p. 53.
16. *Ibid.*, p. 46.
17. Henry, *op. cit.,* pp. 126-33.
18. Emory, *op. cit.,* 1933, pp. 145-49.
19. *Ibid.*, pp. 28, 54.
20. *Ibid.*, pp. 72-74.
21. Henry, *loc. cit.;* Handy, *op. cit.,* 1930; and M. Sahlins, *Social Stratification in Polynesia,* Seattle, American Ethnological Society, 1959, pp. 37-45, 260.
22. Henry, *op. cit.,* pp. 16-17.

Chapter 12

1. T. Henry, "Tahiti aux Temps Anciens," *Publications de la Société des Océanistes,* No. 1, Paris, 1951, p. 484.
2. D. Malo, "Hawaiian Antiquities," *B. P. Bishop Museum Special Publication No. 2,* Honolulu, 1951, p. 6.
3. K. Luomala, "The Menehune of Polynesia and Other Mythical Little People of Oceania," *B. P. Bishop Museum Bulletin 203,* Honolulu, 1951.
4. K. P. Emory, "Pacific Islands: Area 21," No. 1, 1958, *Council for Old World Archaeology Survey,* Cambridge, Mass., 1958, pp. 3-5.
5. K. P. Emory, "Our Reach into Hawaii's Ancient Past," paper presented before the Social Science Association, April 6, 1959, Honolulu: "Origin of the Hawaiians," MS., *B. P. Bishop Museum,* March 1959.
6. *Ibid.*
7. Emory, *op. cit.,* April 6, 1959, pp. 4-5.
8. W. C. Bennett, "The Archæology of Kauai," *B. P. Bishop Museum Bulletin 80,* Honolulu, 1931.

9. K. P. Emory and Y. Sinoto, "Radiocarbon Dates Significant for Pacific Anthropology," *Pacific Science Association Information Bulletin,* Vol. 11, No. 3, Supplement, 1959, p. 13.
10. After K. P. Emory, "The Archæology of Nihoa and Necker Islands," *B. P. Bishop Museum Bulletin 53,* Honolulu, 1928.
11. Emory and Sinoto, *loc. cit.*
12. Malo, *op. cit.,* p. 6.
13. *Ibid.,* pp. 240-50.
14. Bennett, *op. cit.,* pp. 41-49. For additional data see also: K. P. Emory, "The Archæology of Lanai," *B. P. Bishop Museum Bulletin 12,* Honolulu, 1924; and J. G. McAllister, "The Archæology of Kahoolawe," *B. P. Bishop Museum Bulletin 113,* Honolulu, 1933.
15. Malo, *op. cit.,* pp. 159.
16. Bennett, *op. cit.,* p. 35.
17. Emory, *op. cit.,* 1924, pp. 40, 52.
18. Bennett, *op. cit.,* pp. 10-13.
19. *Ibid.,* pp. 105-07.
20. *Ibid.,* p. 54; and Emory, *op. cit.,* 1924, p. 75, Fig. 8.
21. T. R. Hiroa, "Arts and Crafts of Hawaii," *B. P. Bishop Museum Special Publication 45,* Honolulu, 1957, pp. 566-72.
22. *Ibid.* See sections on crafts for excellent discussion of materials and techniques.
23. See Malo, *op. cit.,* p. 52; and M. Sahlins, *Social Stratification in Polynesia,* Seattle, American Ethnological Society, 1959, pp. 13-22 (contains an outstanding summary and interpretation of Hawaiian data).

Chapter 13

1. J. M. Brown, *The Riddle of the Pacific,* London, T. F. Unwin, 1924.
2. G. de Hevesy, "The Easter Island and the Indus Valley Scripts," *Anthropos,* Vol. 33, 1938.
3. K. von Moeller, "Die Osterinsel und Peru," *Zeitschrift für Ethnologie,* Berlin, Vol. 69, 1937; and B. Oetteking, "Anthropologische Beziehungen zwischen der Osterinsel und Amerika," *Zeitschrift für Morphologie und Anthropologie,* Stuttgart, Vol. 34, 1934.
4. T. Heyerdahl, *American Indians in the South Pacific,* London, George Allen and Unwin, Ltd., 1952.
5. For a complete list of all sources concerning Easter Island see A. Métraux, *Easter Island: A Stone Age Civilization of the Pacific,* New York, Oxford University Press, 1957.
6. T. Barthel, "Grundlagen zur Entzifferung der Osterinsel-

schrift," *Abhandlung aus dem Gebiete der Auslandskunde,* Vol. 64, R. B., Hamburg, 1959.

7. K. P. Emory, "Pacific Islands: Area 21," No. 1, 1958, *Council for Old World Archaeology Survey,* Cambridge, Mass., 1958, pp. 6-7.
8. After A. Métraux, *L'Ille de Pâques,* Paris, Librairie Gallimard, 1941, pp. 165-68.
9. A. Métraux, "The Ethnology of Easter Island," *B. P. Bishop Museum Bulletin 160,* Honolulu, 1940.
10. *Ibid.,* pp. 175-82, Fig. 7.
11. *Ibid.,* pp. 187-88, Fig. 13, b, c, d.
12. *Ibid.,* pp. 194-99.
13. K. P. Emory and Y. Sinoto, "Radiocarbon Dates Significant for Pacific Anthropology," *Pacific Science Association Information Bulletin,* Vol. 11, No. 3, Supplement, 1959, p. 15.
14. See M. Sahlins, "Esoteric Efflorescence in Easter Island," *American Anthropologist,* Vol. 57, No. 5, October 1955.
15. Emory, *op. cit.,* 1958, p. 6.
16. A. Métraux, "Easter Island Sanctuaries," *Ethnologiska Studier 5,* Göteborg, Sweden, 1937, pp. 104-07, 122.
17. *Ibid.,* pp. 122-125. See also: H. Lavachéry, "Stéles et Pierres Levées à l'île de Pâques," Sudsee Studien, Basel, 1951, p. 418; and "Archéologie de l'île de Pâques," *Journal de la Société des Océanistes,* Tome X, No. 10, Paris, 1954, pp. 140, 146, 148.
18. Métraux, *op. cit.,* 1937, p. 127.
19. Emory, *op. cit.,* 1958, pp. 6-7.
20. See respectively W. L. Bennett, "The Archæology of Kauai," *B. P. Bishop Museum Bulletin 80,* Honolulu, 1931, pp. 22-23, 105-07; K. P. Emory, "Stone Remains in the Society Islands," *B. P. Bishop Museum Bulletin 116,* Honolulu, 1933, pp. 114-19; and H. L. Shapiro, "Les Iles Marquises," *Natural History,* Vol. LXVII, No. 5, 1958, photos on p. 270, middle and bottom of page.
21. Métraux, *op. cit.,* 1937, p. 116.
22. *Ibid.,* p. 115.
23. *Ibid.,* p. 114.
24. *Ibid.,* pp. 194-99.
25. Statues of this type correspond to the uprights noted by Métraux (*op. cit.,* 1940, pp. 302-03) and Lavachéry (*op. cit.,* 1951, p. 421).
26. Emory, *op. cit.,* 1958, p. 7.
27. H. Lavachéry, *Petroglyphs de l'île de Pâques,* 2 pts., Anvers, Belgium, 1939.
28. K. von den Steinen, *Die Marquesaner und ihre Kunst,* 3 volumes, Berlin, Vol. I, 1925, pp. 130, 170, 188-89.

29. Métraux, *op. cit.*, 1940, pp. 280-82.
30. H. Lavachéry, "Contribution à l'étude de l'archéologie de l'île de Pitcairn," *Société des Americanistes de Belgique Bulletin*, No. 19, 1936.
31. Lavachéry was of the opinion that the Pitcairn occupation came from Mangareva.
32. See Sahlins, *op. cit.*
33. Métraux, *op. cit.*, 1940, p. 22.
34. Emory, *op. cit.*, 1958, p. 7.
35. Métraux, *op. cit.*, 1941, pp. 168-69.
36. Métraux, *op. cit.*, 1940, p. 149.
37. *Ibid.*, p. 43.
38. After Barthel, *op. cit.*

Chapter 14

1. J. Golson, "New Zealand Archaeology," *Journal of the Polynesian Society*, Vol. 66, No. 3, 1957, pp. 271-73.
2. After R. Duff, "The Moa-Hunter Period of Maori Culture," *Canterbury Museum Bulletin*, No. 1, 1950, Ch. VIII.
3. *Ibid.*, p. 258.
4. R. E. Bell, "New Zealand," *Asian Perspectives*, Vol. I, Nos. 1-2, 1957, p. 140.
5. Duff, *op. cit.*, pp. 70-78.
6. *Ibid.*; R. E. Bell, *op. cit.*, Vol. II, No. 1, 1958, p. 91; and Golson, *op. cit.*
7. Bell, *op. cit.*, 1958.
8. *Ibid.*
9. Duff, *op. cit.*, pp. 50-57.
10. *Ibid.*, Pls. 26-35.
11. *Ibid.*, Ch. IV.
12. *Ibid.*, Pl. 14-B.
13. *Ibid.*, Ch. III.
14. For a discussion of the physical anthropology of the aboriginal population of New Zealand, see H. L. Shapiro, "The Physical Anthropology of the Maori-Moriori," *Journal of the Polynesian Society*, Vol. 49, No. 1, 1940.
15. Bell, *op. cit.*, 1957, p. 134; 1958, p. 91.
16. Golson, *op. cit.*, p. 280.
17. Duff, *op. cit.*, pp. 14, 19-20, 243, 251, 299.
18. Golson, *op. cit.*, pp. 282-83.
19. *Ibid.*, p. 279.
20. A. P. Vayda, "Maori Conquests in Relation to the New Zealand Environment," *Journal of the Polynesian Society*, Vol. 65, No. 3, 1950.

21. J. Golson, "Field Archaeology in New Zealand," *Journal of the Polynesian Society,* Vol. 66, No. 1, 1957. See also F. G. Fairfield, "Puke tu tu Pa," *Journal of the Polynesian Society,* Vol. 47, 1925; "Mannga Kie Kie," *Journal of the Polynesian Society,* Vol. 50, 1941; R. Firth, "The Korekore Pa," *Journal of the Polynesian Society,* Vol. 34, 1925; and articles by L. G. Kelly in the *Journal of the Polynesian Society,* Vols. 42, 47, 48, 54.
22. Golson, *op. cit.,* pp. 101-09.
23. *Ibid.*

Chapter 15

1. K. P. Emory, "Archæology of the Pacific Equatorial Islands," *B. P. Bishop Museum Bulletin 123,* Honolulu, 1930.
2. E. S. C. Handy, "Marquesan Legends," *B. P. Bishop Museum Bulletin 69,* Honolulu, 1930.
3. T. and L. Davis, *Doctor to the Islands,* Boston, Atlantic Monthly Press, 1952.
4. O. Aichel, "Osterinselpalaeolithen in Prähistorischen Gräbern Chiles," *Congrès international des americanistes compte rendu de la 21e session,* Göteborg, Sweden, 1921, pp. 267-69; and A. Métraux, *L'Ile de Pâques,* Paris, Librairie Gallimard, 1941, p. 179.
5. P. Humbla, "Steinerne Querbeile aus dem Gebiet Mizquetal (Ozeanisch — Südamerikanische Beziehungen)," *Anthropos,* Vol. XX, 1925.
6. J. Schmeltz, "A Patu-patu or Merai from an American Mound," *Internationale Archive für Ethnographie,* Leiden, 1898, t. XI, p. 165.
7. J. Imbelloni, "La prémier Chaine isoglossematique oceano-américaine," *Publication d'hommage offert au P. W. Schmidt,* 1948.
8. G. Ekholm, "A Possible Focus of Asiatic Influence in the Late Classic Cultures of Mesoamerica," in "Asia and North America—Transpacific Contacts," *Memoirs of the Society for American Archaeology,* No. 9, 1953.

Chapter 16

1. See T. Heyerdahl, *Kon-Tiki,* London, George Allen & Unwin, Ltd., 1950; *American Indians in the South Pacific,* London, George Allen & Unwin, Ltd., 1952.
2. For a report of this work see R. T. Simmons and J. J. Graydon, "A Blood Group Genetical Survey in Eastern and Central Polynesians," *American Journal of Physical Anthropology,* Vol. 15, No. 3, 1957.
3. T. Heyerdahl, *Aku-Aku,* Chicago, Rand McNally and Company, 1958, p. 376.

4. T. Heyerdahl, "The Voyage of the Raft Kon-Tiki," *Geographical Journal,* Vol. 115, 1950, p. 23.
5. Heyerdahl, *op. cit.*, 1952.
6. Heyerdahl, *op. cit.,* 1950, p. 20.
7. S. Ryden, "Did the Indians in Chile Know the Use of Sails in Pre-Columbus Times?" *Southwestern Journal of Anthropology,* Vol. 12, No. 2, 1956. Also for a typical rejoinder see T. Heyerdahl, "Guara Navigation: Indigenous Sailing off the Andean Coast," *Southwestern Journal of Anthropology,* Vol. 13, No. 2, 1957.
8. B. Danielsson, *The Happy Island—Kon-Tiki Isle,* London, Panther Books, 1956, p. 40.
9. See E. D. Merrill, "The Botany of Cook's Voyages," *Chronica Botanica,* Vol. 14, Nos. 5/6, 1954, pp. 263-70; R. Heine-Geldern, "Some Problems of Migration in the Pacific," *Kultur und Sprache Wiener Beiträge zur Kulturgeschichte und Linguistik,* IX, Vienna, 1952; and R. Firth, Review of Thor Heyerdahl's *American Indians in the South Pacific, Nature,* 171, 1953, pp. 713-14.
10. Heyerdahl, *op. cit.,* 1958, plates between pp. 304 and 305.
11. *Ibid.,* p. 352.
12. *Ibid.,* p. 352.
13. *Ibid.,* pp. 334-35.
14. J. A. Mason, *The Ancient Civilizations of Peru,* Harmondsworth, England, Penguin Books, Ltd., 1957, pp. 90, 113, 114, 131, 202, 203, 213, 214, 220, 232, 233.

Index